Trucking
In
English

An

Armchair Emigration

Tale

CAROLYN STEELE

Cover art and design by
Rebecca Poole

ISBN: 1480262811
ISBN-13: 978-1480262812

DEDICATION

For Ben,

who doesn't mind having an odd parent.

.

CONTENTS

ACKNOWLEDGMENTS

Everything happened. Everybody exists.

Some names have changed to spare a few blushes but not all of them. If you recognise yourself anyway and don't like what you read, please know that you may have driven me nuts at the time but without you there wouldn't be a book.

To the fine freight transport companies who took a chance and offered me employment, thank you. Anything you would prefer not to read was my fault and mine alone.

Thanks for the nagging to Julia, Pinky, Ben and all the loyal fans of *Trucking in English* the blog and podcast.

Without Jo's perspicacious editing and Ken's painstaking proofreading the book would be a great deal rougher round the edges. Thanks for your patience.

And without Rebecca it wouldn't have the cover I wanted but couldn't describe. Thank you for reading my mind.

.

PART 1: FROM WANNABE TO ALMOST-AM

IF ALL ELSE FAILS

IT WAS slick, slippery and dark. We were hauling the maximum allowable load, 80,000 lbs gross. The snowploughs had been by clearing surface drifts but snowploughs leave icy droppings. As they passed they mashed the remaining mess of snow, oil and gravel down into a solid layer of scariness.

The road east from Marathon, Ontario was windy, bendy and hilly as well as icy. I bravely managed about 80 kph on the straight runs, a lot less on the hills and bends. I slowed to an irritating crawl on the downhill grades with bends at the bottom. We'd been warned in school, trucks can end up in trouble on slippery hills with bends at the bottom. Apparently they can end up in lakes and/or ravines as well as the vaguer sorts of trouble. Overtly I was being responsible but truthfully I was being pathetic. No, what I was being was terrified.

Other trucks with presumably more experienced and less wimpy drivers flew past us when and where they could. This wasn't frequent. I switched off the CB, not really wanting to hear what everybody thought of my speed, my mother or my physical attributes. After a couple of hours we were stopped by yet another police cordon... another road closure.

A day's worth of Highway 17 traffic was neatly corralled into the nearest truck stop. Should you wish to consult a map with a magnifying glass you may spot Wawa, Ontario, somewhere north of Lake Superior. It has a truck stop. That is all. As we drank tolerable coffee and ate tolerable chips we heard the gossip, a truck had 'parked in the ditch' in front of us. Behind us the road that had held us up all night—having been closed by the police due to snowdrifts and whiteouts—was closed again, a seventeen truck pile-up with fires and people killed. All of a sudden I didn't mind being the sort of cowardly rookie who drives slowly on ice. Not dying seemed to be sufficient achievement, careful wimps might live to drive this awful road again.

The offending truck was winched out of the ditch eventually and we all trooped off in a grumpy conga line of tired and late freight. I waited for the back of the line, who needs more abuse? The road remained slick. It snowed. The whiteouts came and went with every turn into the wind. In brief moments when the visibility cleared, you could see waves on the lake flash-frozen into little grey mountains.

It took all day and most of the night to round the rest of Lake Superior and emerge from the dreaded weather system that is a Lake Effect Winter Storm. We were exhausted, anxious, and late. But we emerged, which is more than some did.

***

Why would a fifty-something, nicely brought-up mother suddenly decide to go trucking? It was a good question and like most good questions it had answers both simple and complex. "It sounds like fun," just made people who didn't know me roll their eyes. I did a bit better with "it's a traditional immigrant job," and with "well, I can earn more money in a truck than I can with a Master's degree." These explanations merely made me sound serious about finding work and supporting my family, not defiantly odd, just a traditional immigrant to Canada indeed. And they were partially true, since emigrating from England I'd struggled to find employment in the things I was actually qualified to do.

My son and I had arrived in Ontario from London posing as entrepreneurs five years earlier. The bed and breakfast I'd bought as my ticket to Canadian citizenship had bitten the dust when I'd realised there was more to running a successful business than looking up *entrepreneur* in the dictionary. I did need a new project but to be honest the trucking thing was more about preferring to play with wheeled toys than do real work. I'd driven ambulances and stretch limos in the past so if I wanted to get bigger and better it was going to have to be something like a truck or a plane.

Trucking school was cheaper, and I'd been eyeing those massive beasties on the roads ever since landing here. I blame my Dad. He wanted a boy. Psychotherapy aside, adding to my list of excuses that it seemed like a great angle for a book helped a bit when explaining to people with no imagination, but not much.

"Ben, have you got a minute?"

"Yes Mum, what's up?"

"You know how I try not to embarrass you accidentally?"

"Yeah, just on purpose because it's good for me. I know."

"Well, I've got this idea."

The seed for my future career as a truck driver had originally been sown back at the B&B. Three lads from England had arrived in search of a year's accommodation, which we provided. They took over our basement and came and went as they pleased, driving their monsters at odd hours and to exciting-sounding places. We spoiled them with random bacon butties when they turned up, temporarily back from Having Adventures. During that year we shared all the tales…we heard about the people, the trucks, the nightmare border crossings, all those great trips, and we enjoyed it all. We laughed, cried and fumed along with Jim, Owen and Mick on their infrequent stops back 'home', agreeing that dispatch were stupid and that Homeland Security were mad but that getting paid to drive over the Golden Gate Bridge made it all worthwhile. And we developed an impression that this job might be fun. (Well, one of us did.) The seed was buried fairly deep back then, a sort of barely acknowledged, *I suppose, if all else fails I can always drive a truck.*

When all else did fail, the idea resurfaced. The B&B was a distant memory and the fifty-something mother found herself empty-nested and wondering what to do next. Why not get paid to see North America? I'd driven for a living before, I'd seen little of Canada and nothing of the States, how hard could it be?

"I've been looking into what to do now you're away at uni most of the year."

"Umm hmm." He gets that look on his face.

"I thought I might learn to drive a truck." The relief is visible.

"Is that all?"

"You don't think it's nuts?"

"Well, yes, obviously it's nuts."

With the familial seal of approval, nuts enough to be interesting but not so nuts as to be embarrassing, I allowed the seed to see the light of day elsewhere. To begin with I introduced it into conversations as a joke, "If all else fails I can always drive a truck (ho, ho)." It was, of course, more of a test than a joke. People who knew me well would eye me strangely, give it a moment's thought and respond, "I wouldn't put it past you (ho, ho)." Frequently these were the same people on whom I had tested out the whole mad idea of moving to Canada and buying a B&B in the first place. As a joke of course.

All of a sudden I was bumping into people from the freight transport industry, I probably had been before then but you know how you suddenly start noticing things when they can serve a purpose. Specific questions began to leave my head via my mouth involuntarily. Which were the best schools? How long was the course? What would it cost? What could you earn? How much work was there out there? Did trucking companies employ women?

It didn't help the growing inevitability when my early questioning unearthed the coincidence that the finest

5

trucking school in town belonged to my old neighbours from the B&B. We'd connected briefly when I'd toured the neighbourhood with bottles of wine to apologise after a particularly noisy pool party but the subject of trucks hadn't cropped up back then. It did now and I got most of my trucking answers from people who knew me and those answers were worryingly positive. Ours, two months, not a lot, lots, lots and yes. They appeared mildly surprised when I asked about the women thing, apparently it's the 21st century and that trail has already been blazed.

I was surprised but encouraged. The London Ambulance Service had taken some persuading to employ me and my fellow lady paramedics in the very early '80s, we had blazed the trails back then in heroic manner. We'd considered our task complete when women began to appear driving ambulances on TV shows and we'd subsequently reserved the right to tell female rookies how lucky they were we'd fought their battles for them. Apparently we hadn't been unique.

***

My neighbours' training school supplied me with a list of the companies they placed rookies with, so that I could call for myself and ask about the female thing. They told me how one qualified for the course; clean driving abstract and police check, medical check-up and mechanical aptitude test. With the presence of mind not to exclaim *mechanical aptitude test* out loud I thanked them prettily and toddled off to continue my research. I allowed the nagging sense that I might have underestimated the task ahead to bury itself under a veneer of bravery and panache.

I called a couple of the companies on their list of employers and left voice messages for recruiters asking about prospects for women on the road. One company called back within hours and I had a cozy chat with a lady called Gwen. She was amused, apparently my concerns really did date back to the dark ages. She also confirmed, independently, that I had chosen the best school. We discussed my background..."Call me when you have your licence," she cooed, "we'll talk some more."

Thus encouraged that paid work might actually exist, I went on-line to Google *mechanical aptitude tests*. Memories of ambulance days flooded back. The aptitude test back then had been to watch someone strip down and reassemble an Entonox delivery kit and repeat the procedure within a time limit. I had visions of being asked to uncouple a rig (or whatever it is they call whatever it is they do) and could see my career on the open road rapidly disappearing into the black hole in my brain labelled *pipe dreams*.

The internet was fairly reassuring though. I found a site which allowed you to download a bookful of sample papers complete with answers and explanations for the princely sum of $19. The book explained that many occupations now use mechanical aptitude tests to check that you are trainable in practical pursuits and that practice could make all the difference.

I cleared a work station on the dining room table, bought myself a toy truck as a visual aid and settled down to do my homework. The questions fell into several categories of IQ type thingy. I was well versed in most of them—spotting series and doing sums, finding the odd one out from loads of nonsensical diagrams—I have always liked that sort of thing, but I did appreciate the crash course in 'O' Level physics.

In no time I was relearning long-forgotten rules for levers, gears and electrical circuitry. The sample tests seemed relatively challenging though. They were aimed at people hoping to be taken on by armed forces to do very clever technical stuff and, not being one of those, I sometimes didn't manage the recommended time limits. I comforted myself with the thought that I was hoping to drive a truck not design a helicopter so presumably my impending test would have to be a bit easier than these.

With the crash revision course in physics under my belt, and bits of paper confirming that I had a clean criminal record and nothing untoward on my driving licence, I make an appointment to be tested mechanically.

The pre-test interview was fairly straightforward. Have I driven big stuff before? (Is an ambulance big? I had thought so but maybe not in comparison to things with many axles.) Have I used a manual gearbox before? (I'm English, that's what we drive.) Am I beholden to alcohol or drugs? (Does an occasional gin and tonic count? See previous question, I'm English, that's what we do.) Have I worked away from home overnight before? (Does shift work count?) Will the family miss me? (Son doesn't care but I'll ask the cat.) The chap who asked all the questions had adopted an almost avuncular smile. When we began to muse about arrangements I might make for feeding the aforementioned cat I had the scintilla of a suspicion I might be being humoured. But very nicely, this is Canada after all.

And then the test. It would take thirty minutes and did I have any questions? I didn't and he left the room, hopefully before my face fell as I opened the booklet.

There were no IQ-type questions at all, just a lot of little pictures of chaps with shovels and buckets and things. Some pictures of trains and dams and drinking straws.

Which is the easiest to push?

Which is the strongest setup?

Which chap will lift the heavier weight?

Which diagram shows what will happen?

Where is the least bumpy seat on a school bus?

The book had been much used and the diagrams were worn, faint and difficult to interpret. Some of the levers and gears and see-saws were things I'd just revised but much of the rest of it was real life. What about that bus? I had to think back an awfully long way. When I was a kid we'd sit at the back for bumpiness, and I thought I'd heard that people who are travelsick avoid being over the wheels, so which is it? A lot of the questions sort of related to hydraulics, which made sense, but there had been none of that on my online papers. The real 'O' level physics was 35 years behind me. Something to do with the size of the pipe affecting the pressure in some sort of ratio, but what exactly?

These questions, the ones that related to life, were taking too long to answer. I was the wrong side of middle age and there was a lot of life to trawl through. What shape made the strongest dam? I could tell you from ambulance days what shape of crowd barrier would crush the fewest teenyboppers...but was spreading out the crush points for people good or bad for water? And the second picture of a train crash meant that I must have got the previous one wrong. I dashed back miserably to the earlier question featuring a little train on a bend, confirming that I'd visualised it backwards.

I got the point of the test. This sort of mechanical aptitude made much more sense for the task ahead than the abstract stuff I had played with, and was a great deal fairer for people without a poncey education, but I had to make a few guesses. That $19 had been a waste of money, the toy truck, ditto. Who the hell did I think I was? "Oh yes, I've decided to be a truck driver you know, because I'm the sort of intrepid, brilliant woman who can do anything she puts her mind to." Silly cow.

The nice chap took my paper away and returned a few minutes later, grinning at the number of Kleenex I had managed to shred during the interregnum. He declared 89% more than ok for aptitude of the mechanical variety, who'd have thought I knew so much about shovels and train wrecks?

Instead of learning from this experience that I wasn't temperamentally suited to trucking, I was sufficiently dazzled by the idea of being eligible for trucking school that I sat and listened to the routine. Medical, registration with the school, receipt of a pile of textbooks, taking the Ontario Transport Ministry's A class licence knowledge test, classroom. Then truck. Apparently one needed to pass the Ministry theory test before they would let one onto the course so the absorption and revision of unladylike facts and figures had only just begun, as had the conveyor belt that is always so easy to step onto and so difficult to get off.

The doc pronounced me fit enough for purpose therefore, a deposit to the school and some signatures later, I found myself the proud owner of three text books to be read in specific order within the next three weeks. I placed them proudly on the dining table next to the toy truck and invited people over for coffee, so they could notice them.

On top of the pile, the *Official Ontario Ministry of Transport Truck Handbook*. Memorising its contents for the Ministry theory test was the first real task, only then would I be able to start school and climb into the cab. Then there was a handbook all about air brakes, to be worked through before day one because that was where the classroom part of training would start. I didn't know air brakes needed a handbook. Then there was a worryingly fat text book for everything else. It would help, allegedly, to look at some of this in advance.

There appeared to be a lot to learn. Who knew? Back in the 'ho, ho' days I'd assumed it was merely a matter of getting used to where the corners were and developing a technique for climbing in. Underneath the bravado I suspected I had finally bitten off more than I could chew. My Dad may have wanted a boy—he might have been prouder on the day I climbed into an ambulance than the day I received my M.Sc.—but I'm over fifty and he is long-gone. What was I trying to prove? And to whom? Surely it would be acceptable to say to myself and everyone else, "I've looked into it and I think that maybe it's not such a good idea after all."

On the other hand, who would want to get so close to a madcap enterprise that you can almost smell the diesel and then wimp out? Driving a truck was now irrevocably on my bucket list, whatever happened next. Sanity and introspection would just have to bugger off and make way for pig-headedness and hubris, especially since I seemed to have accidentally committed too much money to the venture to stop before trying to earn it back again.

The gent who handed me the books had two pieces of advice to give with regard to the Ministry test. The first was to memorise all the numbers, the second was to ask to write the bus-driving test while I was there. Why would I want to write a bus test? I didn't want to drive a bus. This was about toys, not people, I'd been nice to people for five years during the B&B phase and I'd turned into Basil Fawlty. My dreams were of the open road, driving into the sunset with no-one's needs but my own to cater to, the romance of those two beautiful words…long haul.

The book-handing gent told me it was only ten bucks and very easy and you never knew when you might want to drive a bus. But he also touched on the frequency with which burned out executives, social workers and customer service reps passed through his office with dreams of solitude. Maybe I wasn't mad.

I memorised the numbers. Maximum allowable heights, lengths, widths and weights in metric and imperial. That part was easy. Not so simple, the memorising of routines involving jargon and describing bits of stuff I'd never heard of. I had to dip in to the truckers' text book to find out what I was applying, releasing and lining up in order to make sense of the apparently vital coupling and uncoupling routines. Fortunately the book had pictures. Once I knew the difference between a fifth wheel and a king pin I stood a better chance of remembering what got done to which.

The most entertaining chapter of the Ministry book (yes, there was one) related to manners on the road. It listed the things that people who don't drive trucks dislike about people who do. It told me, *Today's truck drivers are among the most visible citizens on the highways, and the motoring public tends to criticize some of their driving practices. So, it's up to responsible truck drivers to influence the public's opinion.*

It also advised, *Be aware that most drivers of smaller vehicles do not understand what it is like to drive a large vehicle such as a tractor-trailer.* Well ain't that the truth? I would appear to be one of them. I didn't even know you were supposed to call the front bit a tractor.

***

Nobody at the test centre looked at me askance, no-one laughed. The lady operating the eye-test gubbins was perfectly nice about the fact that I didn't know it was a bad idea to turn up wearing bifocals. Once I'd twigged that I could see the dancing numbers if I mimicked them with a dancing head we got on fine. The chap who marked my paper congratulated me relatively genuinely.

"Now you're qualified to drive with someone who has an A licence," he observed.

"Blimey, am I? I don't even know how to climb in yet."

"Maybe they'll find you a ladder."

***

And on to the next thing. *Practical Airbrakes: Driver Handbook and Study Guide.* It was written in a friendly, jocular manner with spaces to scribble notes and little self-tests at the end of each chapter. It began nice and simply with line drawings of wheels and thermometers to illustrate a spot more school curriculum physics, friction and the like. I'd just revised this sort of thing so the first few chapters lulled me into a false sense of security. They moved slowly through topics such as how compressed air gets compressed and what valves do. There were helpful pictures of people getting blasts of compressed air in their faces, leaving one in no doubt as to the wisdom of being careful with the stuff.

Then all of a sudden, in the turn of a page, air brakes became a tad complicated. It crept up on me that I was having to concentrate more…and read bits several times. The section I had to read six times and then go back to after a lie down in a darkened room—identifying whether your trailer has a 'spring brake priority' or a 'service brake priority' sub-system if you must know—appeared just about half way through the book, precipitating the crisis. Finally after committing far too much time and money, and after telling way too many people to be able to back out with dignity, appeared the *what the hell have I done?* moment. The *who on earth do you think you are? You cannot possibly cope with this* thunderbolt.

I suddenly recalled that actually I was not and have never been terribly mechanical. I may be intelligent and relatively practical but have spent my life to date choosing to allow others to know about activities that are greasy, dirty and/or heavy. Had I forgotten when I started this caper quite how much I liked to be all clean and relatively fragrant? It now appeared that I was engaged in learning to make inspections of air brake systems on a daily basis and from the little line drawings in my handbook this looked to involve grubbing about under greasy undercarriages.

Did I really want to do this? Did I have a choice? Could I learn to want to? Nobody would mind if I just stopped the madness right now but that wouldn't be very intrepid and I liked it when people told each other I was intrepid. So, maybe I was doing this for them. That would be beyond nuts though, it would be really stupid.

I solved the problem by going shopping. I became the proud owner of a pair of fleecy-lined work gloves and some army surplus overalls. I could maybe climb underneath a truck and maybe keep relatively clean and dry. I liked my gloves a lot, they looked very workmanlike and I considered adding them to the dining table montage but I knew that every penny I expended on this potty scheme would be another reason not to stop.

As I watched myself brick up the escape route I told myself it would be ok in the end. Maybe I couldn't stop now I was on the conveyor but we all knew I'd never really get the hang of it. I'd flunk out of school after a valiant effort and people would be sympathetic. They'd admire my pluck. I could end my days telling grandchildren that I might have been a long-haul trucker if it weren't for the…something.

THERE'S A SCHOOL FOR IT

TRUCKING SCHOOL. Where to start? Imagine a classroom full of enormous cogs, brake drums and model trucks. A room full of toys in other words, toys large and small and people, mainly large. Twelve wannabes most of whom fit the six-foot-square image of a proper trucker, two women and a skinny lad.

I was glad to see another female until Sherrie mentioned that she was actually already driving trucks for Fed-Ex, she merely needed the upgraded licence to drive bigger things. Most of the guys had been made redundant from Ontario's faltering manufacturing industry, they may not have driven these monsters before but they came from worlds where they could at least recognise the bits and understand the jargon. One or two of us appeared to be on the course merely to satisfy the unemployment people that they were sorta-kinda trying to find work. I planned to try and keep up with that contingent.

Week one appeared to be mainly about frightening us,

101 ways to kill yourself and others. We watched videos regaling the overconfident with tales of just how easy it is to lose your brakes and hurtle down mountains to certain inferno or jackknife into shopping malls and school buses. Our instructor, Gregg, who clearly had a cat-like superpower when it came to extra lives livened up the horror stories with a level of detail that led you to suspect he might have been there. And they all ended with his charming little catchphrase, "And you don't want to be doing that, no you don't."

This preamble had two purposes. Both the cocky individuals who thought they knew it all and the game players who just thought it might be fun (I think I fall into the latter category) needed to understand that lumbering about with 80,000 lbs under and behind you was dangerous. We were to comprehend that most other drivers on the road didn't know that 18 wheels can't stop on a sixpence, road safety would be our responsibility. Since we, and only we, would know what trucks could and couldn't do we needed to learn to think for everyone else on the road. Was that even possible?

Week one was also about unlearning all that car stuff. No matter how good a driver you thought you were in your car, or in my case in an ambulance, it was all different now. As drivers, we were starting over.

The preamble, having terrified us, moved into an intensive two-day course on air brakes. I hadn't really understood it of course during my diligent pass through the book. It's just as well the people I'd already bored with this stuff had glazed over. Air brakes are so different to the usual unthinking, 'put your foot on the pedal and the car stops' routine that you have to deconstruct it all and start again. These brakes do a different job and behave in a different way. They require understanding. Moreover, if and when you lose them they stay lost and big things go wrong. It's physics and we must have it hammered into our heads a dozen ways. We trawled through the book I thought I'd understood chapter by chapter, with heavy chunks of cut-away brake chambers to pass around and look at by way of visual aids.

There was a complete miniature braking system installed on the classroom wall which did everything for real, with noisy little puffs of air as pushrods pushed and springs sprung. The only bit I recognized was the foot pedal, the rest was a mystery.

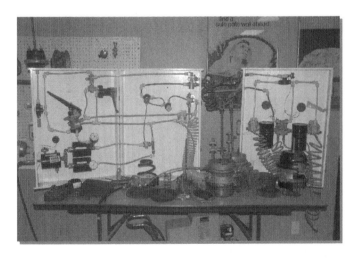

More stories, tales of woe and scary movies punctuated the theory and Gregg talked to us as though we were truckers. I started to absorb how and why you didn't want to be doing that, no you didn't. The fear and panic subsided, I was getting it. By the time the Ministry air brake theory exam came around, a short multiple-choice questionnaire, I'd pretty much got it. In theory I excelled. The classroom was safe enough, theory was comforting and we could all talk trucking just like people who knew how to do it.

There was more to the Transport Ministry of Ontario's air brake qualification though. To complete it and be allowed on the road we had to amble outside to play with the Really Big Toys. Airbrake systems require daily testing, I'd got that bit right. Before our training could proceed any further we had to complete a Ministry-approved practical test as well. Specifically, ten different brake checks, each check to be conducted with running commentary to our instructor's satisfaction.

Out in the yard behind the classroom, in among the training school monsters, Gregg demonstrated them all to us once and then sent us home with a little sheet of instructions. The following afternoon we would have some time to practise once or twice and then we would be tested. This would be the 'Z' part of our eventual 'AZ' licence, the air brake endorsement. Once we passed the road test as well the 'A' bit would kick in and we'd be licensed to drive anything, any size, throughout North America. We would be observed checking for air leaks, testing shut-off valves, timing air loss rates, listening for puffs of air while watching gauges on the dash and measuring pushrod travels. It all seemed a bit much for week one. The terminology wasn't familiar yet, it didn't trip off the tongue properly, cheat-sheets notwithstanding.

"Can we have the notes with us during the test?"

"No, you have to memorise it all for tomorrow but keep the notes safe. The sheet is for you to have in your truck, then you'll be sure you've got it right each day until it's second nature." I think I might laminate mine, second nature could take a while.

Nerve-wracking? Yes, a bit, but it was hard not to have fun practising how to make all those burping and farting noises that make you jump in traffic jams. And the physical exercise was useful for keeping the nerves at bay. What with chocking and unchocking of trailer wheels, taking air supply lines off and putting them on again and opening the bonnet to get at the brake chambers on the front wheels, I calculated that one clambered in and out of the cab exactly twelve times from the beginning of the assessment to the end. And carried some stupidly heavy stuff about. Those wheel chocks look light enough don't they? We've all seen the aircraft version being whisked smartly from the landing gear at the merry yell of, "Chocks away!" Well, that's as may be but the chocks that are supposed to stop a laden trailer from moving about are solid little chaps. They have a helpful ring screwed into the back so that your average trucker can chuck one about with a nonchalant index finger but yours truly can only carry one by cuddling it to her chest as though it were a fretful baby.

Add to that the interesting gymnastics required for getting the bonnet open at all and that's quite a work out. The six-foot-squared thing, it looks as though it might be a significant advantage. Now I know why truckers generally cultivate a serious beer gut, one needs either height or weight to satisfactorily achieve looking at the engine (something else which must be done every day) without making an idiot of oneself. There is a handy little step in the truck's front bumper to facilitate bonnet-opening. The taller of us can just pop a foot into it to brace with and add a little leverage while they grab hold of the fancy chrome ornament on the top of the bonnet and pull. Those of us with shorter legs can use it to climb up, grab hold of the fancy chrome ornament and launch ourselves backwards, legs waggling about in ridiculous manner as we try to get enough momentum going to pull a huge lump of truck groundwards.

I think I can safely cancel my gym membership, this is not going to be the sedentary occupation I had imagined. Still, I fared a little better than the lightest chap in the class, he did fine getting the bonnet open but was taken for a ride in the air by it while putting it back at the end of his exam. And yes, I will have to start calling it a hood at some stage.

Passing the first practical test gave us all a bit more of a spring in the step, a stage on the road 'from wannabe to almost-am' as Gregg so quaintly put it, even if I did discover in the process that only he can get away with calling things doohickeys. Apparently we are not afforded such licence and should, ideally, know the proper names of bits of truck. Even if we can mime what shape it is and what it does quite prettily.

***

Air brake certified and brimming with—not exactly confidence, more a slight lessening of dread—it was back to the classroom to dust off the togs and learn about Hazardous Materials (another ministry must of a test) and Hours of Service. Some things explode. I know that, we learned it in ambulance days. The fire brigade need to know what to spray at you and which suit to put on once you have jackknifed and closed a highway. I've stood upwind and uphill of many an incident checking Hazchem codes against a little pocket reminder sheet, so the switch from the UK Hazchem to the transatlantic Hazmat system enabled that half-a-day to pass in a breeze of 'this is getting easier'. But Hours of Service? Oh dear.

There are rules to stop people falling asleep at the wheel. These rules are different in Canada and the US. If you want to drive across the border you need to be legal in the country you happen to find yourself in at the time. The fines are severe and in the US it's not unheard of to have a night in jail for a log book violation. They are not simple, these rules. In Canada you can drive for 13 hours a day, so long as you don't do more than 14 hours total work and have had 10 hours off. Unless you take 2 hours off in the day in which case you can work for 16 hours (but not drive for more than 13) and take 8 hours off.

In the US you can only drive for 11 hours in a total working day of 14 and no amount of time off in the day can lessen your time between one shift and the next from 10 to 8. Additionally, you can only work for 60 hours in 7 days in the US before taking a day off, but you can do 70 in Canada. A day off is 36 hours in Canada but 34 in the US. (Have you got that? I'll be asking questions later.) This is all to stop us getting greedy and driving round the clock when we should be sleeping.

I like sleep, it's one of my favourite occupations. Do I have to drive for 14 hours a day? Can I do less if I want to? I'd love to never get even remotely near a log book violation, 70-hour weeks sound like a lot of work. And the answer to this is that if you want to drive long-haul it's expected. There are part-time jobs around (and it is beginning to sound as though the usual 40-hour week in any other industry is part-time for trucking) but you won't be seeing the world.

Ah well, it mightn't be so bad, and week one is over. Just like that I'm a week nearer what I already knew to be the daftest ambition ever before I learned about the hours. I've been introduced to a braking system that fails fast if you don't treat it right, a gearbox with at least ten speeds and a clutch that does more than one thing. I am particularly upset about this, I used to be a dab hand at double-declutching years ago, it was the one aspect of trucking I thought I'd have a head start at. But, as with everything else on these monsters, it's not that simple.

Neither is the whole business of having an accident,

apparently. In a car one tends to notice the 'oh shit' moment. You realise that you are about to hit something or skid off the road or whatever but trucks are sneakier, you may not notice the imminent jackknife at all. We are incredulous. How can you not know something as huge as a 53-foot trailer full of heavy things is creeping up past you? Gregg grins knowingly. "You don't feel a thing," he gloats, "until you leave the road…taking cars and people with you." This is the reason we will be expected to check our mirrors every two to three seconds. (Which, as I'm sure you know, is almost twice the Metropolitan Police emergency driving system's expectation of every five seconds!)

"You won't feel a jackknife but you can see it. There's a clue if you look in the mirror and you can read the name of your company down the side of your trailer…and you don't want to be seeing that, no you don't." We are all quiet again. "Don't worry about it now though, you'll all go through a jackknife before the course is over." Blimey, will we? "And then you'll brake more carefully for the rest of your lives." He beams, delightedly, around the room. "See you next week."

Weekend homework? Well, chatting to a chap who was a whole two weeks ahead of us on the course I received a natty piece of advice. He reckoned that a good way to get into your head how an articulated vehicle behaves in reverse was to play with a model. I have treated myself to a new toy truck, a little more to scale than the first, and will be spending some time making it go backwards on the dining table into little bays constructed from coasters. He didn't mention whether it helps to say, "vroom, vroom," as well, but I may feel obliged to go the whole hog.

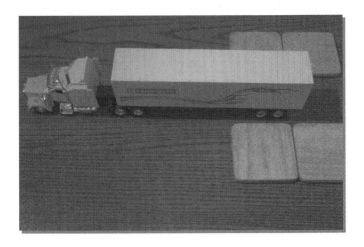

Week two consists of customs paperwork, more getting scared and more getting dusty. Brains, legs and guts all working out 'til they feel the burn. The theory doesn't stop with things that go bang and how to sleep legally, there are complex things to know about moving freight across borders. Specifically, three different systems for processing your trailer full of stuff from one country to another, all with different slips of paper. Some of them have barcodes. And, oh joy, different sorts of paper (and/or barcodes) depending on whether you are travelling from the US to Canada or from Canada to the US.

These bits of paper are almost the same and do the same job but we have to call them something slightly different. Why? Well apparently if we made it all the same then Canada wouldn't be a foreign country and we might begin to think that the US told us what to do, even if we thought of it first and they copied us. For it to be a real border and not a Mickey Mouse international exercise, the rules have to vary on each side.

All this might sound a little dry and in fact it probably would be if it weren't accompanied with a side order of Gregg's little tales. We have heard all about how to avoid being hijacked, how to hit a moose correctly, how to pretend getting stuck under a low bridge wasn't really your fault and how to brace yourself for the one-way trip up a runaway ramp.

Hijacking? Really? Why? This isn't the movies. I am bemused that anyone would go to the trouble but apparently it's big business, I just haven't taken into account the size of a trailer. Well I have, I've walked from one end to the other and thought, *oof, tired now* but I haven't done the sums. A quantity of pretty much anything that is 53 foot long by 12 foot 6 inches high is worth money to someone. Trailers must be sealed and the seals checked every time you stop. Unhooking your trailer in a truck stop so that you can go shopping is a big no-no since anyone can hook up to it and drive it away. There are things called pin locks you can buy to prevent this but it's still frowned upon to leave a load unattended.

According to Gregg truckers will steal anything that isn't nailed down, including hazardous chemical placards. His advice regarding the sudden loss of legally essential signage is to get on the CB and ask if anyone nearby has a spare set of placards for whatever you are carrying. As if by magic, someone in the same truck stop will have a set they can sell you for a little less than the cost of buying them new. This angel of mercy will naturally be the miscreant who stole them last night.

But back to hijacks and the most important piece of advice Gregg had to offer…never tell anyone what you are hauling, where you have been or where you are going. If the conversation on the CB turns to who's going where and with what, change the subject or leave the chat. Never get drawn into such matters at truck stops and make sure, whenever you stop, that you are not being followed. While you are stopped, eyeball the people lurking about, walk with confidence and spot anyone taking too much of an interest in you.

This was all beginning to sound a bit more CIA than freight transport. Mouths were already dropping open around the room when Gregg came out with the next piece of trickery, which rendered us all speechless with its simple cleverness and the worrisome nature of a world that made it necessary.

He squirmed a little, trying to be non-sexist while explaining that although it was good advice for anyone it was particularly useful for the girls. When you walk away from your truck, always turn and gesture, wave or call out to a make-believe person in the cab. "Whoever you are, whether your partner's asleep in the bunk or you're driving on your own tell the truck stop you're being watched." I wrote it down. We all did. The guys resolved to tell their wives and girlfriends, who were happily awaiting the chance to go along for the ride, to do it too. We didn't mind a dose of reality. there was no point in pretending women weren't an obvious easy target just for the sake of political correctness. I'd happily wave at non-existent men if it kept trouble at bay.

We learned a lot about attitudes to women on the road that day. Most truckers are gentlemen it seems, apart from a few dinosaurs. Unless a chap had designs on one's load for nefarious purposes we'd be safe enough from other drivers but should keep a weather eye on the Lot Lizards.

Another hazard I'd not really counted on.

I'd heard amusing tales of Lot Lizards from Mick, Owen and Jim back in the B&B days so I was at least familiar with the vernacular. Truck stops provide a decent source of trade for local prostitutes. Our lads would occasionally get young ladies knocking on the cab door late on a cold night if business wasn't brisk enough, I knew this but now we learn that they can be a little territorial. It honestly hadn't occurred to me that I'd be a considered a threat to trade but according to Gregg the territorial Lot Lizard is the lady trucker's main predator.

We will be assumed to be there for nefarious purposes of our own unless we make it obvious that we are driving as part of a couple. If anyone is likely to play the nasty practical joke of 'pulling your pin', ie disconnecting your trailer so that you drive away without it, it will probably be a disgruntled lady of the night. The pin works the release catch for the fifth wheel, which holds the trailer in place. If someone yanks it open while you aren't looking you will drive off leaving the trailer behind without its landing gear down. It falls on its nose, things get broken, winches are required, jobs are lost.

Gregg pointed out that we would all be well advised to check for such nastiness every time we left the truck unattended, but that women are the usual targets. The chaps in the class bristled on our behalf, clearly most truckers were gentlemen. Sherrie and I took a step closer to becoming little class mascots.

Since there were rules for avoiding hijacks I expected rules for avoiding moose but apparently that's not how it's done. They are sufficiently unavoidable that the rules are for hitting one correctly. I have a page in my little notebook full of scrawled Greggisms headed, *How to hit a moose*. The trick is to stay upright and you do that by hitting it square on. Sounds easy enough but one's instinct from driving a car is to swerve to try and miss it. Swerving is the best way to tip both tractor and trailer over sideways and that is Not A Good Thing. You will not miss the moose, you will catch it a glancing blow and the angled forces will help you over. The moose will still die. You, the driver, will hit the ground from a considerable height and get hurt. The load in the trailer will be demolished and a seriously-sized winch truck will be required to get both tractor and trailer up on their wheels again to clear the road. This takes a long time and costs a lot of money.

If you merely come off the accelerator, allow the load to slow you down, brake gently to minimise the impact and square up to hit the poor beastie head on…you will demolish the tractor, kill the moose and get knocked about a bit (it's advisable to duck) but the trailer and load will stay on their wheels and a normal tow truck can clear the road nice and fast.

None of us yet quite understand why you wouldn't see a bloody great moose in the middle of the road in time to avoid it. "You just don't," advises the oracle. "They stand completely still and absorb the light, you never see them until you're about to make contact." We are sceptical. "You can be lucky if your headlight catches an eye, the glint gives you a bit of warning. But if you try and avoid it, you have no way of knowing which way it will run." This is starting to sound a bit like trying to save a penalty.

My notes declare that the best defence against wildlife convergence will be to slow down a little in areas that have warning notices, especially overnight and at dawn. High beams will help too. They spread your pool of light further sideways so that you can catch the glint of animal eyes at the sides of the roads and thus be prepared for them leaping under your wheels. I'm not sure I've got what it takes to drive straight at an animal, I once got a bollocking from an ambulance instructor for trying to avoid a pigeon on a 'shout'. High beams it is.

***

After the alternation of mind-numbing facts and figures and the unexpected terror of Gregg's little life lessons it was a significant relief to get back outside to learn what is meant in this particular industry by yard work. An odd phrase, on most of this continent it means gardening although to a Brit it is closer to meaning a spot of sweeping up than anything else.

In our context however, it means memorising a full check of tractor and trailer to be performed every day before you take it anywhere. You examine the engine before it is switched on. You examine the engine after it is switched on. You check that all the lights are working. You circle the beast methodically, announcing your findings to a putative examiner. You hit the tyres with a little hammer. You clamber underneath to look at suspensions and brake chambers. You measure brake shoes and tyre treads. You run some airbrake tests and make sure gauges are doing what they are supposed to do. Allegedly an experienced driver can make a full circle check in about fifteen minutes. We are currently running at well over an hour.

Some things are easier to remember than others, we all have blind spots and are getting better at helping each other with the gaps. I have fallen into a little team with the other oldies. It suits us, our memories are similarly dodgy and we work at the same pace. Tim tends to forget to check the free play in the steering linkage, Robert needs reminding to mention the trailer air lines and I have a blind spot with regard to whether the tyre valves are centred and capped. All eighteen of them.

A well commentated circle check is a Good Thing, we are given to understand that examiners and employers alike are impressed by it. "If his (or her presumably) driving is half as good as his check we want him," is the way the thought process goes. It is not only the way to get a licence, it is the way to get a job. We repeat it over and over. It is a little boring and we get very dusty. I find myself examining the undersides of trucks as I drive home.

And then we actually got to move a truck. Not far, only the few feet required to become expert at coupling and uncoupling the trailer, but it was real, live, proper moving forwards and backwards of huge vehicle. They were letting me do this. These people who were passionate about safety and correctness and representing the industry with excellence on the road allowed me to climb into the cab of a real truck and throw it around their yard. They weren't humouring me after all, the avuncular ones who twinkled kindly, maybe they didn't just act all encouraging for the sake of another set of course fees. This was worrying because they were my last line of defence. I had to be able to rely on trucking school to say, "Oh stoppit," and call a halt to the madness at some point and preferably before I had too much more fun.

Fortunately, the giddy excitement of moving forwards was tempered a little by the frustrating lack of accuracy in reverse. I had not expected this, just like the clutch it was an area in which I'd expected a slight head start. Despite being expert at reversing an ambulance I seemed to be totally unable to translate the skill to a truck.

The coupling of tractor and trailer involved quite a bit of being-very-accurate and learning what the mirrors could show you. In my case not much, until I twigged that they were set for someone a few inches taller than me. Moving the driving seat forwards far enough to reach the pedals rendered the mirrors useless. Leaning back a bit and sideways a smidge and just-over-there a tad did bring enough trailer into view that I could now watch myself veer wildly off course as I turned the steering wheel towards where I was leaning.

An inch or two out while trying to line up fifth wheels and king pins is another Not A Good Thing. The fifth wheel's jaws will compensate a little and guide the pin into place but perfection is better. Please be impressed by the jargon, I started using it a lot to cover for the disappointment of realising that nothing I'd ever done before was going to help in the slightest. Talking a good drive was about the only thing I could learn fast and it contributed a little to the truckerly camaraderie. I was frustrated with the lack of instant perfection but since the others were struggling too, I opted to allow myself to learn at the same pace as everyone else. That way, maybe I could have a bit of that fun before the *oh stoppit* moment.

What with the winching up and down of trailer landing gear, the remembering of which buttons to push in and out and how to disconnect air lines without having masses of compressed air blow surprisingly in your face (ah yes, there was a picture of that in the text book) and the aforementioned reversing, week two of trucking theory passed in a blur of exams, clambering in and out of trucks, frustration, dust and—finally—fun.

"You'll be going out with your driving instructors on Monday morning," grinned Gregg. What? Now? Are you sure? Can't I play in the yard a bit longer? Have another week spouting jargon? That clutch still feels a bit heavy and I'm not quite sure I've got all the buttons sorted out...yes, a million excuses. Half a lifetime ago I seem to recall writing that it must be good fun to drive a truck. I think that might have been a little naive. What it actually is, is complicated and terrifying.

NOT EXACTLY DRIVING

THERE ARE four of us in a truck made for abusing. A Mack, for the aficionados out there, with a thirteen speed gearbox. Thirteen seems quite a lot. Our on-the-road instructor, Jeff, is quietly spoken and calm. From beneath a baseball cap that appears to be welded on he exudes a gentle confidence that we are all really truck drivers on the inside and his job is merely to bring our innate truckerliness to the surface.

He smiles enigmatically as he stows his cooler containing a somewhat endearing Tupperware of kiddies' breakfast cereal and little tub of cold milk. He gives no sign that he has, this month, drawn the short straw. The geriatric bunch. The grouping of our class into threes for each instructor has been an interesting study in social engineering. The guys-who-have-been-around trucks have been placed together in one little team, the boy racers who might need bringing down a peg in another. We are the forgetful old farts and we made life easy for the course administrators by finding each other last week. We learn at about the same pace. We appear to have been given the instructor with the most patience.

As we clamber into the rear of the cab where what was once somebody's bed has been turned into some rough seating, two things are observable immediately. Despite being a relatively normal height Jeff settles into the driving seat by lowering it to the floor. I would like to ask why but it's hard to get a word in. Tim has not stopped chattering since we all espied each other in the early morning gloom.

We wait politely for a pause and I consider buying him a coffee tomorrow since there would then have to be a break in the wittering for sips and slurps. Jeff, once installed on the floor, his nose level with the bottom of the windscreen, baseball cap snug over his eyes, regards the three of us. Robert is paying quiet attention, I am twitching with the effort of trying to get a question in edgeways and Tim is still telling us about, um, something. We all stopped listening a while ago. We know it's a nerves thing.

The silent eyes upon him, Tim realises that he is still talking. He apologises and tells us he will stop and listen now. This takes several minutes, which Jeff uses to complete his air brake tests and fill in his log book.

Robert fades further into the background, he appears to appreciate the absence of attention. Taciturn by nature, we will all learn over the weeks that the more anxious Robert is the quieter he becomes. There will be times when the driving seat seems almost to be occupied by a black hole whereas, impossible though it appears on that first morning, Tim will actually get chattier as his stress levels rise. Me? I will stop breathing.

"Just watch and listen," Jeff advises us with a slight

emphasis on the word 'listen' and a beady eye on Tim. "I'm going to describe everything I do, you'll have to do the same when you're driving." He pulls smoothly out of the school yard, into the traffic and off down the road. He counts out the beats as he changes from gear to gear, leaving that perfect gap between slipping the gearlever in and out of neutral as the engine drops its perfect 300 rpm. We are sitting in a moving truck. It is a glorious thing.

As Jeff drives us to the quiet industrial area where trucks can get into trouble without causing trouble, he talks us through every move, every observation and every decision. This is the sort of commentary drive we will have to produce on Ministry test day and the demo version is polished, calm and unhurried. Everything sounds quite straightforward. Gregg's gleeful final words to us from last week recede into the background. "We won't be dignifying what you do on Monday with the word 'driving'." What does he know? It looks easy enough.

Jeff's plan for the nursery slopes is that we will drive round a simple right-handed circuit relatively undisturbed, practising gear changes and the like. I offer to go first. This gambit seems like the best way to ditch the nerves early, then I might stand a chance of learning something watching the others instead of wasting the time dreading my turn. I adjust the seat upwards, which is odd taking over from someone taller than me but that question will have to wait, it has flown out of my head in the tailspin of trying to remember everything else. I take my time looking around, reminding myself where all the knobs and levers are. This is approved of, you can call it 'checking your gauges' if you like, and you can pretend you recall what they should be telling you.

Setting off is a piece of cake, we have done this before in the yard. Of course the spot of moving to and fro that we are used to from learning how to hook up a trailer only involved one gear, all that timed double-declutching to match the engine revs is yet to come. I'd tried to practise it in the car on the way home of an evening with limited success. However, I am in the driving seat of a real live truck and we are moving, therefore I am queen of the road. The sun is shining and we will have fun.

It would appear to be time to change gear.

"Are you going to spend all day in second gear?"

"No, I'm checking my revs."

"And are they telling you anything?"

"Yes, they're telling me I have to change gear."

"Go on then…"

"Ok, um, I'm in second gear." I announce it with pride, as if to compensate for not quite being in third yet. I am getting the hang of this commentary lark.

"1400, one...two into third gear, come on, do it now".

"Right, I am changing into third gear, one, two, oh..."

The crunching, grinding and juddering come as a shock. I have no idea what went wrong, the truck is still moving, we are not in any sort of gear. I am looking aghast at the gear lever and not the road. We shudder to a halt.

Trucks don't have synchromesh on their gears like cars do. Each gear change has to be effected with two dips of the clutch (but not all the way to the floor, that's only for when you stop and is A Bad Thing otherwise because of something called a clutch brake. Which I have yet to completely understand.)

The first dip should happen when the engine reaches exactly 1400 rpm, for changing up and 1100 rpm for changing down. The second dip must be precisely 300 rpm down for changing up and 300 rpm up for changing down. (I didn't know it then but different trucks have different 'sweet spots' for optimal gear changing and what's more, some like different rpm depending on which range you're in, but we're getting ahead of ourselves here and it's brain numbing enough already.) So changing up is easy enough, you just need to develop a bit of muscle memory for the rhythm, the perfect 300 rpm delay as the engine slows. I am reliably informed that saying "one…two" out loud really does help to get it right. Presumably if it's accompanied by an absence of crunches one feels slightly less silly.

"It'll take a while to get the timing right, don't worry," the patient man opines, "but try to get out of the habit of looking at the gearlever while you're going along." I am crushed. That was the first thing they had to tell you about learning to drive a car wasn't it? Just how far have I regressed?

Robert and Tim are trying very hard to be very small which isn't easy given that they are both strapping chaps. I appreciate the sensation that there is no-one really sitting behind me though, it's kind of them to behave like mice for me despite the fact that their innate chapness will ensure they won't go through this embarrassing hell as well.

We set off again. This time the first gear shift goes relatively well, only a bit crunchy. More Malteser than Almond brittle. The next is even better, minimal crunch, and things look up. Until the corner. I am only half registering Jeff's instructions because the panic has shut down my hearing. I do know that the next trick is learning to turn right and I do see the road on the right approaching…

"Go straight, it isn't a car, you can't make the turn until your mirror meets the kerb otherwise you'll clip the sidewalk with your trailer." I only hear, "Go straight." I miss the rest and think that Jeff has changed his mind about making the turn after all. We sail past the road that I am subliminally aware we might have had to turn into, I am just happy to be in the right gear.

"Why didn't you make the turn?"

"You said go straight." Jeff sighs.

"I know I said go straight, but…" he gives up on the explanation as we all see a major road heaving into view.

"We're out on the main road now, I wasn't planning that for today but you'll have to do it. Listen carefully. And don't look at the gearlever."

I listened, we survived. Gear changes happened, some of them entirely unregarded by the person who should be looking at the road. I began to understand why Jeff spoke so softly, you had to really concentrate to hear him and that concentration cut through some of the blind (and deaf) panic.

All three of us messed up in similar ways, which was faintly reassuring. My assumption had been wrong, chapness made no difference. Sometimes a gear shift went well, the occasional not-unsuccessful turn, we could hold it together for whole minutes at a time commentating like experts. Then an old car habit would reassert itself—too deep on the clutch, revving through a gear change, mistiming the double declutch, a turn of the wheel too soon—and the mind imploded.

To an unconcerned observer it may have looked as

though we all blanked in the same way, the hands and feet flailed helplessly whoever was driving, but we came to understand that different portions of hell waited for each of us.

Robert's blanks were quiet. As his commentary dwindled to nothing we'd realise the black hole was driving. "Talk to me," Jeff would urge. "Tell me what you're seeing and doing, if you say it, you'll do it. Come on, which gear are you in? What can you see?" Robert just wasn't a talker. He had a family full of kids and grandkids, there had never been any necessity to fill the air with sound for himself before. He was trucker-shaped and capable, he was everything a future knight of the road should be except verbose. Asking him to say anything under stress was to torture the poor man and we all knew the examiner would demand just that on test day.

Tim's meltdowns were predictably chatty. "Ah yes I see now that I should have changed gear a bit sooner but it's taking me that bit of time to read the tach and make sure it's exact because Gregg said that you have to change at exactly 1400 revs so by the time I've realised that I'm at 1400 and go to think about the gear change I'm actually closer to 1500 and then I'm not sure what to do about the gear change but of course I realise that next time I just have to do it all a bit quicker..."

We all watch the red traffic light draw closer. Tim is still reliving the previous issue, it's a commentary of sorts but trouble is looming. "Leave it behind you and concentrate on the next thing. Tell me what you can see now, not what you did before." Jeff experimented with different ways to intercept the never-ending sentences. Just as Robert had to learn to talk it out, Tim had to learn to shut it up.

And me? I learned to verbalise my personal circle of hell relatively precisely before stopping breathing. Which may or may not have been useful for Jeff.

"I can see the light change and I know I have to gear down, however I have forgotten which gear I'm in," at which point my world would diminish down to an area a few inches in diameter around the gear lever.

"It's the same gear that you just told me you were changing up into," Jeff coaxes me, pointlessly.

"I know that."

"You said it out loud, remember?"

"Yes."

"It'll be easier to remember if you don't hold your breath."

"Yes."

"So you're going to change back down from…?"

"I've still forgotten." He gives up, tells me which gear I'm in and reminds me again to breathe in and out and look out of the windscreen as well.

***

By the end of day one, things were approaching encouraging. I could 'upshift' through the gears almost reliably with nary a crunch or a judder, I could turn right without mounting the pavement with my back wheels. Some 'downshifts' were getting there too, even though they were more complex.

It's the same engine ratio thing in reverse, the rpm has to go up by 300 instead of down for the cogs to settle into each other. That requires an extra movement, a little 'voom' on the throttle as you watch your gauge to bring the revs up exactly the right amount, while you are patting your head and rubbing your tummy at the same time. Difficult enough to coordinate in isolation but well-nigh impossible along with reading the road, slowing for traffic lights or sizing up a turn. But I chose to celebrate visible progress, conquering the most complex of all gearboxes was under way and I was back to being queen of the road. I'd have those pesky downshifts mastered during tomorrow's turn in the quiet industrial area where we could go round in undisturbed circles. Another week making gentle right turns on deserted roads and you'd definitely be able to dignify what I was doing with the word 'driving'. That gearbox was as good as beaten.

Day two dawned and we gathered in the yard for more of the easy, quiet driving. I'd bought coffee for us all and confidently volunteered to do the circle check. I was glad I'd gone first yesterday, I would be less anxious sitting in the back until my turn today. I knew what we would be doing and I was making progress, I'd not waste the first hour of driving time being all scared. I checked the lights and kicked the tyres like a real trucker and made a mental note to ask Jeff why he put the driving seat down on the floor when he did it again today as he got in to drive us to the nursery. But he had other plans.

He climbed in the wrong side, stowed his cereal and milk and informed us that the first driver of the day was going to take us out of the yard and into traffic.

"We can't do that!"

"Of course you can."

"No but, we need more time turning right."

"You'll turn right today."

"But, I haven't practised downshifting enough yet."

"Don't worry, you'll get plenty of practice."

"But…"

Each of us in turn underwent a very personal nightmare. We knew those bits of stuff that had gone tolerably well yesterday would evade us totally when there were a hundred other things to look at on the road. And they did.

"Talk to me," said Jeff. "If you say it, you'll do it, remember, and it'll help you concentrate."

"Waiting until my mirror is level with the sidewalk, making the turn, observing my trailer wheels, I've completed my turn, checking my mirrors, my trailer is safely round, one-two into fifth, gosh that didn't crunch, I am observing that pedestrian…and I've forgotten which gear I'm in."

We each had our unique blind spots, old car-driving ways that we just couldn't shake off. The more overwhelmed with information we were, the easier it was to relax into a familiar habit. Robert had trouble only pushing the clutch part way in to change gear, Tim couldn't unlearn accelerating through an upshift. I mastered both of these but still couldn't retain in my head which gear I was in for longer than a nanosecond, despite saying them all out loud as I went along.

Changing up became instinctive relatively quickly but the car driver in me had to unlearn thirty years of block downshifts. Changing down one gear at a time, an essential trucking skill, challenged me to recall where I was in the system, where the switch from high to low range fitted in and whether the gearlever had to go the wrong way or not.

We slogged through the local traffic, arms, legs and

brains in overload for hours. By the end of day two, some whole minutes went by when I could read the road, commentate on it and breathe in and out just like the star emergency driver I used to be. But inexorably, that moment when it would all fall apart was lurking, ready to pounce. The world would slow down, I would go deaf…"I've forgotten which gear I'm in." I drove home dejectedly to tell friends that I might have to give up this stupid idea and take up needlework instead.

"How's it going?" asked one of the pals who had already declared an interest in reading the book.

"Not great, it's a lot harder than it looks."

"I'll bet, but that's why you're doing it, right?"

"I suppose. But I don't think I'll ever get it. I'm too old, it's not coming together as fast as it used to."

"How long have you been learning?"

"In the cab? Two days."

"That's not very long. How long was your ambulance driving course?"

"Two weeks."

"Well then."

"But, I thought I was a good driver…"

"Ok, here's a question. How many of the blokes do you think are fretting over not being perfect on day one?"

"They'll get it though."

"And so will you, you just think you need to be bloody superwoman all the time. You don't have to be the best, just good enough."

"I want to be best though."

"You're impossible."

"You just want a book to read."

"Well, yeah."

***

Day three introduced the famous buttonhook turns. We were deemed to have learned how to turn right and left the easy way, with lots of space and plenty of lanes. We would now learn how to make turns without enough available road space for a 53 foot trailer. I'd heard the theory, Gregg had described this technique in class complete with little toy trucks and pictures of roads. If you are going to turn into a road which is too narrow for a normal turn, you do it by making your truck look like a buttonhook first.

It might have helped to have seen a buttonhook possibly, I have no idea what one looks like so can't advise on the accuracy of the representation. It sounded relatively straightforward though, all you had to do was be in the right gear before you started (hah) and then you had plenty of time to think about things like occupying both lanes to stop cars trying to undertake you, signalling right when you were going left, turning left when you were going right, and completing the turn without flattening street furniture or causing other drivers to reverse away from you in horror. Frightening other road users would be an instant fail apparently.

It began well enough. I'd been a bit hazy over the point of it all with the toys but remembering the theory and suddenly understanding it as Jeff demonstrated the turn was a real high. Today was the day when I wouldn't forget what gear I was in. I'd had my pep talk, people with no idea what driving a truck was like believed in me and Jeff thought we were ready to learn a new technique. There had been progress, there would be more. I would produce a sudden and radical improvement, and restore my faith in my ability to learn stuff. I might be over fifty, with a failing memory and a spot of arthritis in my clutch knee, but I could still be brilliant. Hey, I could be the best.

"I've forgotten which gear I'm in." Jeff is a patient man.

We were all in the dumps. Robert, Tim and I united in a combination of disappointment in ourselves and relief that the others were struggling too. We heard from groups in other trucks all about the fun they were having. "Oh, buttonhook turns, we've got those down, we're using the Jake on grades now." I was at one and the same time proud to know what using the Jake on grades meant, but mortified that my buttonhooks still left plenty to be desired. "If we're never going to get it, would you be telling us by now?" Jeff grinned. And told us we would be reversing tomorrow. I relaxed a little. Reversing meant a big empty compound and no traffic, time to really get to grips with stuff. Maybe that would help.

***

The reversing yard was huge and almost empty. It sported a few trailers and some lines of tyres and bollards and stuff, things to manoeuvre around but at least they had the decency to remain stationary. Jeff demonstrated what we were to do, merely reverse the trailer in a straight line and into a parking bay directly behind us. It looked simple until you tried it, whereupon the old difficulty of unlearning deeply ingrained habits came back into play. The back of a trailer goes the opposite way to the back of a car and magnifies the slightest error hugely a couple of seconds after it's too late to correct it.

My first go produced some strange shenanigans in my mirrors (and presumably 53 feet behind me) but somehow something clicked. The agony of the school yard had taught me something, I knew not to steer the way I was leaning and I was grateful for the lesson. The next run worked. And the next. I could reverse in a straight line and into a parking bay. Not only that, I could breathe in and out at the same time.

"You've got that pretty well," mused Jeff, "try the bay next to it, just turn here and straighten up there, see how it goes." It went haywire the first time, then a bit better and then I appeared to be parked.

"Ok," Jeff enthused, jumping onto the step outside my driver's door for the ride. "Here's how to execute the parallel park you need to learn for the Ministry test. Right lock when your trailer wheels get to here, left lock when your mirror gets to there, straighten up, stop at the sign, look at the hockey stick." Hockey stick? Why am I looking for a hockey stick?

"The angle your trailer makes with the tractor, it's the shape of a..."

"Got it...thank you."

There were several more sightlines to master, turning this way and that as items appeared and disappeared in various mirrors. We had a bit of a language barrier over bollards and pylons but then things improved. I'd like to be able to tell you that I got it right away but actually I had to write down each stage and draw myself a diagram of what it was supposed to make the trailer do, turning the paper around and waving my hands in the air quite a bit. But then, move by move, section by section, I got it right.

By the end of the day it was almost there. "You're still

leaving it a little late to straighten up," Jeff was getting picky now, "that's why it's slightly crooked, but you're ahead of the game. Most people are still trying to do a straight line. There are three more days here before the test, you'll be fine."

A switch flipped in my head. I had got a thing faster than some, I was the best at being a rookie reverser. Something looked as though it would be fine for the test, on day one! There was now a thing I wasn't frightened of which meant that I wasn't frightened of everything. Before that session of throwing a trailer backwards around an empty yard I had actually been frightened of the truck itself. I realised that I hadn't been driving it, it had been driving me. But now things had changed. I was in control. I could do it and tomorrow would be better. No really. This time there would be no blanks, no panics, I would become a confident driver again as opposed to a pathetic heap of incompetence with a fixation for observing the gear lever instead of the road. Superwoman had done her pirouette.

Day five dawned bright, the end of week one on the road. The sunrise bloomed red and gorgeous over the expressway as I drove to school. I imagined myself trucking through similar fabulous scenery as dawn broke every day of my new career. I took my seat at the wheel of our truck with a smug smile.

"Second gear to exit the yard, hazards off, right signal on, traffic is clear and I'm making the turn. Rpm at 1400, one-two into third, one-two into fourth, watching the pedestrian and stopping with room to spare."

"Turn left at the next lights, it's a buttonhook."

"Left buttonhook? But I've only done right ones."

49

"Principle is the same, just the other way."

"Um, ok, I'm signalling left, taking this lane, no that one, am I in the wrong lane now? Where am I turning again? I've forgotten what gear I'm in."

We stopped for a post-meltdown coffee. Honestly, what was the point of pep talks and getting a thing right and having switches flipped in your head and remembering to breathe if you were still useless? It had been a whole week and I was still, well, a rookie. Someone who had only been driving trucks for a week. The humiliation was utter.

As I got back into the driving seat Jeff adopted a psychological persona, which tussled a bit with the baseball cap.

"How anxious are you? On a scale of one to ten? About eight or nine?"

"Can't be quite a ten because I was worse on day one but not much. Hmm, eight-and-a-half-ish."

"It's good to be a bit keyed up, keeps you sharp, but not too much. Bring it down to about a six...breathe out now." I breathed out, and actually did bring my anxiety down to about six on a ten point scale. Then I drove. Really drove.

"Red light ahead, I want to be in fourth before I get there, I'm in seventh now so I'm downshifting to sixth, one...two, watching the parked cars, lights still red, double down to fourth, 1100 revs, blimey it went in, taking my position in the left lane, lights have changed and I can take it through, junction clear, no pedestrians, my trailer is safely across..." It went on and on. I lost a few gears along the way but more went in than not and I didn't go deaf or stupid even once.

Jeff knew his stuff. This taciturn trucker who'd hauled

dangerous loads of sheet metal for 25 years turned out to be a real psychologist, headgear notwithstanding. He would spot the light bulb going on and then pinpoint why you thought it had gone out again. The see-saw of emotions that made sense on the inside was about as relevant to actual progress as rerunning the last gear change while you were approaching the red light, but only he knew that at the time. I was grateful and slightly embarrassed. I wasn't normally that mercurial and I was officially done behaving like a hysterical girlie.

As our first week of driving drew to a close it was entirely possible that I might be able to do this after all.

***

Another whole week went by and to be honest my driving was only a little better but my commentary was coming along a treat. The gear changes were erratic, some perfect, some awful. The buttonhook turns, ditto. Nothing was consistently good but talking it through helped me to leave each screw-up behind and concentrate on the next thing. The chaps put it down to women just generally talking too much but they smiled as they teased. We were all pleased when someone found a coping mechanism.

The only remaining concern commentary-wise was whether the examiner would accept English English, I was under enough pressure without remembering words like intersection. These were destined to remain junctions just as my hazards would never become four-ways. Level crossings were staying level crossings, I couldn't say 'railroad tracks' without feeling like I was auditioning for some sort of movie. Apart from anything else, my versions were quicker to say and made for a snappier commentary. I'd had to cave in on the vexed topic of 'pavement' and that was as far I was prepared to go. (That's what they call the tarmac over here so digging my heels in sidewalk-wise had led to some worrying misunderstandings.)

Jeff noticed the big change before I did. An irrepressible grin had started to plaster my features as soon as I took my turn in the hot seat. I liked being up there seeing it all happen. The fun was under way. The more I relaxed, the more I noticed and the more I noticed, the more I relaxed. That grin got wider and wider. The glee took over every time a simple turn signal from me produced exaggerated reactions in the drivers round me.

The things that Gregg had said about truckers controlling the road started to make sense, as soon as you let it be known that you wished to make a turn or change a lane things happened. People reacted. Drivers either dropped back to let you in or accelerated to race past you.

I wasn't sure whether this was because we were in a truck *per se* or whether it was because we were in a truck that said TRAINING in very big letters on all sides but I wanted to find out, I really did.

"Can you taste it yet?" asked Jeff during one of his regular pep talks. He had begun to play tricks and crack jokes, to chat and to be light hearted. By this time I knew that nothing this man did was without a reason, I was being manipulated into a new mindset. He wished me to know that it was possible to chat and joke at the wheel, that this could be an enjoyable life. Of course as soon as the chatting took over too far the gear shifts went to pieces but, "Now you're getting sloppy...concentrate," was all it took.

I mentioned to Jeff that I was writing a book.

"You're in it of course."

"I bet, what as? 'The arse who trained me?'"

"Not at all, I've been very complimentary."

"Hmm, I quite like that, I wouldn't mind being 'the arse who trained me.'"

***

We finally had our dates for our Ministry road test, precisely a week and a half away. What with Thanksgiving long weekend in the middle that left seven more driving days to get competent enough for an external examiner. Two of those days would be in the reversing yard. (My parallel park was just top hole by then but the backing into bays, which was a lot closer to the sort of thing we'd have to do for real, left a little to be desired. It was neat enough, but fairly random as to which actual bay it was neatly enough in. I did a good line in reversing perfectly into the bay next to the one I was aiming for. Freight companies may not like that.) Two from seven left five more drives. Could one go from happy but sloppy to good enough in a week? Jeff seemed to think so.

It was the Friday before Thanksgiving. I was determined to enjoy my drive and put thoughts of tests back in the box labelled *worry about that another time*. The vehicle was inspected and ready to go, just the brake tests before we set off. Trailer spring brakes tested, tractor spring brakes tested. Trailer service brakes tested, tractor service brakes tested. Off we should have gone but the vehicle wouldn't budge.

What had I done? All the brakes were off surely? I just tested them. "Maybe we didn't put the chocks away," suggested Robert. I clambered out of the cab to check the chocks (partly because I liked saying it) but there was no sign of them and then Tim remembered putting them away so I tried again. Elaborately rechecking that all the brakes were off I popped effortlessly into gear and attempted to pull away gracefully. Nothing happened. In desperation I looked at Jeff who was apoplectic with amusement.

"What have I done?"

"Nothing," chortled the arse who trained me, "I've got my foot on the dual control brake."

.

THE MAN FROM THE MINISTRY

THANKSGIVING came and went, a long weekend spent brimming with confidence and enthusiasm and telling all and sundry that I was a trucker, as good as. Goodness my friends were impressed. Even falling off a horse during an ill-advised holiday Monday trail ride and cracking a rib didn't dampen the hubris. I was a trucker now. I was all tough and could handle anything.

Then came the interim evaluation. The school's final check to ensure we were making sufficient progress to be worth putting in for that road test. It was an unwelcome dose of reality, a reminder that the fun wasn't really the point. We needed that licence to be able to work and the school needed to uphold a sterling reputation by keeping potential failures back before they made everyone look silly.

I sat at the wheel of my truck all calm and smirking a little. The painkillers had kicked in and I'd managed to climb into the cab with panache, exactly as though I wasn't an old lady with a cracked rib. My running commentary was smooth as silk. "Second gear for the yard, go deep to avoid the building with the trailer, hazards off, right signal on, watch the trailer wheels, keep straight, wait for the traffic to clear." My turn from out of the school was textbook. Then I attempted the first gear change. My rib kicked me, exactly as though it was another horse, and everything fell to bits.

Nothing went right. Nary a gear fell into place, the commentary lapsed into occasional squeaks, we coasted through intersections, we clipped kerbs with trailer wheels...and we omitted to mention lurking pedestrians. Admittedly I'd skimped on the painkillers, not wanting to get drowsy at the wheel but that was no excuse for a professional driver was it? The final tally of awfulness, a spectacular fail laid bare on Jeff's score sheet for all to see, wiped out all the progress I thought I'd made. I was clearly the most useless driver this continent had ever seen and ought to be shot as an example to others.

I burst into tears. In thirty years I have never cried at work. Women trying to make it in men's occupations despise such appalling weakness, it shouldn't happen. It's an insult to the sisterhood. I was even more ashamed of breaking the rules for feminine trailblazing than I was of failing my evaluation.

Comfort came from all sides. Instructors I hardly knew and had never spoken to appeared from nowhere to dry my eyes and reassure me that everyone has a bad day and that I was doing fine. That maybe having a broken rib was some sort of excuse after all. I was a decent driver having an off moment, they said.

This helped a bit but not much. I did know of fellow

students who weren't being encouraged. One had already been advised to leave the course before he'd ever tried to turn a wheel due to not having a hope in hell of ever making it. A couple of others had been interviewed by the head honcho about their lack of progress. The rumour mill had generated sympathy and encouragement for them as the class became a cohesive unit despite our bizarrely different backgrounds. But the school remained firm, some people would require more time. These trainers didn't appear to mess about with putting total incompetents in charge of eighteen wheels. (And, let's face it, I was totally the wrong age and shape for any hidden reasons for such ministrations.)

So the fact that everyone thought I could do it and the school was going to put me in for the test anyway despite a dreadful evaluation should have made it ok. But now at the last minute after the emotional rollercoaster of the previous weeks there were several new hurdles to the vital business of getting licenced.

I had to process the fact that this was no longer a lark, I really wanted to succeed. I had to get my confidence back from somewhere. I also had to find a combination of painkillers that would deaden the discomfort enough to be able to move my body without deadening my concentration into the bargain. I had to work out what on earth was going on with those once reliable gearshifts and, most vitally, I had to live down the heinous crime of tears before bedtime. Truckers just didn't do that.

Putting it all back together took every minute of our remaining driving hours. We were now officially 'getting ready for the test' and the rest of our time was devoted to teaching us the test routes and their traps and tricks. There were two AZ examiners at our local test centre and each had a favourite circuit. Jeff planned to take us round them both. We sneaked in to the test centre early one morning before anyone else arrived and each spent some time trying to convert the reverse parallel park manoeuvre we'd learned in the backing yard to the space allotted for it behind the Transport Ministry offices.

"It's an identical set-up," said Jeff, "just do what you did before." Tim verbalised what we were all thinking,

"Actually, it looks a lot narrower."

"That's an optical illusion," Jeff reassured us, "just because you're between buildings instead of pylons and they're taller." I knew by then that when he said pylons he really meant bollards, so the fact that buildings aren't taller than pylons didn't upset me the way it would have done a few weeks earlier. And daring yourself to stick to the formula—full lock here, count to three, full lock the other way, stop by the door—did work despite the illusion that you were about to smack a building. And the obvious added complication of not wanting the first building you smacked to be the Ministry of Transport of Ontario's DriveTest Centre.

Then we went off round the first test route. The lady examiner's favoured circuit. Robert drove it while Tim and I sat in the back craning our necks to see the difficult bits. The first complication was getting out of the test centre itself. It was located in a normal shopping plaza with a car park full of people living their lives. There was a blind corner to negotiate as you emerged from behind the building (remember to say you're looking for pedestrians), followed by an awkward turn out of the plaza during which it was easy to mount the pavement (must state:

"Sidewalk clear!") Then came a left turn into a three-lane road on a blind bend and a hill (whatever you do don't encroach on the far lane). Within feet, another left turn at traffic lights (must cancel left signal and then put it on again). The route got simpler briefly, a spot of normal driving onto the expressway and off again to demonstrate one's merging skills and then...three consecutive buttonhook turns.

"It's not too bad," Jeff opined, "they're not quite as tight as the ones you've been doing." (That would be the ones none of us could quite achieve yet without clipping the kerb and frightening people.) "Only thing is, there are telephone poles right on the edge of the sidewalk so if you do misjudge one you won't just clip the kerb, you'll get your trailer wedged on the pole. One guy did that and the examiner had to take over and reverse him out." Good to know, as I think teenagers now say.

We all began to obsess over the details.

"How many crunchy gears can you get away with?"

"Oh they might let you get away with one."

"One? That's inhuman."

"How many of your students pass?"

"That depends on you, I can only teach you what to do, you have to concentrate and do it."

"Can you forget to say 'intersection clear' once maybe? If you remember it all the other times?" We are nitpicking now.

"Just tell him everything that you see, think and do, you'll be fine."

***

Another early morning, another test route. The gentleman examiner favours a route somewhat longer but less sprinkled with buttonhooks. Just the one, although there are some dodgy lane changes to negotiate instead. Tim drove this one with Robert and me doing the craning.

We finished a little early so that afternoon I popped out in the car, headed up to the test centre and drove round in several circles. Twice out onto the blind bend and back into the test center to get the layout of those initial turns into my head, then I drove the short test circuit followed by the long one. I noted down the best places for lane changes, the sneaky speed limit alterations, the distance from the kerb of those terrifying telephone poles and took one more look at the optical illusion created by buildings replacing bollards in your mirrors.

I sat in my car in the reversing bay behind the ministry for a little while. People looked at me curiously, my mouth may have been moving. I was commentating drives in my sleep by then so I was probably talking to myself without realising it. I was also waking in the night in the middle of a downshift from fifth to fourth on a regular basis, I could tell by the shape of the duvet and the disgusted cat that I was hitting the throttle for real.

The phone rang one morning when we were scheduled to start a little later. I was enjoying a luxurious second cup of coffee at the time. It was Gwen.

"Have you got your licence yet?" I was being head hunted. How bizarre.

"Not yet, another week before the test and then some short courses, it won't be long." I sounded more confident than I felt.

"Call me."

And yes I would call Gwen, if all went well. I had been researching trucking companies. Her outfit, Challenger Motor Freight came out well on all comparisons. They had a comprehensive apprenticeship scheme, a decent reputation and they paid good money. They were also very local. The chap who sat next to me in class used to be one of their mechanics and he had told me all about their maintenance routines, they sounded safe. Best of all, they provided chaps to grub about under your truck checking brake adjustments while you sat all warm in the cab. I knew enough by then to understand that these details can matter.

They were also, in the financial climate of rocketing fuel costs and the collapse of smaller outfits, buying up the little people. Big may not necessarily be beautiful under all circumstances but a large company with a secure future seemed attractive just then. It looked like I almost had a job, I really did have to pass that test.

Time concertinaed. There were better days and worse days and in the blink of an eye it was the day before my appointment with the Ministry and Jeff was asking, "What would you like to practise on your last drive?" I opted for having a go at the turn out of the test centre—I'd done it in the car but not in the truck—and then some churning relentlessly up and down through the gears.

"That's the wrong lane," said Jeff as I chose a spot to exit the test centre from, "and so is that, you can't do that tomorrow you'll fail before you even leave the parking lot." I took a hapless guess at the positioning for the next left turn. "What are you doing now? That's much too deep, that's a fail too." It all looked different from higher up. I was inconsolable. What was the point?

"Leave it behind," Jeff adopted 'ology mode, "we'll do it again later. You can drive, you've been doing it all your life, just drive now." And drive I did. Every gear change fell into place and as I worried less about the gears I saw more of the road. I was driving, making decisions, watching my trailer wheels instinctively instead of because I'd been told to, commentating up a storm, getting safely from a to b, and yes, feeling like a real truck driver. At last everything fell into place with mere hours to go. I'd forgotten in all the learning of new stuff that driving was something I knew how to do. We returned to the test centre to do the exit again. I saw the lines on the road this time, realised what needed to be done and did it.

The school calculates that it takes 32 hours to rip your driving apart and put it back together again. I had needed every last one of them but it did finally look possible. It was feasible that things might go ok the following day. I would need an absence of bad luck—none of it was quite hard-wired enough to withstand the unexpected—but, well, not-bad-luck might happen mightn't it?

I woke at five the next morning and couldn't get back to sleep. I rehearsed vehicle checks in my head, ran through the reversing routine and upset the cat by changing a few gears. "How anxious am I now on a scale of one to ten? About seven. That's ridiculous, you're not there yet and you need somewhere to go later with this. What's reasonable for being in bed before you are anywhere near the test centre? Threeish? Yes threeish. Ok, deep breaths and down to three." It worked. "Now you can get three more anxious later and still be functional."

The cat settled down again and I gave up on sleep. Logging on to the internet, I looked for someone to chat with. An old pal from England was online. I told her how nervous I was and explained that I could do it all if I thought about it but that it fell to bits when something unexpected happened. Jo and I share some skills in training and instructing various things, it's one of the hats I wore before emigrating. "Ah," she wrote, "conscious competence, that's fine."

An alert in my head went beep. I knew all that stuff, the competence chain. Conscious competence was where most of my decent students had got to when they went for their assessments. They did fine if they kept their heads. I had a label for my progress and that meant it was not just feasible but actually quite likely that I could do it.

I thanked her profusely for reminding me that training theory did not cease to exist just because I was on the other side of the fence. I got up, dressed and cruised into school to collect Jeff and the truck with my anxiety level still at about a threeish. People appeared from offices and classrooms and I received a resounding chorus of 'good luck's from all and sundry. Except Gregg.

"I'm not saying 'good luck' because I know you don't need it."

"Thank you. I think."

After a decent drive up there, we had a bit of a wait. The chap before the chap before me was performing his circle check. We watched from a discreet distance. It appeared to go fine. We watched him uncouple and recouple his trailer. That looked ok too. The examiner pointed, that meant the reverse was next.

You would know if you had passed the yard work portion of your test if the examiner actually climbed into the truck. If you screwed up before that point the test would be halted and nobody drove anywhere.

"He's taken that turn a bit early, he might not make it," Jeff told us, just as a loud yell rose from behind somewhere. The examiner emerged beckoning to the unfortunate student's instructor. This test was over, the yell had been to prevent some wall-smacking. We all shuddered a little and I realised I had been holding my breath on the hapless chap's behalf.

Next up was our class star, the guy everyone knew would make it from day one. His check, coupling and reverse were rapid and perfect. The examiner climbed in, they were going driving. Twenty minutes later they were back and shaking hands. It could happen then, except that now it was me.

The gentleman examiner. That meant the single buttonhook and the lane changes. The pre-trip inspection went smoothly, I was talking, I could do that. I remembered the tyre valves ("Centred and capped, sir,") and even called the bonnet a hood. We knew that you could tell it had been a good check if they stopped you half way round, working on the principle that one side of a truck is pretty much like another. It meant you'd remembered it all and didn't need a chance to redeem yourself.

"What might you check on the other side of this truck?"

"The landing gear handle must be safely stowed sir, and the inspection certificates must be in date."

"Very good."

We were on to the next thing, uncoupling and recoupling the trailer. My biggest anticipated problem here was reconnecting the electrical cable. It was high up, awkward to get to and very tight-fitting. I didn't have either the height or the upper body strength to just pop it home like the chaps did, so I had to resort to squeezing my body between the tyre and the mudguard to get my entire weight directly behind the stupid thing. This looks absurd, you have to contort yourself round the wheel like some diesel-encrusted version of that TV show, *Hole in the Wall*. (I now know that nobody ever really does it that way, the hard way, ever again. The Test tests things that haven't been necessary for decades.)

The examiner thoughtfully stayed out of sight. I looked daft unobserved, adrenalin gave the cable an extra bit of oomph and another successful chunk of test was out of the way. Next, the dreaded reverse. "Remember the chocks, remember to get out and look." These had been mantras all night and all morning. I remembered the chocks and I got out and looked. It was perfect. No, really. Perfect!

"Ok," said the examiner, "let's go for a drive." Adopting a tone which was aiming for polite but which came out ludicrously solemn I advised him that I might be referring to things in the English vernacular, confessing to reverting to my old language when nervous as though I were seeking absolution. His face was difficult to read. As I covered my embarrassment by 'checking the gauges' he settled down next to me with the exam form, a pen and a huge pad of lined notepaper.

The blind corner (no pedestrians) behind me, the difficult left turn (sidewalk clear) over with, the next left perfectly in lane, I began to relax. I was driving and it was fine. The gears were going in. The commentary was sounding relatively professional, if a little English. The examiner put down his form and began to write on his notepaper. This was odd, I thought they just put crosses in boxes. Perhaps that was just the training school way, maybe the Ministry required longhand notes for trucks. There were an awful lot of longhand notes though, he was writing lists and whole sentences, he seemed to have a lot to say about my driving. Every so often he looked at another booklet too, something coloured. I didn't want to take my eyes off the road to see what he was up to so I tried to blot it out. I was driving and it seemed to me as though not too much was going wrong, what would be would be.

I ramped up the commentary to take my mind off his voluminous jottings. "Watching the cyclist, passing my point of no return, checking the crossing guard, keeping an eye on those children..."

The buttonhook came and went. We cruised on and off the expressway and he lifted his eyes briefly from his writing pad to check the mirrors for my lane changes. The traffic was kind. The gearbox cooperated for the main part, a few slightly crunchy ones but no more than you'd expect in a box of mixed chocs. In no time we were approaching the test centre again and I relaxed even more.

One more set of lights (remember to straddle the lanes) one more turn (sidewalk clear) and....I'm in the wrong gear for the final turn into the test centre. I have left it too late to gear down. I'm used to stopping at the last set of lights but this time they stayed green. Taking the right turn in fourth would be ok normally but now I must manoeuvre into the car park. The truck begins to complain. In my panic, I miss the sidewalk comment. As we judder to an unprofessional stop I add, "Oh, and that last sidewalk was clear," somewhat cravenly in the hope that this will help.

He is still writing. He puts his longhand notes away, picks up the test form and pops an x in a box. He seems a little distracted.

"That's a pass," he mutters, as though I would already know this.

"Thank you," I stammer a bit bemused, "is it really though?"

"You did very well."

"But what were you writing?"

"Just ordering some spring bulbs for the garden."

"Oh, I see. Um, yes, thank you." He hands me some papers and tells me to take them inside, "They'll give you your licence."

It hits me as I get out of the truck. The Snoopy dance of glee begins much to the amusement of passers-by. Jeff, waiting anxiously, sees my face and grins. The hug almost knocks him off his feet and all of a sudden everyone is there congratulating and smiling. I've passed my test, I've got my licence.

The examiner takes Jeff to one side to tell him how well I did. That my reverse was perfect first time, that he put the test sheet away because there was nothing to write and spent the time ordering tulip bulbs instead. Because he likes tulips. It's that time of year. (I will never view a tulip in quite the same way again.)

We look at my copy of the test sheet. There are two crosses…two minor errors. One is the totally inappropriate gear for the final turn. The other is something to do with brakes neither of us is quite sure what, but apparently two paltry little mistakes is an unheard-of success. It is Very Good with knobs on.

Back at school we run into Gregg, who interprets our faces.

"There you are, I told you so."

We dig out the test sheet for his perusal. "Hmm, four-way brakes on starting, oh you didn't forget to test the brakes before you moved did you?"

"I don't know, I think I did them. Maybe I didn't. I have no idea now you come to mention it."

"Do you remember any of it?"

"Not really."

Grins and hugs. The delight seems genuine. Who knew that truckers had soft centres? As I wave farewell to Gregg and Jeff and hop into the car to dash home and share the news, I realise that I still haven't asked Jeff about that sitting on the floor thing.

SHIFT THAT TRUCK

SCHOOL WASN'T quite over, there were a couple of short courses left. Those of us who were now in possession of our AZ licences (and I really wanted to be stopped by the police so that I could show mine off) moved relentlessly on to the final week. This part sounded enjoyable enough to be a small reward for making the school look good. We would spend the first two days messing about with forklift trucks, even though we are highly unlikely to be required to load our own trailers. The rationale went that we will be around forklifts much of the time so knowing how they worked would be A Good Thing. And we could also safely load up our own truck at a pinch.

Then…a glorious road trip. A proper jolly with someone else driving. We were heading over the border to Michigan for a spree disguised as skid school. There would be meals out and a night in a hotel. With the tension over the larks could really begin and expectations ran high for a week of frolicking before the serious task of job hunting.

We'd had to sign all manner of waivers and provide ourselves with steel-capped boots ready for this final part of the course. Safety footwear is apparently mandatory for initiation into the arcane rituals of forklift (or as I now know one should say to be totally correct, counterbalance forklift) truck safety. Now, safety boots are expensive and I am a bit of a cheapskate at heart. I know they are pricey because I'd had to buy a pair for my son. I'd been somewhat surprised at the time that one needed safety gear for a Theatre degree course but now that we had a pair in the family I opted to borrow his rather than splash out on my own. The last time we'd shared footwear, snow boots for shovelling the drive, our feet had been about the same size.

I threw the purloined boots over my shoulder all ice-skate-like as I headed out of the door to present myself in a freezing cold warehouse at seven o'clock on Monday morning. When the time came to dress for safety I discovered that his feet had grown in the last few years. My boots were most definitely steel-toed but not necessarily safe. At four sizes too big for me they flapped about like clown's shoes, I had to take stairs sideways to fit the bit of boot with my foot in on the step.

Feeling more like Charlie Chaplin than Smokey and the Bandit I tried hard to absorb all the theory but it was disappointingly boring. I wasn't having fun yet. We had to learn rules for propane tanks. Liquid propane that is, not the vapour stuff that runs your barbeque. The difference is apparently important. As is how cold it is, how much it expands when let loose and where it likes to hide. We would be tested on all this.

Forklifts also have a tendency to tip over easily. They kill and injure people. We learned much geometry and discussed centres of gravity in grave and serious manner. After half an hour of high school maths, calculating what kind of weights can be carried, from which side, depending on their shape, we were informed that usually there's no real way to tell what your load actually weighs. Some irritable shifting of bums on seats began. Why make us do the sums if it's all pointless?

What did most of us take away from our theory session? If your truck tips over stay in the seat, brace yourself and enjoy the ride. Do not under any circumstances climb, jump or fall out of it. For this reason it's imperative to check your seatbelt before you climb in. And then wear it. We would be tested on all this. Enough already with the safety stuff, we get it. Can we please drive one?

And then, as you will have guessed, it was all a lot harder than it looked. More habits to break. The pesky things steer from the back wheels which meant that all of us had instantly lost the ability to drive at all, the bloody machine just would not go where you thought you were putting it. There was a lot of detailed iteration of when not to do this, that or the other. Tip your forks forward when parked, level them off 80% over the shelf you're putting things on…always pootle about with them tipped back to four inches above the ground. This last bit stuck with me because the reason was something I already knew, if you hit someone their lower leg will heal a lot more quickly than a shattered ankle. Your victim is thus back at work faster. I would be destined to check forklift trucks for their observance of little this rule in every warehouse I entered from that day forward.

Since pallets of stuff are moved about tipped back slightly and then straightened up when your forks are level with the shelf they have to be put on, there was rather a lot of looking at things from strange angles. Specifically, looking at things from above that were a good distance away, and looking at things from below that were relatively close. The most vital piece of safety information had been missing from our preparation notes, *do not, under any circumstances learn to drive a forklift while wearing bifocals.* Why did no-one mention this?

"This is crooked."

"Is it?"

"That's too close to the ground."

"It looks ok to me…"

"It's six inches short of the shelf!"

"Oh dear."

I got the impression that beetling about on a forklift could be highly enjoyable, it certainly looks it when someone who knows what they are doing shows off but half a day was just not enough time to start getting it. Another few hours with sensible specs on and things might have been different but I really don't think I'd load a trailer with much confidence. The job hunt will involve applying to companies that don't expect it and I'll stick to being an irritatingly fanatical four-inch checker.

Still, we were spat out of the warehouse door half way through the day, which left lots of time to get prepared and in the mood for the much anticipated road trip. Collecting US dollars, travel insurance and identity documents segued nicely into an early night and a predawn scrambling into minibus for the six-hour drive to

Marshall, Michigan.

Fortunately for those of us with ageing bladders, the driver was a smoker so comfort breaks were frequent and pleasant. We were, I will admit, as skittish as schoolchildren on their first field trip until the hours bouncing around in uncomfortable seats quietened all but the hardiest souls and we began to wonder what we were in for.

The venture had been planned with military precision. Arrive late afternoon, rooms booked in a nearby hotel, supper at Applebee's and meet in the vestibule at 7.40 sharp in the morning for the bus to skid school. There were dire warnings not to drink too much. Anyone appearing dozy, dopey, sleepy, hung-over or smelling of beer would not be allowed to participate. I will refrain from the obvious gags about new names for dwarves here and deposit you with us in a chilly, prefabricated classroom in the middle of a large expanse of wet concrete miles from anywhere and dotted with orange traffic cones.

Two distinctive groups of people huddled at opposite ends of the class. Nine were champing at the bit to get out there and skid things, the other six were displaying resentful and aggravated body language. How could anyone not want to be here? This was going to be Fun.

Two large, loud, baseball-capped and bewhiskered personages inhabited all the rest of the available space. They introduced themselves as our instructors for the day and shouted at us for having started on the registration forms laid out on our desks without waiting for instructions as to how to fill them in. The forms weren't complicated but the tone for the day was set...'do exactly what we tell you, when we tell you, and nobody will get hurt.'

We were apprised of a few more rules. Anyone unable to shift a truck at reasonable speed would be thrown out. Anyone who didn't listen to instructions and follow them to the letter would be thrown out. Anyone displaying a perceived disregard for safety would be thrown out. Anyone landing a truck down the twelve-foot drop on all sides of the skid pan would get hurt (and thrown out) and anyone losing the contents of their digestive system (from either end) would clean it up themselves. (And be thrown out.) The personages gleefully held aloft, as if by way of proof that this happens, one industrial sized bottle of vehicle upholstery shampoo and another of chemical deodorant.

Next to be held aloft equally gleefully was the huge pile of pre-printed certificates for participation in the course which had been withheld from previous attendees for various reasons such as being thrown off the pan, refusing to participate, losing their lunch and passing out.

The enthusiastic rookies quietened down a bit. Some lost a little colour. The resentful huddle glowered. The large whiskery chaps grinned, they clearly loved their work. It was their job to frighten us before they taught us how to survive and they did it well. We began with video montages of truck accidents and much theory about momentum and locked wheels. We learned in many and various ways that there is no such thing as an emergency stop in a truck and neither is it possible to swerve to avoid things. The tricks we were to learn would enable us, if the time ever came, to choose the safest alternative place to put the beastie and get it there without tipping over. More importantly, we would be leaving even more convinced than ever that it paid to be a bit safe, slow down and leave a good gap from the vehicle in front.

Light dawned as to the provenance of the glowering huddle. All from the same firm, they were seasoned truckers who had transgressed in some way and were being compulsorily retrained. Hopefully they would have fun too once the action kicked in.

The first practical exercise wasn't too difficult—threshold braking—pah, done that before. "Bring your speed up to 30 mph, wait for the red light and then come to the shortest possible stop in a straight line without locking your wheels, driver." Of course it's not easy to keep accelerating when you know you're going to stop in a minute, most of us received whimsical teasing and jolly abuse on the first pass for chickening out of going fast enough. With radios in all the trucks, everyone got to hear everybody else's abuse and this was a tool of the trade in itself. "Wow you professional drivers are being put to shame by the rookies here, next time, driver, put your foot down." Followed by a series of strange noises which turned out to be chicken impressions.

'Driver' is a general term, much used by truckers to each other. It is a sign of comradeship and respect. For a rookie it's actually a bit of a compliment and yet, these guys managed to turn it into a snide insult. We rookies though, we all stood a little taller and added a slight swagger to the gait, we were about to outshine the pros.

Back into class we went, to learn about steering. Specifically the impossibility of turning a moving truck through more than 15 degrees without its wheels locking. Unless you learned the next skill…chopping your steering. The video showed a chap working very, very hard. The trick is to turn your 15 degrees then centre the wheels again, over and over and as fast as you can, it's as close to a swerve as a truck can get. The steering wheel on the video now looked like some sort of mad exercise machine.

We would be entering the skid pan at exactly 22 mph this time and negotiating a chicane without the use of brakes. It looked impossible. We would all get two passes at this insanity with the standard abuse coming out of the radio.

"Shift that truck driver."

"If you go any slower you'll be going backwards."

"Oh, there goes a cone, that's a child under your wheels."

"Watch your trailer, did you forget it was there?"

"Let the rookies show you how it's done, driver."

On the first pass I gamely attempted the steering wheel manoeuvre and made a sort of decent fist of the whole thing. As I did so some vague physical memory came back to me from a skid pan twenty-five years earlier, I'd done this before. It had been two ambulances chasing each other around in a figure of eight back then but the steering was the same. I let go of my apprehension on the second pass and trusted to instinct.

"Look at her go, that's the way to do it, good job driver."

"Not just the rookies showing you up now guys, the women have you beaten."

"Why send a man out to do a woman's job?"

"Oh, and by the way driver, if I say 'good job' you earned it."

This was both a good and a bad thing. Bragging rights notwithstanding I now expected myself to shine next time out but unbeknownst to any of us we were about to be had. The next exercise was set up to be impossible. We'd been working with two people per truck so far but the next time out of the classroom we were divided into two groups. One bunch would drive each truck solo and the others would stay with our coaches and 'observe' through the classroom window. The observers were given distractingly pointless things to time and measure. The aim of this little piece of subterfuge was to make sure nobody twigged that the task was impossible until after they'd tried it.

A set of lights was strung over part of the skid pan. Bollards represented a central obstacle and lanes to veer into on each side of it. The task was simple enough. The obstacle represented a school bus. We would approach it at the prescribed 22 mph. At exactly 75 feet away, that's one tractor-trailer length, the lights would tell us which way to turn to avoid killing the children. One 'lane' would have a red cross over it and the other would have a green arrow. Abuse would ensue if you 1) didn't approach fast enough 2) turned the wrong way 3) guessed which lane to take before the lights activated and 4) demolished any bollards.

The abuse flew. Bollards were mangled. People slowed down, turned too early, panicked, and swore. I tried, I really did. I thought that maybe I couldn't see the lights because of the sun, that they were on really and I just couldn't see them. One moment I had no idea which way to turn then suddenly the green and red flashed and the bollards were already under my wheels.

"That's a bus full of children driver, what's the matter with you, you had 75 feet to react in." What was the matter with me? I didn't know, it was terrifying. I wanted another chance to not kill the bollard children but we only got one pass each this time. Nobody managed it.

Our debrief began as the exercise had done with pacing out the distance from the lights to the 'bus'. It had seemed perfectly adequate for thinking time when you were on the ground before trying it. Then they told us that it just wasn't. Whiskers aquiver with amusement.

I didn't know it then but the lights had been acquired from a highway truck inspection station and I would encounter the same set of lane directions numerous times in the future. The lights over the lanes at weigh stations would always give me sufficient warning but I was destined to hyperventilate at them anyway.

After a slightly heavier lunch than was probably wise we reconvened in the chilly classroom hut to find out what horrors came next. After a little physics lesson about friction on bends we stood to attention back outside for demonstrations. One of the fierce chaps clambered into a rig to show us what to do while the other commentated in charismatic style, including the useful information that what we were about to see was the trick that tended to make people regret their lunch. We would be observing an intentional jackknife.

The truck and trailer approached us at a solid 22 mph. It steered left, then right, then applied the trailer brakes to lock the rear wheels. A bizarre dance followed, almost beautiful in its huge, inexorable demonstration of the laws of physics. The trailer swung around the tractor almost as far as it could go without disaster. "He can now see his trailer in the left mirror," the commentary had lost its jocular edge, they were concentrating now. The trailer swung back the other way like a pendulum, almost a full 180 degrees, "the trailer is visible in his right mirror, he's aiming for the next turn and accelerating gently." And it was over. The truck took the lane out of the pad as straight as a die and silence descended on a group of open-mouthed wannabes. We weren't going to do that? You needed to be a loud, whiskery expert.

And then another vehicle was approaching us. A tractor 'bobtailing' without a trailer this time. The next demonstration. "This is what happens when you don't control a drive wheel lockup." Approaching at 22 mph, turning left, turning right, locking the brakes, and another dance. The bobtail spun and spun describing several circles. It rocked from side to side and looked at one point as though it would topple right over. "We want you to feel what that's like before we teach you to control it." Oof, really? We couldn't maybe take your word for it? The next pass was positively tame, lock the brakes, skid a bit, then drive away.

"Any questions?"

"Are we going to do that?"

"Yes. Any more questions?

"Will you tell us what to do?"

"I will be talking to you all the time, commanding every move. Listen and do as you're told. You'll be fine." Grown men are looking a little pale. The girls (two of us) huddle together slightly for reassurance. "We've been watching you all carefully. If you couldn't do it we'd have thrown you out." The joker is serious now and he has timed his change of mood exactly. I've been here before too, on that other skid pan 25 years ago and it was the same game then. The teasing and abuse are about knocking the confidence out of you so you'll really listen. Overcoming natural instincts requires that the voice outside of you is more important than the voice in your head. Now they were telling us we'd learned that lesson and were sufficiently capable of doing what we were told to learn the big trick. They trusted us. That meant something.

My partner for the day went first like a perfect gentleman. Sitting in the passenger seat while he jackknifed and then drove away was a little surreal, I couldn't see or feel anything at all. Apart from his face. The business end of the event was happening silently in his mirrors, nothing in the feel of the ride changed in any way as the massive trailer danced about behind us. Gregg had been right. You had to watch other people's passes to see what was going on. This unnerved me totally. We'd heard it in class on the 'you don't want to be seeing that, no you don't' day, but until I sat there, oblivious, it hadn't quite sunk in.

My turn came. Along with the merest hint of panic attack. We'd been told the story of the young lady who jackknifed her rig perfectly, parked it neatly, removed the key and radio as instructed, climbed out using the approved three point contact...and then passed out cold in the middle of the skid pan. All my big talk had evaporated, I just didn't want to be the next amusing anecdote. Some breathing exercises helped a little on the approach, I got to 22 mph, chopped the wheel left, then right. "Hand valve down…" came through the radio. I tweaked the trailer brake slightly and then let it off again in terror. My body was screaming at me to panic and hit the brakes. We wobbled a tad but it was hardly a jackknife.

What seemed like a minute or two later the radio came back to life. "Hand valve back up now, what was that driver? A waste of time, you'll do this as often as it takes." I'd chickened out of my first pass and we all knew it. The next one needed to be right. Did I trust them enough? These chaps who trusted us? No-one else had died doing as they were told.

The next pass came with a little more determination, I wasn't going to be the one to let the girlies down. 22 mph, left, right, "Hand valve down…" I did it this time. "Hand valve up, look in your mirror." There it was. The trailer loomed around, a purely visual sensation. I could see the writing on the side. "Steer for the exit, keep your throttle steady." Again, my body was desperate to hit the brakes but back in the zone of being told what to do I accelerated instead. The trailer disappeared then there it was in my other mirror, it disappeared again and I got traction. We were pulling through the last turn of the course. "Nice work driver," the radio told us I'd done it.

And on to the bobtail. We spun and we skidded, we corrected our wheels in the approved manner, laughed, joked and played. The adrenalin flowed and when it was time to stop we all wanted 'one more go'. But the surreal nature of that jackknife had everyone spellbound. Even though you'd done it for yourself you could still only comprehend what had happened when watching someone else. The terrifying event that happened with no physical warning had spooked us all. Would we have the presence of mind to accelerate if we ever again saw our trailer where it shouldn't be? "Oh yes," said both instructors at the end of the course. "You'll never forget this, you'll do it if you need to."

They were all smiles now, these larger-than-life-and-twice-as-scary chaps. We each got a sincere, bone-crushing handshake and a genuine, "Well done." They knew what they'd put us through. The drive home was a tad quieter, all nine of us uncharacteristically subdued. The companionable silence was broken from time to time as someone turned to someone else and asked, "Did I really just do that?" The nods were friendly and understanding. We'd really done it. And it was quite something.

ALL CHANGE

SCHOOL'S OUT. The twilight world of wannabe truckers is over and it's time to set about finding work. The final piece of the preparatory jigsaw was a trip to the border for a FAST card. That's Free And Secure Trade, natty acronym eh? The card is a way to accelerate your progress at border crossings…it means you are neither a terrorist nor a criminal. Moreover, you are a certified Good Egg therefore possession of such a card makes one extra employable and I was still under the impression that I'd need as much help as I could possibly get.

I had sent in all the paperwork (photocopies of everything enlarged and in duplicate) several weeks in advance along with my $50 processing fee. All that remained was the drive to a border crossing with a FAST office to produce the originals of all the documents they had already seen. Candidates for international approval then needed be interviewed by representatives of both nations, fingerprinted and generally checked for being kosher. It smacked a little of job creation scheme but I didn't mind, it was a sunny day so I packed a picnic and headed off to Fort Erie in high spirits.

After twenty minutes or so of sitting in the wrong waiting room (clearly our initiative must be tested as well as our bona fides) I finally fetched up at the right window, the lair of the receptionist whose job it was to hand out The Forms. Name, address, date of birth, easy enough. Height, weight, colour of eyes, colour of hair…back to the window.

"Um, which hair colour do they want? The real one or the name on this month's box of dye?"

"The one we can see," she advised.

"Because really it's grey." She smiled.

"That's ok, ma'am, so's mine but this is for recognising you at the border."

"But suppose I change it sometime?" The face behind the window went blank, I was annoying her now, "Auburn it is then." I made a mental note not to experiment too outrageously with new hair colouring while being an agent of international commerce.

Unsettled and resettled by the hair colour question I moved on. Location Of Tattoos. The form offered a brief list of likely body parts for me to tick. Now I do have a small (and tasteful) tattoo on my left hip. But hips weren't on the list so I had to settle for Left Thigh which set me to wondering; if all this information was about recognition at border crossings would I be required to drop my trousers every time I hauled freight into the US? And if so, in what way was having this card quicker than using a passport? It was beginning to feel as though I had entered the lair of the world's biggest jobsworth. My ponderings meandered down the mental cul-de-sac of whether terrorists did or did not tend to have tattoos and whether they would lie about them if they did.

My tattooed-terrorist-related musings were interrupted by the next step, the bizarre shenanigans that are modern fingerprinting. Now correct me if I'm wrong but I'm sure we used to stick our fingers on a pad of ink and then onto a piece of paper. Just the once for each finger. Then CSI types could identify the baddie from a tiny smudge of blood on a wineglass. So how come the world's greatest superpower's Homeland Security department, utilising the latest in digital technology, has such trouble taking fingerprints?

"Are your hands clean and dry?" asked a chunky and faintly frightening woman whose Homeland Security uniform did her no favours.

"I think so." She pressed my fingers gently onto what looked like a laptop touchpad and a smudgy image appeared on a screen.

"They're a bit greasy. There's a washroom in the waiting area, please go and wash and dry your hands." I did so obediently. Repeat of previous routine. "Hmm, it's still not good enough, rub some of this on your hands." She presented me with a dispenser of hand sanitiser and I dutifully squirted some onto my fingers. "Rub it in like this." She demonstrated the preferred technique with a mime. We were now waving wringing hands at each other just like a lesson in sign language. I gestured towards the touchpad again but she stopped my precipitate haste in mid-air..."No, not yet, you have to dry them." I'd thought they were dry but now the scary lady in ill-fitting uniform was waggling her fingers in front of an ancient and creaky desk fan, suitably directed towards the technological wizardry. "Like this." I waggled my fingers as enthusiastically as I could considering that I was, by then, an odd combination of amused, irritated, intimidated and incredulous.

I decided against mentioning that the RCMP already had my fingerprints on file, sent from Scotland Yard back when I applied to immigrate. They'd used ink and it hadn't taken long at all. "Let's try those prints again." Yes, let's. Fingers on screen, images appeared. She declared these acceptable although, to be honest they didn't look any different. Except one. A thumb must be redone. More of the squirting and waggling, honestly, if CSI was like this they'd take a whole series to catch one baddie.

The interviews themselves seemed a bit of a letdown after all that excitement, the American and the Canadian just took it in turns to tell me the same rules. I nodded obediently and looked honest. They took my picture, handed me the card and a pile of booklets and that was it. No-one verified the tattoo. It was an educational introduction to the strange and pointless phenomenon that is US Homeland Security but more tales from the lair of the world's biggest employer of jobsworths anon. I was one step closer to a real job.

***

Challenger Motor Freight. Somehow over the weeks they had become the company I really wanted to work for. I called Gwen, who made an appointment within days for me to go and be interviewed and test driven. I enquired, as instructed by a handy set of 'how to get a job' hints given out with our school certificates, as to the sort of gearbox I'd be handling for them. "Ten speed," advised Gwen, who was beginning to transmogrify from friendly and reassuring to slightly intimidating. I had learned all I knew on a thirteen speed gearbox so it was back to school for one more drive. A thoughtful piece of reassurance offered by Tri County Truck Driver Training to its graduates was the undertaking to let you practise the precise gearbox you will be required to test drive for a job. I will love them forever.

I appeared for my practice hour brimming with confidence. I was a real trucker now, not even an almost-am, all that anxiety was behind me and I could do anything. Well, I wasn't too sure what I would do if I turned out not to be the superior driving material that Challenger advertised its apprentices must be but mind over matter had worked on test day. It wasn't going to let me down now. It was good to see Jeff again too, I made a mental note to ask about the floor thing.

The new gear-change pattern was a little odd but not insurmountable. I seemed to have undergone a personality transplant since the test, or possibly since the skid pan. I was driving. Really, properly, with confidence and finesse. Even I could see it. "I'd hire you," said Jeff, "and you're fine with the gearbox, we've got half an hour left, how about some reversing practice?" He knows me so well. The test reverse had gone perfectly but the 90 degree manoeuvres were still dodgy. He showed me how to stop a ropey reverse from getting worse if you catch it in time. What else could go wrong? Apart from forgetting all about the floor thing again.

They were all smiles when I arrived, the recruiting

people. They sat me down in a fancy-schmancy waiting area, all grey, silver and glass, and offered me coffee. Then they produced a 'little theory test'. Gwen, who really was quite intimidating in person despite the endearing giggle told me to pop in to her office when I'd completed it. No-one had mentioned a theory test. I'd done no revision. Yes I'd averaged 99% on the theory papers in school (and won a natty baseball cap for so doing) but that was with revising, short-term memory tricks and the ability to look things up. None of it was still in my head.

There were questions I should have known but didn't and questions about things I'd never heard of. I sweated and tried to work things out logically from first principles but I knew it was unlikely to work. We were dealing with border crossing rules and ways in which Canada and the US insisted on doing things differently merely in order to feel like foreign countries to each other. There was no logic to be had. I sat and fretted for a while, made some desperate guesses and poked my nose apologetically through Gwen's door. "Um, I've done my best."

She twinkled, gestured to a seat and set about marking my paper. Some of it appeared to be right. She made no comment about it, just asked to see my passport, driving licence, certificates and FAST card. Did that mean I'd passed the test? There were a few questions about convictions and stuff then it was out to meet the charming young man who would be taking me for my test drive. I thought that probably meant I had squeaked through but I hadn't quite recovered from the serenity battering. The slightest niggle was still all it took to turn the confident driver into the gibbering wreck.

We found our vehicle and I clambered in. I spent the

advised few moments acquainting myself with where all the controls were and the charming young man spent a few moments telling me how the lower range gears liked to be changed at 1200 rpm and the upper range at 1500. I was used to changing both ranges at 1400. As I processed this additional challenge I depressed the clutch to turn on the engine. It snapped back at me like a bolt out of a crossbow. "Ah yes, and the clutch is a little heavy." Heavy? It's a Rottweiler, how the hell can anyone double declutch that? Did I say that? I think my face possibly did. "You'll get used to it," purred the charming young man.

It was not a textbook drive. Rattled, confused and unsettled I clipped a kerb or two, missed a downshift or several and reverted to English for my running commentary. Fortunately we weren't out for long. In what seemed like no time we had turned back into the company yard and I assumed that the CYM had given up on me and cut the test drive short so as to be safe a little sooner. But no, I was being shown a bay to reverse into and he hopped out to watch. Maybe things could be redeemed with my newfound ability to retrieve disastrous reversing. But Jeff's handy new trick was for correcting a turn taken too early…I turned too late. And ended up neatly in the bay next to the one I had been asked to occupy.

I looked at the CYM, who just waited politely for me to put it right. I pulled forward again and did the stupid thing with my hands that told me which way I want the back to go, steered this way and that, being right royally bitten by the clutch all the while, and ended up back in the same spot. Twice. Eventually he took pity on me and issued some instructions. Somehow we ended up in the required bay. He climbed back into the cab and I waited to be told that I didn't have a job but he merely asked me to drive up there and over here and around there and park in here. Forwards. Thankfully.

He made some notes and I waited, again, to be told that I didn't have a job. He asked me a few questions instead. "How would you conduct an in-cab check?" I knew that inside out, I might not have a job but if he was going to insist on completing the whole bloody shooting match before putting me out of my misery I'd show him there was some stuff I could do. I rattled off all the relevant checks, added a few more and editorialised like mad. "Ok, let's go back and see Gwen." Ah, now I get it, they're not allowed to tell you that you don't have a job one-on-one in the truck in case you turn nasty, it has to be in the building where there's backup.

Despondently I trailed after him back into the building. People waved and said, "Hi," as we walked in. It seemed like a nice, friendly place to work, I think I could have liked it here. Hearty joshing appeared to be commonplace. "I didn't think we were test-driving girls anymore," quipped a chap with a nice smile. (Girls, hey, thank you.) "He certainly won't be after this one," I managed by way of jolly banter despite my disappointment. Everybody laughed. Nicely. Then I was placed back outside Gwen's (empty) office and the CYM plonked his notes on her deserted desk. "She'll be back soon to see you." I couldn't take it any longer.

"Um, are you allowed to tell me whether it was ok or not?" I muttered, unable to look him in the eye.

"Oh yes, I've recommended that she hire you."

"What, after that reverse?"

"Oh, we can fix that, everything else was fine."

"Was it?" He looks surprised that I am surprised.

Gwen returned to a nonplussed applicant. She asked some questions about attitude, availability, future plans, all the standard recruitment stuff. I expect I probably answered them. She said that if I had time to attend a medical that afternoon I could start on Friday. This was Wednesday. I think I probably went for that medical.

Suddenly I was pacing about packing and repacking my kit for starting work. Challenger gave its apprentices two weeks learning city work with a local trainer before sending them to head for the hills, so I would begin my working life sharing a smaller cab. There was no need for all that sleeping and storage space if you went home every night. I tried to pack all the things I thought I might need into a more nonchalant and less ridiculously comprehensive array of bags. I'd found a nifty document thingumy for all the log books, maps, manuals, guidebooks, lists of rules and regulations, hazmat codes, checklists, envelopes and forms. Then another smallish sports bag for all the safety gear; hard hat, goggles, gloves and earplugs. It was too small for the steel-toed boots as well.

I looked at the boots. Challenger insisted on them, their clients wouldn't allow anyone onto their loading docks without full safety gear. My borrowed four-sizes-too-big-boots took up a whole bag on their own as well as not being safe, maybe it was time to spend some more money. I dashed out and found a half-priced pair of cute, powder-blue safety trainers. They would be more practical, I could drive in them. Not only was I one bag down, the extra weight might help with those Rottweiler clutches and my son could have his boots back.

Then there were the emergency rations. A backup

muesli bar and/or standby peanut butter sandwich, fluids and sweeties. And the 'handbag or pocket?' debate for valuables. I had enough ID cards, fuel cards, border crossing cards and company credit cards to perform tolerable magic tricks and no time to dash out again for a wardrobe full of cargo trousers with myriad pockets. A handbag mightn't look the part but it would enable me to add all the stuff that would normally be permanently stowed in my own truck but would have to travel to and fro for the next little while. Vital kit such as tissues, baby wipes and hand sanitiser. I had spent long enough resembling Pigpen by the end of a working day, I was going to begin my new career with a little more panache.

I knew it probably wasn't going to matter to anyone what I took with me on day one, they had to be used to rookies getting it hopelessly wrong but it took my mind off the fact that yet again, for the umpteenth time since this whole daft enterprise began I was truly frightened. No-one in school had said, "Oh stoppit, you stupid woman," like they were supposed to. The examiner hadn't, Challenger hadn't, they actually wanted to pay me to do this, it wasn't a game any longer. I didn't want to think about who was going to turn up for work on day one...the newly confident, internationally-approved truck driver or the quivering heap of idiocy whose meagre truck driving abilities were too fragile to transfer from one vehicle to another.

***

I still wasn't sure which version of me was going to inhabit Challenger's latest rookie when I presented myself at the wrong dispatch desk at dawn. The long-haul dispatcher regarded me kindly, masked any residual amusement and directed me to the city desk. The city people looked at notes and told me Janice was around somewhere and to sit and wait, she'd appear soon. Which she did. The long, curly, blonde hair bounced this way and that as she finished a lively conversation with someone and grinned in my direction. We were in a hurry to get going apparently so the introductions were brief and I followed her out to her truck at a frazzled trot.

Janice was confident that she could turn me from a training school clone into a Challenger superstar within two weeks even though I would be unlearning everything I'd learned and starting again from scratch. We would be turning corners differently, handling traffic differently, using different following distances and changing the carefully rehearsed coupling procedures. My buttonhooks and hockey sticks were laughably passé, this was the real world and nothing that had been drummed into me for the Ministry test was now the least bit relevant.

All this might have heralded the return of the quivering heap of idiocy had it not been for the fact that Janice was also in love.

She drove for the first part of day one so that I could see how it was done. She demonstrated new ways to turn corners, which looked to me pretty much like the old ways. She showed me how to zip through the gears without the clutch in heavy traffic, which I'd been told in school was a bad habit, and how to set up for a reverse using something I didn't understand called a 45/135. "Make the trailer dance..." she trilled, as though this was a meaningful piece of advice. But mostly she told me about her life.

There was this new man you see, one of Challenger's long haul drivers. I was her final student because they were going to drive team as soon as I'd moved on. There was an ex too, and some kids and a Mum. It was all upsetting and complicated and there had to be many phone calls and texts during the day to and from each of the players in this drama, each call processing everyone's feelings about all the other calls and who had said what to whom this time.

I began to be a little miffed by all this. If there was going to be any drama surrounding my learning to handle a truck it should be all about me. I felt entitled. But then maybe I'd been spoiled by Gregg and Jeff, maybe industry trainers didn't explain themselves like training school trainers did. At the same time I twigged that I was getting off lightly, earning money to be an agony aunt for two weeks. I tended to do that for nothing most of the time, I've always had that sort of face. Oddly enough my confidence grew since clearly it didn't really matter whether I got better or not, perhaps the whole training thing was just company flimflam and I'd be able to do as I liked eventually. I'd bloody well buttonhook if I felt like it as soon as I was set free.

"Off-track that next turn."

"I'm still not quite sure what you mean by 'off-track,' where do you want me to…"

"Hello Mom, where are you? No that's ok, carry on, what did he say to you? You didn't off-track again, I keep telling you."

"And I keep asking what…"

"Hello darling, did Grammy put you on the phone, what's the matter?"

"Please Janice can you show me with a diagram or

something, I really don't get off-tracking at all and I understood buttonhooks."

BINGLEBINGLE. A new noise. We had the CB at full volume, ditto the radio, I'd had ample opportunity to become familiar with the mobile ring tone but what new hell was this?

"Oh look, how sweet is that? Listen to this Carolyn, he's texted that he loves me and he misses me and he can't wait 'til we're driving together, what shall I text back, how does this sound?"

The first week trailed uncomfortably on. Some things improved, some things fell apart. New complications emerged and I worked most of them out for myself. In school we'd been driving trailers with carefully judged amounts of concrete in the back to give them just the right kind of heaviness. In the real world, every trailer has a different weight and they all behave differently. Heavy trailers drag you back going up hills and push you forward going down them. Empty trailers have less traction, they can skip about if you don't change your ways for them. Each and every drive requires a slightly different set of rules. Why do we consign this task to the blue collar world? Doing it well is like brain surgery.

People asked me how work was going and I went all vague and changed the subject. They might have been relieved by this—I'd become a bit of a trucking bore before I knew I couldn't drive one—but I knew it wasn't a good sign. Neither was the grin test. I might have evaded the anticipated falling-to-bits but the grin test was infallible and I wasn't grinning yet.

During week two the love triangle crisis came to a head. There were dramatic issues with the ex and the new man was out of contact somewhere between cell phone masts in Saskatchewan. Each day's developments had to be relayed, in quiet corners, to numerous friends at Challenger's head office every morning. I sat for longer and longer at dispatch with my little bag of stuff, feeling like an unwanted evacuee at some remote railway station as I waited for the bouncing curls to emerge from an office deep in urgent and whispered conversation. Then we would be late for our delivery window and there was no time for my slow, methodical vehicle checks. In fact on some days, there was no time for my slow, methodical driving either.

"I'm too stressed to train you today, it's easier to drive myself, just watch what I do."

"Ok, but you did say we'd do some reversing before we left."

"We'll do it later, there's no time now."

"I came in early though."

BINGLEBINGLE.

I'd climb dejectedly into the passenger seat not sure whether my whinging was more or less annoying than that cell phone and ticking another day off my mental countdown of opportunities to get used to Janice's way of handling traffic. And this was something I knew I really did have to change. We'd been indoctrinated in school with the seven second rule. The laws of physics dictated stopping distances and they approximated to a second for every ten feet of vehicle length. At 75 feetish therefore, seven to eight seconds was the minimum safe following distance at highway speed. Gregg used to call the seven-second gap your 'living room'. I was used to how it looked and it felt all comfy and safe.

Toronto traffic however will brook no stupid seven second gaps. Highway 401 is a permanent 100 kph traffic jam and you will bunch up like the others unless you wish to spend all day almost travelling backwards as vehicle after vehicle cuts in front of you. The trick is to hit 100 kph and maintain it come what may because as soon as you slow down the loaded trailer will eat up your momentum and you'll take forever to speed up again. There are delivery windows to meet, we are no longer out for a jaunt. Especially when we seem to have accidentally set off an hour late.

As an added complication, Ontario trucks are equipped with speed limiters, it's the law. Each truck's engine will stop itself accelerating at a speed somewhere near 100 kph. The exact speed that each limiter kicks in at varies from vehicle to vehicle however, so maintaining the maximum speed your engine will allow also entails overtaking things that are only going very slightly slower than you. You don't want to start all that until you are quite close up behind them otherwise it takes all day. This requires one to bear down on the stuff in front, assessing your alarming closing speed and diminishing living room all calmly, while you signal to overtake and wait to see if the traffic beside you will drop back politely or race you for the hell of it.

I took Janice's point that it was the only way to get efficiently from a to b, I really did. But I wanted my living room back. I was starting to hold my breath again and my toes were scrunched in permanent curls of terror.

We are back at the yard at the end of the day.

"Can I do the reverse?"

"Yes, you need the practice."

"I know, I need to draw a diagram as well, I still don't

see what you mean by lining the wheel up with the landing gear."

"I keep telling you."

"Yes, but I keep not understanding, I need to get out and…"

"Hello Mom, what's that? He's called you?"

I set up as best I can. I've lost my fragile instinct for the hockey stick by now and I am lining up the wrong things in my mirrors for Janice's system. I have got that the cab and the trailer must make a 90 degree angle with each other but not how to achieve it.

"Is this right?"

"Just dance the trailer."

BINGLEBINGLE.

The second week dragged by. On days when my driving wasn't too stressful and when we weren't too late I began to learn to check our weight from the paperwork before the trailer's behaviour caught me out. I had whole moments of driving without white knuckles and toes in a tight little ball at the end of my cute, blue safety trainers. I wasn't quite grinning yet but I began to take an interest in the trivia of life delivering freight. The sort of trivia that make life worth living, like learning that there really is real chicken in Campbell's Cream of Chicken soup.

I hadn't given soup much thought until we hauled a trailer full of it to Toronto. On the way I learned that a trailer full of tins of soup is heavy enough to put us at our legal maximum weight, which was only mildly interesting in a trucking-bore sort of way, but once we arrived I learned, amazingly, that each tin contained actual meat. Who'd have thought? There are rules for bringing meat over the border you see, it has to be inspected and cleared by people in uniforms on both sides. This load had been delivered to Challenger's holding yard from somewhere in the US by a long-haul person, short of one piece of paper. We were missing a meat inspection certificate from Canadian Customs and that was clearly a disaster.

We sat for an hour and a half waiting for the office wallahs back at Challenger to look for it. And when they couldn't find it we were turned around, still soup-laden, to return our load from whence it came. Because it was a shipment of meat. This all set me to musing on the mechanics of inspecting the meat inside a trailer full of tins of soup. I'm still not sure how they would do that.

Other things came together slowly. My observation skills reasserted themselves, I learned my way around the yard and the buildings, discovered that Challenger's canteen made a mighty fine BLT and started to walk about with a confident, almost truckerly air.

***

An odd thing happened on our last day together. Reverse parking the trailer as we returned from another tediously terrifying jaunt to Toronto and back, it went into its bay first time. There was a bit of jiggerypokery and some messingabout to get it quite straight but I worked it out for myself. Was that dancing the trailer? Janice grinned, "I think you're ready for Highway Training."

I was glad she couldn't see my toes. I had a sneaking suspicion that her assessment had as much to do with wanting to be rid of me so that she could hit the highway with the new beau as it was with any actual progress…but my mouth stayed firmly shut. I was sick of Toronto, I wanted to hit the highway too. And maybe, just maybe, she'd left me to get it all by myself for a reason.

PART 2: TEAMWORK

BARRY

MORE PACKING. How many extra bags would there be room for in someone else's truck? I had no idea but worrying about it worked very well as a displacement activity. I already had my safety stuff bag, my silly handbag full of wet wipes, the emergency lunch bag and daft document case. Now I had to add bedding, clothes, a bag full of showering things, waterproofs, overalls, torches, the laptop and a lot more food.

I knew my trainer was called Barry and that he drove a flatbed, beyond that I knew nothing. Would he be a 'getting out of the truck to eat' person or a 'picnic in the cab to save time' person? I needed to take provisions just in case but not stuff that required a cooler because he might not have one.

I had dutifully noted down everything Gregg advised us to squirrel away and now it was all in a heap. My hallway resembled base camp for an assault on Everest. There were the flip-flops for showering in so that you didn't have to put your feet on a yucky floor in a less than hygienic truck stop. There was the sonic attack alarm for traversing dodgy truck stops in the middle of the night. There was the decoy wallet full of Canadian Tire money to give to potential highwaymen, and a lot of muesli bars and apples.

Barry was less intimidating than I anticipated, although his truck effectively filled the intimidation void. It had 'super single' tyres which no-one had yet mentioned, corners in new places and lots of shiny chrome bits to get in the way of being able to see out of the windows. I didn't know it then but reducing your visibility with unnecessary chrome would appear to be a ubiquitously macho thing to do to one's truck. Barry was patient and encouraging to begin with though and in receipt of a glowing reference from Janice. He explained some of the ways his truck was different to what I was used to and I understood some of it. I would discover later that he was less patient with uniformed jobsworths but we managed to evade arrest. Possibly only just.

Our cab was a relatively snug home from home, we had a fridge, microwave, little oven, TV, you name it. Add a cat and it would be indistinguishable from the real thing. All my junk seemed to fit in somehow although it would be three nights into our first real run before I got the chance to settle in properly and look around.

Barry drove on our first day out. This was a little trip to Michigan and back, a gentle run to initiate me into the new horrors that come with a flatbed trailer. I watched a lot of time-consuming athleticism as strange-shaped items were chained, strapped and tarped. I tried to be useful, handing things up onto the trailer and such but my total inability to lift anything heavier than a scrap of carpet got in the way somewhat. I was surprised that we needed scraps of carpet to be honest but I now know they are useful for cushioning things with.

We chatted, I made notes. I tried to pay attention to things like the significance of the super singles and a 'ten-one spread' but a lot of Barry's explanations were a little over my head. I twigged that the tyres held the road differently and that the ten thing referred to a bigger gap than normal between the trailer's two rear axles but not exactly how or why I needed to care.

On our way back to the yard, dispatch asked Barry if he fancied taking a container to Baltimore tomorrow. He agreed enthusiastically, it would be great for me to learn all about containers. The only downside was that we wouldn't get back to Challenger until around four-thirty in the morning. Since we'd have to leave again by ten, we weren't going to get our legal sleeping hours off. "That's ok," Barry told me. "We'll say you drove tonight, then I'll start in the morning and we'll both show ten hours rest on our log books." This didn't sound legal but I didn't like to argue, what with it being my first day.

***

Our container full of truck parts was heading for Australia via Baltimore docks. It had to be there to meet its ship between eight and three the following day. Leaving at ten would allow plenty of time for a rookie to get it there and even supply a legal rest on the way. But it had a complicated customs designation, being a thing that was passing directly through the US. Faxes had to be sent to brokers and back before we could set off. The day became an object lesson in that obscure rule of physics that decrees, *once a thing begins to go pear-shaped, it just keeps on getting more piriform.*

Who can say whether the faxes really never arrived or whether the broker was having a party but our proof that the container was correctly bonded for customs purposes didn't turn up until three in the afternoon. Leaving so late, we would be arriving uncomfortably close to the end of our delivery window even without further rookie-behind-the-wheel type delays.

I'd hated watching so many daylight hours disappear before we set off, we were driving in the dark before the interesting landscape began. And by interesting I mean the Appalachian Mountains. The romance of the open road wasn't working for me yet, it was icy and terrifying. I had no idea whether it was the super-singles, the weather or my driving but I knew we weren't holding the road very well, even before Barry's yelling added the bit of the jigsaw that I'd not popped into place yesterday. The big thing about ten-one spreads is their rampant enthusiasm for jackknifing on the slightest little bend. There is a reason that I should have understood but I'll postpone the physics for now.

Of course we got lost for an hour and a half in Baltimore trying to find the docks, why wouldn't we? Presumably signposting dockyard entrances would make life too easy for the terrorists. After driving round in some bad-tempered circles we fetched up at the dockyard security checkpoint with twenty minutes to go.

We thought we had just made it, and apparently I'd done ok really what with the mountains and the ice and stuff, yelling notwithstanding.

We had reckoned without Homeland Security. There was a yellow slip of paper to be had before you could drive onto the docks. Said yellow slip of paper must be obtained from a mobile checkpoint that we had allegedly already driven past. It was about two miles back. Allegedly. Just past the blue underpass there would be a police car, "Look to the right, you'll see the light," advised the uniformed jobsworth. Barry attempted some pleading, but the uniforms bristled. These were clearly The Rules.

We went back, found the underpass and looked not only to the right but in every direction. No police car with lights on, no mobile security point. Back to the docks. Same chap, same directions, "Everyone else has found it." The smirk rankled a little.

"Past the underpass is just a concrete wall opposite a parking lot," Barry protested, visibly irritated.

"Look for the light."

"Are you saying light, or lot?"

"In the light."

"A parking lot?"

"Yeah, like I said, look for the light." He regarded us in amused manner as though we were a little simple, or it could have been the amusement of enjoying giving us the runaround. Difficult to tell. We concluded that we were looking for a parking lot and not a police car with lights on and tried again.

The mobile security point was indeed in a car park but just before the underpass, not just past it. No lights at all. It was a trailer, there was no police car. Normally I'd blame my English ear for the language barrier but Barry heard it all that way too. We hung about in the freezing cold for half an hour or so while another guard took our driving licences into the oddly scruffy trailer with a stupidly piddly little Homeland Security logo on the side. There was, allegedly, a real policeman on the inside who would peruse our driving licences at his leisure and then scribble some nonsense on, yes, a yellow slip of paper.

Now, all this is undoubtedly a worthy attempt to prevent terrorists from depositing unauthorised goods in a container bound for Australia but Barry and I both already had FAST cards. Unlike our driving licences, they proved that we had been assessed within an inch of our lives for terrorist tendencies. Homeland Security already had our fingerprints for goodness sake, so quite how a chap in a caravan—who doesn't even pop his head outside to see if we look like the photos on our licences—is providing an additional layer of safety for innocent US citizens who wish to sleep safely in their beds is beyond me.

People came and went. Yellow slips flew in all directions but ours, clearly foreign driving licences were extra difficult to process. We arrived back at the docks with our vital little bits of paper a few minutes after four o'clock. Customs closed at four. Our load was not just an hour late now, it would have to wait for the following morning.

The uniformed jobsworth who'd given us the wrong directions twice was beside himself with glee. Barry's body language altered slightly, "Shame on you, do you realise that by doing this you are costing your country money?" he began. The body language among the jobsworths altered slightly. Somebody was about to explode with something and these people had guns. I tried to make myself very small. Our jobsworth thought about it as his hand moved towards his belt, then made the decision to explode with mirth. Clearly there was less paperwork that way.

***

The next day we arrived at the security gate bright and early and proffered our yellow slips.

"These are yesterday's."

"Yes, we missed customs getting them so we're here today."

"They're not valid for today."

"But we're the same people…" It was no good. We must re-attend the scruffy trailer in the lot-not-light.

We waved yesterday's yellow slips hopefully at the Homeland Security guard, saying, "Look, you approved us yesterday," but the implication that this might mean we were still non-terrorists today was clearly lost in translation. Yesterday's slips were discarded and our driving licences recollected. We waited. Lots of other people arrived, handed in their licences and waited. The lots of other people all received their yellow slips. We waited. Ontario drivers were clearly still too foreign and annoying for rapid processing even though they weren't terrorists yesterday.

With slips in hand we were finally allowed, a mere 24 hours late, to venture onto Baltimore docks with our container full of bits of dumper truck bound for Australia. There was a telephone arrangement at the first of several barriers. It wasn't easy to hear the disembodied voice but through the crackling and the accent I discerned, "What are you doing today Challenger?" I would have thought it was obvious that since I was sitting at the barrier to their dockyard with a container behind me I was probably delivering a container for shipping. But you are not allowed to be facetious with these people, we learned that yesterday. "I'm delivering a container." I advised, as respectfully as I could muster in the circumstances.

"What are you delivering?" Well, that made more sense as a question.

"Dump truck parts for *Hitachi*, going to Australia."

"What's your booking number?"

"Um, I don't know, where will I find it?"

"It's in the top right hand corner of your crackle, mumble, rhubarb."

"Didn't quite catch that? Which document is it on?" (We were in possession of half a tree of paperwork and booking numbers were a new one on Barry, who generally knew everything.)

"The crackle, mumble, rhubarb." I read her a few numbers off the top right hand corners of various documents. None of them were right.

"Can you tell me how many digits it's supposed to have, that might help me find it?"

"No, ma'am, I can't do that."

Barry and I swapped seats at this point, clearly my English ear was costing us valuable time. He couldn't hear well either and none of the numbers either of us read off to the disembodied voice would satisfy so we were instructed to proceed to Customer Services. We asked for directions but the voice was only authorised to tell us to go there, not to tell us how. On to the next barrier. A person this time, a person who wanted our driving licences not any blooming yellow slips. We waved our yellow slips anyway but no, they were already redundant, presumably we could have been hijacked between the caravan and the gate by a yellow-slip-forging desperado. The second-barrier person did, however, have clearance to direct us to Customer Services. The Customer Services person took our driving licences again (but not our yellow slips, again) showed us the errant number on the paperwork and sent us off to Customs with the cheery words, "Come back here when you've cleared Customs."

Paperwork, messing about, identifications, little stamps on more paperwork and finally we were clear to find a numbered bay among rows of little mountains of containers and await the crane which would unload our trailer. At no point did anyone want to see our yellow slips. Then we made a third trip to Customer Services who had managed to hold on to a piece of paper that Customs needed—don't these people understand their own system—back to Customs one more time, one more driving licence check on the way out and we appeared to have escaped Baltimore docks without being arrested. They let us keep our yellow slips, we could have handed them on to anybody.

With relief we called in to tell dispatch we were empty. A new load would be a new start, this one could begin on time and not go even remotely pear-shaped. But dispatch had had a job ready for us since that morning. What with all the messing about, by the time we received it, refuelled and got across Baltimore to collect four tractors bound for three different destinations in Quebec, time was pressing on. We arrived just before five, as the manufacturer was closing. The quickest of handovers went, "The first two are one drop," followed by a flurry of paper. Various people drove the tractors onto our trailer in a neat little line and then we had to pull out of the yard to chain up in the dark because they were all going home now.

I tried to help. I knew enough by then to hook the right bit of this to that but Barry was effectively on his own trying to work out how to secure four tractors safely and legally for being driven about by an amateur. This all took a while. We had been messing about with stupid bits of paper all day and now the drive would begin in the dark. I was learning that this was a pattern, sit about all day watching the sun move across the sky and count the daylight driving hours you are losing while someone else does their job badly. It's rough having to start a long journey when you're already tired but we had to get some serious miles behind us if we were to make the first delivery by close of business on Friday. If all went well, if the weather didn't close in, if I managed to keep my speed up and there were no delays at customs we would just make it. Tight but doable.

I did my best. It snowed a bit and the roads were icy. Barry took over for a while when the visibility dropped and my eyes gave up. When we stopped for the night we were just about on target to arrive on time but only if the border crossing didn't hold us up. The papers we'd received from the shipper had to be faxed to a customs broker for pre-processing so that we could trundle merrily into Canada unimpeded.

Normally we'd do that from the shipper's office before we left but they'd been locking up and going home, so we used the 'driver facilities' (ie a phone and fax machine) at the truck stop we overnighted in. The paperwork didn't look quite right to Barry and, not wanting any time-consuming mistakes, he decided to call the broker and check. His end of the conversation went along the lines of, "I'm calling you before we send the fax to find out exactly what we need to send...no, I'm calling you first...no, because I'm not sure what to fax yet, that's why I'm calling...can I tell you what I have here, then you can tell me what to send...may I speak with your supervisor...no, I'm calling you before I send the fax..." Well, you get the idea.

Eventually, after several more, 'I'd like to tell you exactly what I have here so that you can tell me exactly what you need.' type exchanges, he gave up and faxed what they thought they wanted. We hit the road in daylight and got to the border bang on target. "Your pre-processing has failed," advised the customs officer in the little booth. This made us instantly nefarious. "You'll have to be X-rayed." Now I do understand that all manner of dodgy things can be carried over the border in a truck but we were hauling a visible collection of tractors. Where were we likely to be hiding the contraband?

Barry ran through the rules, quickly and sotto voce, for behaving correctly whilst being x-rayed. Step out of the truck immediately and back away from it with your hands visible. Stand where you're told, say nothing and make no sudden movements. We watched a mobile X-ray unit pass very slowly up one side of our tractors, round the cab and down the other side of the flatbed. There could have been packets of contraband taped to the tractor seats of course but it would probably have been quicker just to clamber up and look for them. It was a bit cold. I shivered. Was that a forbidden movement?

"We have to make a cab search now," said a chap with

a gun. "Do you want to get your coat?"

"Um, no it's ok thanks, it's way up on the bed and I don't want to delay you." I guessed it was permissible to answer direct questions but while I was trying to be polite and helpful Barry was asking the other chap with a gun to remove his shoes. Barry is fanatical about no-one wearing outdoor shoes in his cab but I wasn't sure that this was the time or the place for finicky housekeeping.

One guard took his shoes off as the other fetched my coat. Why were they being so nice? And what were they looking for? Did my Swiss Army knife show up on the x-ray? Would they confiscate my vitamins for women over fifty? Did this always happen when a broker screwed up? After a couple of minutes, during which nothing much could realistically have been looked at, they emerged and waved us away. Barry's grin began while we parked and widened as we walked across to the broker's office to find out what had gone wrong with the paperwork. He dealt with my perplexity. "The cab search was to save face. They knew they shouldn't have sent an open flatbed for X-ray so to cover for the first guy's stupid mistake they pretended to find something interesting inside."

"You faxed the wrong paperwork," began the conversation with the broker. I'll gloss over the next few minutes as the pressure cooker that was Barry's frustration level began to do what pressure cookers inevitably must, but will add a note of admiration that it waited for someone who couldn't arrest us and didn't wear a gun. The hours passed, papers were shuffled, stamps were stamped. The other trucker in the waiting area with us, they'd screwed up his paperwork too, produced from his pocket the fattest paperback book I have ever seen. I made another mental note. When we finally pulled over the border into Canada we were too late to deliver any tractors anywhere.

We drove to a truck stop an hour from our first delivery address and settled in for the night. The plan was to be outside the company's gate for eight o'clock on Saturday morning. Then, with both of the next stops open until lunchtime, we should just be able to drop the other two, each 100 kilometres apart, and start back by the afternoon. We could be home by Sunday.

Saturday began well. A truck stop with beautifully clean showers, decent coffee and an early start. The first two tractors dropped at the first customer as per orders from the shipper and on to the second drop. Nice weather, daylight, good roads, this was trucking. My sunglasses were on, the scenery was nice, it was almost a Yorkie Bar moment. The traffic in downtown Montreal was a little hairy but I only had to do it one more time and then we would be on clear roads again and heading for Ontario to tell of grand adventures.

Drop two. We'd unloaded tractor number three, got the paperwork signed and sent a satellite message to dispatch when a worried-looking chap came back out of his farming supplies shop to speak with us. We'd delivered the wrong type of tractor, not the one he'd ordered. Much shuffling of papers ensued. We read and reread the bills of lading trying to interpret which catalogue numbers related to actual tractors and which to accessories. We matched weights to items and finally the horrible truth dawned, the customer expecting two tractors was the last one we had to go to, not the first one we'd already left.

"He said, 'The first two are one drop.'"

"Maybe he meant the 'first two' on the trailer."

"The ones at the front?"

"Yes, he drove them on the trailer first but they'd be the last off."

By dint of not treble-checking everything we'd been told we had managed to leave, 100 kilometres behind us, the tractor ordered by the chap standing in front of us now. The one we had just offloaded for him was destined for the next port of call and they would want two of the buggers, not the single one that now remained on the trailer. Customer number one must have been over the moon when we offloaded two tractors after he'd ordered and paid for one.

Back onto the flatbed the wrong tractor went. We re-secured it and settled down for a planning meeting. We were still in possession of the two tractors the last drop had ordered, we could deliver them that day if the third destination would stay open for us. Then we could be back at drop one first thing Monday morning, bring tractor two back to drop two early and set off for home before lunchtime. We'd have to do downtown Montreal traffic again twice in a Monday rush-hour but that wouldn't be as bad as getting nothing done today. Barry called drop three and begged. They agreed to take delivery after twelve and gave him a mobile phone number to call when we arrived, someone would be with us to take receipt of the tractors within ten minutes of his call.

More Montreal traffic. The French clearly drive the same the world over but Montreal makes it extra difficult by being partly on an island. There are a limited number of bridges and all traffic passing through or around must do so by way of onto said island and off it again via said, horribly narrow, bridges. Knuckles white and toes curled we finally made it to drop three with their two tractors. The shop was locked and in darkness. It was also next to a junction combined with level crossing, there was nowhere to park that wasn't potentially lethal for someone. The mobile phone number didn't work. It wasn't just not getting answered, it wasn't a phone number.

We knew we were stuck for the weekend. We had no option but to find somewhere to park up and sit it out until Monday morning. There was no chance now of getting home before Tuesday and I was running out of clean clothes. There were no nearby truck stops but we consulted maps and guides and found an unprepossessing shop/restaurant of sorts with space for a truck to park outside. There was food, that is all. Abandoning the trailer and bobtailing off somewhere nice wasn't an option since the remaining tractors were in full view, very shiny and nicely nickable. Sunday passed in a blur of sleep, boredom and bad temper.

Monday began at six in the morning and ended at two o'clock on Tuesday. What did I learn with Barry? Two big lessons and a shameful little secret one. Never trust anyone to know their job, if you are leaving Ontario stick a bottle of vinegar in your handbag for the chips...and I might just be a bit too old for all this.

DAVE

WHEN I intimated that I might be a little old for all this, I did leave out a few salient details. Details which Barry chose to commit to paper and present to Challenger's Safety and Training department as reasons to chuck me out.

Details like, the more behind we were arrival-wise the more stressful I found the driving. The more stressed I got the more tiring it was. The more tiring it was the more stressed I got. By about half-way through our disastrous trip back from Baltimore my driving was worse each day rather than better. Reading the road became harder and harder as my death grip on the steering wheel got tighter and tighter, as I fought off exhaustion, forgot to breathe and fell to bits.

The final day of my last run with Barry may have begun at six in the morning but I didn't take the wheel until four-thirty in the afternoon, fully aware that Montreal had to be fought one more time and that we would be driving all night. I hadn't spent the day resting.

I'd tried hard, I'd negotiated the narrowest of Montreal bridges at rush hour in nose-to-tail traffic but by the time we hit the highway it was dark and I was already spent. I drove for four hours and then told Barry I needed a break, at the least a run round the truck and some blood sugar. We ate a dismal meal, Burger King I think. I carried on driving for another couple of hours but the stress, tiredness, dark and opposite-of-progress defeated me in the end. My exhaustion affected my focus, we gradually slowed down as I tried to drive within my vision and I knew I was no longer safe. Barry had to do the last, miserable two hours through a worsening blizzard. He said little but intimated that my stamina left much to be desired. Which of course it did. I had hoped that I would at least get a brownie point for being aware that it would be unsafe to continue, we'd been told in school that this was kinda admirable but in the real world it was a pretty useless asset.

In my defence I had sort of expected that training runs would involve getting used to marathon driving distances a bit at a time after legal amounts of sleep. I had wanted the opportunity to work up to things, getting stronger as I got used to the vehicle and instead I had been sleep deprived from day one. If long-haul work involved farting about all day while other people screwed up until you were knackered and then trying to drive all night, well, maybe it wasn't for me anyway.

I was called in to see the new training department Big Cheese. Barry seemed to think that I wasn't cut out for long-haul work, what did I think? I replied that I thought he might be right. I'd been a little disappointed, I added, that the work we'd undertaken had been so tight for time. I skirted around the details, not wanting to complain directly. The truth might have made it look as though Barry had coerced me into running an illegal logbook. Because of course, he had. Big Cheese asked a few more pressing questions about our timetable and I squirmed a little blaming bad luck that there had been no opportunity to ease in more gently, suggesting rather than saying that the lack of sleep had seemed a little OTT. I really didn't want to become the sort of arse who blames poor training for their own lack of ability but I did feel aggrieved as well. I'm not a happy snitch but it looked like my job was on the line here. Big Cheese pressed for details and I bleated that I was now in a difficult position since I had no wish to blame others for my shortcomings. Big Cheese got it anyway, called for the logbooks and examined our driving times for himself.

I received an apology, a confirmation that training runs should be unpressurised and that easing gently into the hours was the usual way to build up one's stamina. I was informed that neither the screw-ups nor Barry's insistence on rushing once we'd been delayed were my fault, that legal rest mattered. Big Cheese suggested that another trainer take me out 'round the block' for a test drive to see whether Barry's assessment had been fair. I was so pissed off by then that I didn't much care what happened next. Test run? Ok, why not? Let's get it over with. Then when they threw me out I could go home and sleep for a week. And cry for another week. Then I might feel better. In fact, right then I'd have preferred a good cry to a test drive but even if I was a crap trucker I could still refuse to let the side down gender-wise, so I didn't.

Dave, the arbiter of my future career seemed like a nice enough bloke. He smiled in friendly manner and told me not to worry about the politics of my recent interview. He opined that Big Cheese wasn't silly and had probably heard similar complaints before, that politically I was in the clear. Barry was famous for using trainees to run an illegal log book. Dave was easy to talk to. I told him that I did fear being too weak for the hours, that I had hoped to build up the stamina for driving all day slowly but that stress had made me get worse and not better.

I told him all this as I drove. I appeared to be handling his truck without any trouble. The gears were going in, the corners were neat and tidy. We chatted, I drove. There were one or two tricky lane changes and I switched into commentary mode as I negotiated them because it helped me concentrate. "Well, don't worry about the politics for now," Dave advised, "I'll tell you what I think in a minute."

We pulled back into the yard and parked. I shot him an enquiring look. "That's the best test drive I have seen for months," he grinned. "You are already a better driver than the guy I've had with me for six weeks, I'd say in the top 25% of people I've ever tested and that includes experienced truckers. I'm going to ask them to rearrange my schedule so I can take you out long-haul myself. After two weeks with me you will have what it takes to excel if you choose to."

And that is what he did. Which is how I ended up with a new trainer and a new truck. The trainer; into classic rock, Monty Python, Angel and Howard Stern. Of those enthusiasms, I only shared Monty Python so we bonded with a few classic sketches as we headed through New

York State and on to Pennsylvania with a trailer full of beer. The truck; a Peterbilt which is, I'm told, the ultimate in truck driving luxury. "Everybody wants to drive a Pete," was a refrain that began in trucking school and I was still trying to work out why.

It was certainly easier to drive than that bloody super single nonsense, although in my not-so-extensive experience anything with normal dual drive wheels would hold the road better than they did. The mirrors and corners were in friendlier places but still the peculiar addiction to huge chrome silencers behind the cab doors, ideally placed to get in the way of seeing anything while reversing. And one specific oddity, the dashboard was set very high up. I found myself trying to raise the driving seat higher and higher to get the visibility I was used to but then I couldn't reach the pedals.

"You'll get used to it, all Petes are like that."

"Isn't it dangerous? I mean I can't see as much of the road."

"You shouldn't need to see that close to your cab, your blind spots are a bit extended but as a good driver you need to have seen everything further away anyway. Anything this close is already under your wheels. You'll get used to seeing what's coming up behind you, and knowing exactly where they have got to, it's part of observing everything sooner than a car driver does."

"Hmm, it doesn't feel right."

"It will, don't worry. You can always tell a Pete driver, they have to put the driving seat down to the floor in any other truck to get their visibility feeling right."

"Oh!" Another penny dropped. I'd never asked Jeff my question but now I knew the answer.

Beer is a complicated thing to move. Not only do you need to take extra care to seal up a 'high value load' and have extra alcohol-related paperwork for the border, but the stuff needs all manner of overnight babysitting in foul weather to stop it freezing. Previously frozen beer is deemed unacceptable to consignees (which you'll know if you've ever popped a bottle in the freezer to chill quickly and then forgotten about it) so Challenger's system involves installing portable heaters in the backs of trailers at their holding yard overnight to prevent the precious cargo from being ruined by the Canadian climate. There is a set routine for making sure that you don't drive merrily off into the sunrise trailing a heater behind you, it involves mechanics and seals and double checks and all manner of fuss.

The system had been intuitively sensible for once though and therefore easy enough to learn. There were now a load more things I understood and I had reasons to be cheerful. We'd had enough sleep, our timelines were manageable and I had just learned that it was entirely possible to cross the border without incident. Nothing much had gone wrong so far, we were heading for a whole trip with nothing even remotely pear-shaped about it, which left me freer to look about and wonder at the oddness of the highway we were travelling along in rural, Amish Pennsylvania.

On the right side of the road, each house boasted a little washing line strung out by the hard shoulder, with a few hand-made quilts apparently for sale. On the left side of the same stretch of the same road, a string of 'adult entertainment' establishments. This bizarre mix begged at least two questions of course. Firstly, who in their right mind, even if they suddenly developed an urge to impulse-buy a handmade quilt, would buy one that was already full of dust and diesel fumes? The second question was obviously that if this is wholesome Amish quilting country where did the customers and in fact the staff of all these exotic establishments hail from?

***

On our first run Dave managed to teach me that one could sometimes drive from a, to b, to c and back to a, with nary a crisis and that getting enough sleep meant you could arrive home not resembling a dishrag at all and feel a bit more optimistic about going out again. After a legal rest of 36 hours at home our next enterprise was going to be Georgia and back before Christmas.

Winter doesn't normally begin for real in southern Ontario until early January but we set off during the beginning of a much heralded 'snowmageddon', a series of blizzards which would pound most of the continent in the week before Christmas. Since we were heading south we hoped to get out of the snow belt between hits and then sneak back in similar fashion. It was sunny as we set off and the roads had been freshly ploughed and salted. The main issue facing us as the journey began was how far to venture that day and where to settle for the night. Barry had been a 'picnic in the cab to save time' person but Dave was a 'get out and eat at a proper table at least once a day' type, so choosing great places to stop was an integral part of his journey planning. This was fine with me, I had a subculture to introduce myself to.

The fifteen hour drive divided nicely into six hours the

first day and nine the next, which would not only allow for paperwork and border delays, it would enable us to stop at one of Dave's all time fave truck stops, Jane Lew's in West Virginia. The plan made us both happy, all we had to do to stick to a manageable schedule was get a trailer full of crackers across the border. The Ritz type, not the exploding sort.

I was mightily disappointed that the border guard didn't ask what we were hauling. They seemed to like firing off a few daft questions like, *Where are you going?* and, *Where do you live?* even though they had advance electronic notification of everything, except possibly what you'd eaten for breakfast. I'd asked Dave what the point of all this redundancy was. "They just like to observe your demeanour while you answer stupid questions, the ones who get annoyed are the ones that get searched." That was good to know. This chap asked, "How do you two know each other?" I attempted to reply, "We work for the same company," without a trace of sarcasm, entirely as though it really was the sort of unfathomable conundrum you'd need to ask about. I would have quite liked the follow-up opportunity to tell him, *crackers*.

With Howard Stern for company we drove our manageable six hours, with regular coffee-and-wee stops, and presented ourselves at Jane Lew's truck stop for the night so I could see what all the fuss was about. I was getting used to the assortment of different ways the average truck stop could style itself. Some tried to be modern travel plazas with food courts and computer games, others went for the down-homey feel of wood panelled walls and resident patrons who could wear cowboy hats unironically. There were corporate chains like the incomparable Flying J, where the person who cleaned your shower before use left you a little choc or a peppermint on your clean towels, but Jane Lew's had to be a total one off. This one had personality. Dave collected truck stops with personalities, the weirder the better, they made for a more interesting drive, even if some were mildly schizophrenic.

Jane Lew's appeared to have been constructed from a combination of church hall and several outhouses. Someone had gone to infinite pains to decorate the interior with individuality and panache, leading to an imaginative mix of lilac and green colour scheme, gilt chandeliers, a huge mural along one wall depicting the truck stop and environs, a real fireplace topped with triptych stained glass windows...and lace curtains. There was also a random aquarium and the ladies' loo sported a red fabric potted geranium. It was all disconcertingly charming, as though some colour-blind person who was only allowed to use the contents of a jumble sale had really, really cared about making it as nice as possible. Oh, and of course the festive season was in full swing so add to your mental picture one wall covered in home-made felt Christmas stockings and one—yes one—string of red tinsel.

The food was on the imaginative side too. I was almost tempted to the battered and deep fried macaroni cheese, just to find out how you can manage to fry macaroni cheese and stop it falling to bits, but I settled for a sandwich in the interests of overnight digestive comfort. I feel duty-bound to add that the adjacent shop displayed a range of Christian T-shirts in one corner (*My Lifeguard walks on water!*) and an equally wide range of inflatable dolls in another. I may discover down the line that parts of West

Virginia are quite normal but dear Jane Lew (I remain unsure whether she is a place or a person) has amused me enough to become a permanent mental State mascot.

**

We passed through West Virginia, Virginia, North and South Carolina and into Georgia in the course of the following day. To a Brit, whose last memory of driving in England was taking seven hours to cover the two hundred miles from London to Blackpool, managing that sort of distance in a single working day was just bizarre. We'd left Ontario under several feet of snow and here the grass was green, the sun was warm and sunset was a whole hour and a half later. Changeable weather is one thing but a movable sunset? We'd shifted a bit of the globe here. Apparently a thousand miles due south will do that.

The unruffleable Dave had managed to teach me how to drive all day. The trick was to stop for a break every two-to-three hours without fail, whether you were tired or not. My previous technique of stopping when I was already knackered was apparently always going to be doomed to failure. People took years to work up to that sort of thing, who'd have thought? But it didn't matter because now I was managing ten hours at the wheel, with another emergency hour left in me if required. This was the standard. This was what could legally be expected of long-haul drivers, effectively my first full day's work. Thanks to Dave and his sage advice I felt a bit more as though it might be achievable more than once.

We partook of supper and showers at a slightly more normal truck stop, almost generic in its ordinariness, although I ought to add though that normal for Georgia involved an odd thing called chicken-fried steak and a shop that chose to juxtapose hand-made jewellery and a selection of crossbows in the same display case. What else can I tell you about Georgia? Nice people, friendly, hospitable and overwhelmingly polite. Lots of eye contact and smiling. Totally incomprehensible though, you wait a week for them to complete a sentence and you're still none the wiser. Did they understand me? Difficult to tell, what with the smiling and all.

Divested of crackers we awaited our instructions for returning, the details of where to go to pick up what for bringing back over the border. This was a little frustrating since Dave had given undertakings to various people-who-must-be-obeyed that he would be home the day before Christmas Eve without fail. The longer we waited before setting off the more of the thousand miles home would have to be driven in the dark. This could be the hiccup that set my new-found confidence in my ability to drive for ever back a bit. Night driving just was generally more tiring, I might be able to drive all day but all night could take a bit more practice. And heading north we'd be barrelling back into later sunsets and fouler weather. Still, I wasn't late for anything and hanging around with coffee, laptop and Dave's beloved DVDs of Angel on the telly had its compensations as a way to be at work. I was learning to snooze whenever the opportunity arose.

A couple of episodes of Angel later we received news of a pile of sofas sitting in Tennessee awaiting our attention. We headed north right away to find them but it was dark by the time we located the relevant factory and the little man in the guardhouse was tired and grumpy. He gave me a set of very precise instructions for where to drop our empty trailer and exactly how to proceed back past his fiefdom with the full one. He had the demeanour of a man who chooses not to say things more than once.

Fortunately I had the Amazing Dave by my side who was a little more tuned in to the southern American accent. Left to my own devices I'd have driven round in circles all night, since going back to ask the grumpy man to repeat his directions would have been a pretty fruitless enterprise. Sofas safely loaded, we eventually began the long trek north still hoping to be home the night before Christmas Eve. We took the driving in turns to try and cover as much ground as possible in the time, and where did we find ourselves stopping for the night? I'll tell you where...Berea, Kentucky. This little spot in the middle of nowhere was about to become famous in Dave's personal folk history of trucking as the weirdest truck stop he had ever seen. Please bear in mind that we'd stopped at Jane Lew's so that I could be shown the weirdest truck stop Dave had ever seen to date, I was honoured and delighted to be present on the night he found a weirder one.

If Jane Lew's had been schizophrenic, this one was a psychopath. We could only see diesel pumps and a scruffy little shop from the outside but there was a sign up that said *restaurant* so we asked where it was. A young woman with the most impeccably elaborate makeup I have ever seen nodded towards a sort of annexe which contained a few plastic tables and chairs. We wandered in to find a long, thin room constructed from bits of old trailer. A sprinkling of people sat silently watching a huge flat screen TV in one corner, each person alone at a separate table. There was a row of electronic slot machines along one end wall and a sort of church screen thing along the other. Comparing notes later we discovered we'd both had the mental soundtrack of *Duelling Banjos* and had expected that moment in the Western when you push through the swing doors and everybody turns to look at you as the atmosphere chills.

We sat at an empty table sporting crumbs and a bottle of Home Style Fancy Ketchup while makeup lady took our order. Nobody spoke. Nobody looked at us. We took in our surroundings. The screen was decorated with a selection of fabric, um, items; a small hand-made quilt, a flour sack and a fleece blanket urging one and all to support the troops. Livening up the long trailer wall was a small bookshelf full of apparently random knickknacks, and a tiny Christmas tree. A sign advised that the slot machines paid out tokens for use in the shop. The wall we hadn't previously been able to see contained a peg board on which were hung a multitude of different sized bungee straps. Across the doorway from the shop hung a piece of string with some wooden clothes pegs on it. Hanging from a couple of the clothes pegs were brightly coloured but somehow bedraggled triangular bandannas. Next to one piece of red tinsel.

A chap turned to regard us. He addressed Dave. "Yumpiver?" Dave nodded. Chap gestured to me, "Shumpiver?" Dave nodded. Chap turned silently back to the TV again. It's difficult to look quizzical when you are trying not to laugh but Dave twigged that I needed a translation. "He wants to know if we're truck drivers." His face was fighting with itself to keep the mirth inside. "I almost told him no, we come here for the atmosphere."

In need of a fit of the giggles I wandered off to the loo

but that just made things worse. Another bit of chopped-up, recycled trailer. The plumbing had obviously been put in as an afterthought since the toilet was situated up a couple of steep and rickety plywood steps on a sort of dais, most throne-like if a little wobbly. The inner wall had been painted but only in patches and there were a couple of sheets of fake tiling attached randomly here and there. It wasn't terribly clean, I made an instant decision to forgo the opportunity of a shower. I badly wanted to pop back to the truck for my camera but thought behaving like a tourist might offend. I didn't want to find out what happened when this silent roomful of people took offence.

On my return, clearly my amusement was leaking out because Dave immediately decided to check out the gents. He returned almost bursting with merriment, face still fighting. He whispered, "Was yours up some steps?" I nodded and we both sought diversion in the somewhat greasy BLT and chips which had finally appeared on our table. We were hungry enough to devour every scrap but it wasn't very nice. Oddly enough the best bit was the ketchup. I don't really like ketchup as a rule but had decided against returning to the truck for my bottle of vinegar (for reason, see above) but this stuff, the Home Style Fancy Ketchup, was actually not too bad. It rendered the meal edible which in hindsight wasn't the advantage I took it to be at the time.

Back in the truck, we could finally give vent to the hysteria. There were several perplexing questions. Who buys all the bungee straps? Were the bandannas for sale or hanging up to dry? Who were the silent people? (There were no other trucks in sight.) Why would anyone play slot machines when all they could buy with their winnings was more bungee straps? And what about the perfect makeup? This wasn't a bit of slap, this was Hollywood expertise, artfully applied and meticulously maintained. Was she waiting for the Johnny Depp of truckers to happen by in his beautifully tricked out Pete and whisk her off into the night?

Popping back inside later for a final wee I managed to answer at least one question. A huge CB setup lurked next to the till in the shop so that makeup lady could chat to passing truckers all night. Presumably her siren call of 24 hour restaurant service, greasy but with great ketchup, and all the bungee straps your heart desires might bring the right man within earshot someday. The mike was attached to a dislodged polystyrene ceiling tile with…another bungee strap. It had a jolly red Christmas bow on it.

In fairness, I should add that both makeup lady and her sidekick were utterly charming, especially when the combination of ill-advised late-night BLT, grotty bathroom and incubating flu had me throwing up for quite some time the following morning. I probably looked the least likely trucker they had ever seen, especially after having turned green, but they refused payment for my reviving coffee with a kindly, "Merry Christmas," that I actually managed to understand.

The blizzard began just south of Detroit. The roads deteriorated for hours as we took it in turns to fight our way home. The race to get Dave back to his loved ones in time for Christmas began to resemble a crummy country song with dead dogs in the next verse. But we made it. And he says I'm trained now. Apparently I can do it. Who'd have thought?

COMPANY WAYS

AND WHAT do you suppose happens at the end of Highway Training? Orientation, that's what. A chance to learn all the things that you really could have done with knowing before they put you in the cab. How to do things right, in other words.

A week of tours, inspections, lessons, lectures and *oh that's what we should have done* moments, during which I finally learned exactly how out of date the training school ways had been. It's not their fault, school ways are mostly to get you doing things Ministry ways, it's the MTO who are the really out-of-touch shower of dinosaurs. I now know that the bizarre and long-winded trailer coupling routine that caused me to replicate a TV game show harks back to the days when some trailers didn't have spring brakes. Even I know that's stupid but the digital age has moved things along pretty fast too, as have terrorism and the onward march of Homeland Security. (Tell me about it.) So, some nonsenses aside, the syllabus would have to change monthly if they tried to keep up.

Before all that however, a guided tour of Challenger's remarkable facility to make sure the newbies can find their way about and won't be annoying all and sundry by parking in the wrong place.

We began with the inspection bays, the part of the operation that had most appealed to me way back when my training school pal explained all about staying warm and dry while other people clambered around under the workings. Separate from the main building stood a little covered island comprising diesel pumps, sunken pits, clusters of tubes hanging from the ceiling for the dispensing of oil, washer fluid and the like…and dozens of mechanics.

All I knew so far was that we had to drive through the island and over an inspection pit every time we returned from anywhere. I knew that the mechanics checked our brake adjustments and fluids because I could see them opening the bonnet and hear them yelling *BRAKE* from beneath the undercarriage. Now we had introductions and a short lecture about everything else they checked for us while we were idly fuelling up and otherwise keeping warm. Our tame mechanics did so much on our behalf that our own daily check dwindled down to nodding at the lights, kicking the tyres and making sure that the brakes held.

From the inspection pits we were shepherded to the truck wash, partly automatic for the trailers and partly more people in boiler suits with foamy brushes on sticks who leapt out of nowhere and scrubbed you down while you, yes, sat about keeping warm. I was starting to feel quite spoiled. On round the huge yard to the repair shops and more introductions. Tractors scheduled for repair parked here, trailers for repair parked over there and if you just wanted something looked at on your way out you could park in this bit. But not there. That was the quiet zone where trucks had to power down because other people were sleeping.

And you could only park in that other bit over there if you were transferring belongings from your car, that was the temporary truck park. Next to the cars. How clever. Then there was another temporary parking area by the dispatch offices and main building, you couldn't idle your engine there either.

Trailers had to be parked in strictly defined rows, loaded in one place, empty further along. One trailer row was devoted to loads needing heaters, such as our beer. Flatbeds were this side, containers were there. All the tractors parked in rows where the block heaters lived. It made so much more sense once the explanations kicked in that I almost wasn't overwhelmed any more.

Finally we trooped over to the natty snow remover. On the way out from the rows of trailers sat an odd contraption which turned out to be a big brush for driving underneath. It scraped snow off the roof so that you didn't drive down the road depositing huge drifts onto the windscreen of the vehicle behind you. It seemed that these people had thought of everything.

Or maybe not. The last lecture of the day took place at the gatehouse. Electronic gates guarded the way in and out of the compound, they were manned by security staff who quizzed the driver of every load entering or leaving the compound. I was used being stopped to declare who we were, where we were going and what we were hauling.

Now I learned that they were checking that we had actually hooked the correct trailer, that it was sealed correctly and that we had applied the really important additional padlock. "No trailer leaves this yard unless it is securely padlocked," a jobsworth admonished. And I sort of knew that because we'd had to supply ourselves with a padlock as part of our kit…and prove that we had it, along with our hard hat and high visibility vest, before we'd been allowed to head out on day one.

I'd been dutifully toddling about with a dirty great padlock in my pocket ever since but I hadn't used it yet. Janice hadn't used one because padlocks didn't apply to local deliveries, they didn't get left unattended. Barry didn't use one because you can't padlock a flatbed. Dave had used a padlock, after a fashion. He'd hang it loose on the trailer door to drive past the gatehouse and then take it off again at the first coffee stop. I'd asked him about this baffling routine.

"Never really padlock the doors, the locks freeze and you can't get them open again."

"Why do you put one on then?"

"So long as the guard can see a padlock on his monitor as you drive by, he doesn't moan."

"Don't they ever check it?"

"No, it's cold out here." I was beginning to regret buying myself an industrial-sized, heavy duty, weather-resistant padlock. It now appeared that the little one floating around the house since it fell off a suitcase would have done.

After a guided tour of the dispatch department we were deemed to have learned enough for one day and it all seemed fairly simple. City dispatch here, long haul there.

(Another thing I could have done with knowing on day one.) Three of the dispatch teams looked after the single long-haul drivers and another little crew took care of the team drivers. We were introduced to this corner of the room. As a rookie, I would be team driving next. Two of us would hit the highway, taking it in turns to drive, and these people would be our link with the company by satellite message and by phone.

They smiled politely and said "Hello," but their faces were difficult to read. Teaming is hard work and not universally popular. Most companies want more teams than they have because they cover the really long distances in tolerable time, keeping the truck rolling round the clock as one person drives while the other sleeps. So dispatch may have been delighted to meet more rookies. Or they may have been dismayed to meet more rookies, rookies are hard work too. They remained inscrutable.

***

The first day of company training had been fairly gentle. I'm not sure whether they deliberately left scaring the pants off us until we at least felt at home enough to spot the difference between a trailer maintenance bay and a quiet zone, but starting day two with 'how to be hijacked' was a bit of a wakeup call. Until then, all I'd known about was how to try and not be hijacked. Recalling Gregg's version of not-being-hijacked, it went along the lines of never disclosing to anyone where you were going or what you were hauling. Whether it was a chat to pass the time on the CB radio or a chewing of truckerly fat at a truck stop your contents and destination were off limits, end of.

I'd rather assumed that keeping one's head down and not talking to anyone anyway would do the trick.

We are in straitened times however and this is no longer enough. Hijacking is bigger business than ever. We now know that most thefts happen from unsecured yards overnight while juicily loaded trailers are snoozing unattended but the violence is out there as well. Two drivers were shot during hijacks in Ontario during 2008 and the figures get more alarming over the border. The rules for not being hijacked have therefore expanded from Gregg's blanket embargo on disclosing information, we must now assume that everyone has their eye on our putative high value load and try not to stop in unlit or deserted places. We must notice behaviour on the road as well as at truck stops and get as good as Starsky and Hutch with regard to spotting that we are being followed. And padlock our trailers.

The rules for being hijacked as opposed to not-being-hijacked are simpler, partly because we are not allowed any weaponry…you can't take anything more dangerous than a sonic alarm over the border. Not that it would do me any good, I don't know one end of a firearm from the other and although I have wielded a pretty menacing crowbar in my time if I had to use one these days I would probably miss. But that won't be necessary since Rule 1 goes: *Try not to stop.* And Rule 2? *If you have to stop, co-operate!* You may be safer on the move but if there are mountainsides to avoid falling off or school buses not to demolish and you have no choice, make nice. Let them have the stuff. Company policy states that a driver is more expensive, long-term, than even a high-value load. Isn't that nice? I'm glad it's relatively simple, one wouldn't want to forget the finer points of hijackery in a crisis.

Then it was on to Challenger's version of customs paperwork, nothing to be scared of here. Except for the knowledge that the mug at wheel at the border is entirely responsible for the in-orderness of all paperwork made out by every other grunt in the chain. If anyone, anywhere in the system messes up, the mug behind the wheel gets arrested. You are the individual importing the goods therefore you are the criminal if it's not done right. I finally found out, after an entire afternoon looking at bits of paper, not only how and why Barry and I should have handled the great tractor faux-pas, but that we were bloody lucky not to have landed in a great deal more trouble than a few minutes shivering and a day and a half driving round in circles.

There are bills of lading. They are legally binding between the shipper and the consignee. There are customs invoices. These are legally binding between the importer (that's the mug behind the wheel) and customs. There can be real invoices too. These only matter if they exist but mustn't be confused with customs invoices. There are also sometimes packing slips. These only matter if they exist. There may be certificates for meat, for alcohol, for dangerous goods and all manner of other things…they may matter but not exist. As with tins of chicken soup. We must learn to shuffle through half a tree of paperwork, check that everything that matters is there, and that everything which may be there but doesn't matter is correct anyway, because even if it doesn't matter it must be right if it's there.

We must recognise the customs invoice above all other things. It may say *Customs Invoice* on it. It may not because it doesn't have to. Whether it is called the customs invoice or merely is the customs invoice, it must contain some very specific details which the person making it out may not understand, therefore we must. It must contain the total value of the load and its total weight. It must state whether the value is in US or Canadian dollars and it must state whether the weight is in pounds or kilos. The simple omission of the three letters l, b and s can scupper the best laid plans, delay freight and cause mayhem.

Having filled our heads with all these dire warnings the customs expert delivering our lecture goes on to tell us we can relax a little, since heading into the US is easy enough nowadays. Much of the routine is electronic and firms as big as Challenger have their own customs office wallahs who sort out all that stuff. We will receive not only all the paperwork, checked and double-checked, (yeah, right, talk to me about chicken soup) but a reference number which confirms that the details have been sent in advance to the border and approved. Lovely. Coming back however, we are on our own. So we do need to understand it all after all. A sticker with a bar code has to go on the customs invoice, once identified and checked, and then the whole caboodle has to get faxed to the right broker for, well, for doing whatever it is that they do. There are dozens of brokers and we are issued with more lists.

Now then, what was wrong with those tractor papers?

One company purchased all the tractors on behalf of, and for delivery to, three different franchisees. So the manufacturer only wrote one invoice because he was only selling to one person. But they were thinking money invoice, not customs invoice. We needed to stick three separate barcode stickers on three separate invoices for three separate deliveries, one barcode on one invoice for one purchase just didn't cut it with customs. Barry had been right of course but nobody would listen. He had suggested putting three stickers on the single invoice we had with us, which might have done the trick but the broker's jobsworth hadn't understood the problem. It never occurred to me for a moment that being a truck driver would require knowing the jobs of all the people who looked down on you better than they did and fixing their mistakes for them.

Our day of being frightened rounded off with a demonstration. We must be initiated into the arcane mysteries of Chaining Up. We were heading up mountains in a Canadian winter and there were rules about chains. These rules varied from province to province and state to state and we were issued with another pile of paper full of little diagrams of the mandatory axles to chain in each region. If you decide to bother. Although it is compulsory to carry chains through most mountainous areas in the winter months, actually putting them on would be a choice in most circumstances. The steepest of roads had thoughtfully-located lay-bys for sitting out the blizzard when a chain-up order went out, but that could take days. It was prudent to be competent, just in case.

The instructor laid the chains out for us to look at. Singles and doubles. The diagram would tell you which ones you needed where but if you were driving long-haul and cross-border you had to carry enough for the fussiest state, California, and a combination of chains which would allow you to please everyone else as well. A single chain would wrap around a single tyre on the front steering axle. Double chains wrapped the dual tyres everywhere else and were more of a pain in the bum to apply. They all had an inside and an outside and would eat up your tyres if you applied them outside-in. There were rules for which direction you laid them out in, depending on whether you were pointing up or down a hill at the time. There were rules for which bit to connect first and in what order to tighten them up.

There were also dire warnings. If you didn't get the cross chains dead straight they would loosen as soon as you began to move. They would fly off the wheel doing untold damage to tyres, equipment and unwary onlookers. They could, of course, rupture your air lines on a really bad day, leaving you with your brakes stuck on in the middle of the road half way up a mountain in the snow. This would not make you popular. If you didn't tighten them evenly across the whole wheel assembly, ditto. If you successfully tightened the chain which anchored between the dual wheels, and maybe even the one on the outside—but not the inside anchor, the one that was really hard to get at— then the chains would fly off and wrap themselves happily around the axle between the two wheels. Another way you could be stuck in the middle of the road half-way up a mountain in the snow. And unpopular.

The demonstration involved a lot of lying upside down between wheels and puffing and oomphing with arms raised at ninety degrees trying to lift and hook together a mess of recalcitrant chains. We couldn't actually see anything except the instructor's legs. It all looked very heavy and tiring, bearing in mind that this was under cover and the chains were relatively clean. On the road they would be covered in grease and snow. In fact come to think of it, on the road you'd be lying in grease and snow.

While no-one was looking I had a little go at lifting a double chain. Yup, impossible. I planned at that moment to sit out chaining-up weather in lay-bys, I'd carry chains because it was the law but you wouldn't catch me using them. If I'd concentrated a little more carefully anyway I could have saved a load of trouble down the line but I didn't know that then.

The orientation was almost over. One day left and just a quick overview of the hours of service rules and a play in a simulator to go. Then we'd be off for real. I knew all about hours of service, I'd learned them and passed exams on them. I'd even complained about them for goodness sake, what else could there be to know?

And of course, there is always something else to know. This time, team driving. There are exceptions to the rules. If you drive in a team the 24 hours must be divided up fairly between the two of you somehow. There are several ways to do this, the most obvious system is to drive for 12 hours each and then swap but that means one person is always doing the same time of day, or night. Some people prefer night driving and others prefer the manoeuvring and paperwork, so some teams find this system fair but others resent doing the same section of the day all the time. It means their partner has a perceived easier time of it, every day.

Some teams drive 10, 11 or 13 hours each so that in the course of a run the hours change a little, nibbling away at the daylight or darkness. Others prefer a strict, 6-on, 6-off routine so that you each drive two 6-hour blocks in the day. This works as far as the fair division of day and night is concerned but it also means that nobody gets their full 10 hours rest. Or even their full 8 hours and another 2 another time. But, for teams, it's legal. Don't ask me why.

Challenger rookies drive team. It's deemed to be the safest way to get you out there doing it for real but not quite alone. If you mess up, the other person may well be asleep and highly miffed at being woken to get you out of trouble, but at least they are there.

The company went to the somewhat endearing trouble of producing a helpful document entitled *Forming a Team*. It contained important nuggets of advice, such as:

Agree that you will both wash/shower daily.

Agree you will share equally any credit received from doing a good job or blame if things don't go right. (Huh, that never happens.)

Don't lose your partner. If you've been away from your truck, check the bunk before driving away.

Never attempt to switch drivers when the truck is moving. Now, as a rookie who is desperate for advice from experienced drivers I devoured my booklet from cover to cover but really didn't need to be told any of this. Perhaps we don't have to be so bright after all.

With no time to fully process the implications of trying to sleep in a moving vehicle or tolerate a stranger in your personal space 24/7 it was on to the final session. The dreaded simulator test. Quite what this would show them that actually driving a truck didn't, I couldn't fathom until I realised that they would be simulating roads rutted with snow and riddled with black ice. They could watch you in a Canadian blizzard without losing the truck. That at least made some kind of sense.

The test did not go well. "This is a two lane highway," said the instructor. He meant one lane in each direction but I heard differently and headed straight for the wrong side of the road.

"Use your mirrors more," he encouraged.

"I would but they're making me seasick." He flicked levers and buttons and my seat squirmed in a way that felt exactly like the drive wheels skidding this way and that. Things appeared in my peripheral vision from nowhere and the visual sensations continued to weave and leap about instead of behaving like things do in a real mirror. The nausea was unexpected and unsettling. I wasn't sure if throwing up in the shiny new simulator would be an instant fail but it seemed likely. I only kept my lunch down by not using the not-mirror mirrors. I passed, but only just.

"Do people often get seasick?"

"Oh yes, all the time."

"Why do you do it then?"

"They spent a lot of money on the simulator."

***

I've finally met my team driving partner. Mark is another Brit, he has driven lorries in the UK for fifteen years but is new to Canada. He is softly spoken with a West Country burr. We smile politely and eye each other warily. He is much favoured by dispatch...new to the company he already has a reputation for getting wherever he's going on time. I have been left in no doubt by Janice and Barry that my slow deliberations can be annoying. Dave seems to think that careful is ok but will Mark? Having been Canadian for several years, I am hoping to contribute my vast experience of geography and climate to the team and to not spoil his apparently flawless record. I am trying not to think about how easy it will be for him to sleep with such a total rookie at the wheel, I'm not sure if I could.

We will set out on our first run together at midnight. We are delivering a UPS trailer from Mississauga to Montreal followed by a mail run to Calgary and then, who knows? It is bitterly cold with record-breaking wind-chills. There are Alberta Clippers in the forecast and I am pleased to be able to tell Mark what this means. I may be a rookie around trucks but after driving through eight Canadian winters I can at least offer some weather expertise. Alberta Clippers dump huge swathes of snow across the country from Alberta eastwards and especially around the Lakes. Mark advises me that he knows all about snow because he has been skiing. Did we just get off on the wrong foot there? We make safer small talk as we check our chains.

MARK

OUR FIRST run as a team began relatively well. Mark volunteered to drive the first leg, partly because he knew the layout of the UPS depot housing our first load and partly because he quite likes to drive at night. That suited me. I'd not been able to sleep well during the afternoon, essential for a midnight start, so the chance to grab some more sleep before having to drive was welcome. We decided to experiment with driving 6 hours each at the start of a run, then switch to 12 and 12 once both of us had got some rest in. We agreed to review the arrangement once we'd given it a try, we both seemed to be being flexible enough to make the partnership work.

I stayed up for the first couple of hours to observe the UPS routine. The depot was huge and set back from the road with an entrance nowhere near the street address detailed on our paperwork. I hated to admit it but Mark was right, I would never have found it. There was a one-way system and a whole load of rules about what safety gear to wear, where to walk, what to do with all the piles of paper…and who to talk to. There was definitely a touch of *only speak when you are spoken to* about the whole enterprise, who'd have thought there was a pecking order among people who shuffle parcels? Thanks to Mark's tutelage I learned my UPS place, which was a mixed blessing. The tone was set. Mark was the one who knew stuff.

Once our load had been sealed and the seal checked for, well, sealedness, we hit the highway to Montreal and I tried to get my head down in the bunk for some rest. This was the moment when I finally got to grips with the biggest team-driving problem of all, the one that everyone from Gregg onwards had warned us about. Trying to sleep in a moving truck.

The sensation is comforting in a way, a bit like being on a combination of train and boat but noisier and bouncier than either. The motion is pleasant enough but it's impossible to shut your mind off sufficiently to doze off. You may be lying down but you're still driving in your head, sensing moves up and down through the gears, spotting hills and corners, wondering at stops whether the brakes will make this sound or that according to whether we are at traffic lights or problems. Old hands reckon that some people never manage to train their bodies to sleep in a moving truck whereas others develop an eventual inability to sleep in beds that keep still.

Additional complications in the bunk of a moving truck involve the whole sorry pantomime which is efficient negotiation of the safety net. This cross between football goal and mosquito net anchors into a series of seatbelt fittings slung from the back wall to the side of your bunk. It is meant to stop you rolling off in case of sudden unpleasantness of a deceleration variety, although it looks like one could have an additional strangling/tangling crisis of one's own, independent of any up-front disasters, if it was ever tried out in anger. The net is floppy and heavy and it lays in wait for unwary fingers and toes if you happen to be an exuberant turner-over. There were many things I had anticipated having difficulty with on this and subsequent runs, but getting eaten by my own safety equipment had not been one of them.

I took over the driving in Montreal which rapidly lived up to its reputation as a truckers' nightmare. Well, more accurately as this trucker's nightmare although in my defence, Mark's GPS contributed part of the trouble. Being a normal, car-type GPS we knew to check its suggested routes for impractical roads but weren't quite prepared for the confusion it created around road works and diversions. I only missed one exit from the highway, due to it being coned off, and then we were at Mrs. Garmin's mercy for a route back to where we needed to be for our next pickup. And this, M'lud, is how I managed to get a 53 foot trailer stuck in the middle of a junction trying to turn right under a bridge that was too close to the kerb, in a road that wasn't wide enough to make the turn.

Mark was awake, luckily, so he jumped out to direct traffic as I took up the entire junction reversing this way and that to make the turn that wasn't designed for trucks without creating a concave trailer.

"It's just as well I was here, you'd never have managed that on your own."

"Yes." The teeth gritted slightly. "Thank you."

"When you're as experienced as I am you'll size up that turn better."

"Maybe. But I did suggest stopping to check the map for a truck route round, might have been even better."

"I told you there wasn't time. Anyway we've got GPS."

"It's a car GPS, and I don't think we'll get there any quicker now."

"That's your fault." I gave up. The dynamic was now set in stone.

Interpersonal irritations and not-enough-sleep aside, all went comparatively smoothly during our first foray out west. We left Montreal, turned towards the setting sun, took turns on the Trans-Canada Highway and reached Edmonton, via Calgary, entirely as though this was a normal thing to do. The scenery changed dramatically day by day. It would be dusk as you passed the hilly, lakey, evergreen-and-rocks appearance of northern Ontario, then the sun would come up from under the prairies, flat as far as the eye can see and extremely boring. It would still be boring when the sun went down again…and then dawn would light up mountains in the distance and we'd gone so far that it was getting early later.

We drove through a time zone a day, which made dawn disconcertingly confusing. When your body is at its lowest ebb and you are waiting for the sun to come up between seven and eight because dawn will make you feel better, there is a huge surge of disappointment when it doesn't. When you realise the night will last an hour longer the depression is total. Yet again I am gobsmacked at how much of the planet you can cover in a day.

***

There isn't much to keep one amused driving across Canada. Entertainment consists mainly of road signs along the highway, which get rarer the further west one travels. Northern Ontario still has some people in it so there are adverts as well as side roads off to small places. Not many though, I had several hours in which to ponder the significance of *Mikey's Smoke House, Wild Meat Processed*. I knew this was hunting country but hadn't given the mechanics of hunting sufficient thought before to twig that it would mean eating what you kill. Yes, presumably someone has to skin, gut and chop up the still warm deer but wouldn't you want to do that for yourself? Isn't it all part of the experience? You'd think so. But on balance and after about a thousand kilometres of thought I decided that, yes, I'd want Mikey to do it for me too.

Through Manitoba and into Saskatchewan I can't report much other than place names. Manitoba had some. We passed signposts to places and it helped the time pass to watch them get nearer, see them drop behind and then wait excitedly for the next one. Saskatchewan didn't. Have places that is. Which didn't leave one much to think about, except for one very exciting road sign...Qu'apelle Lake. Now my French is a little rusty so correct me if I'm wrong but surely that's the French for *Wossname*? It sounds quite fancy but I spent another few hundred kilometres wondering who on earth decided that was a sensible name for a lake.

As we neared our first destination I still wasn't sleeping. The trick, I had been advised, was to get so totally dog-tired that you'd fall asleep standing up given half a chance. I was hoping the transition wouldn't be too much longer, I had to be exhausted enough to make the trick work soon.

Maybe it was the lack of sleep but the cracks in our patience with each other were beginning to show.

On the surface we played nicely enough. Mark hated paperwork, found map reading and bills of lading difficult and struggled a bit with all the code numbers for fuelling up. I didn't mind in the least doing all that stuff but I wasn't too steady climbing about on the engine to clean the windscreen so Mark happily did that bit. I still wasn't completely confident reversing so he'd jump out and 'spot' me backing into a bay. He liked to drive through sunset and I liked to drive through dawn, so we developed a system of swapping at four in the afternoon and four in the morning. It should have suited us both.

The rot began with our differing attitudes to timekeeping. Mark brought a British sense of urgency with him, compounded by the apparent inability of his wife to cope without him for very long. He was in a hurry to do everything, his only personal gear was hurry-up. I remembered this way of being from my previous life as a Brit but had thankfully replaced the resultant stress with a Canadian sort of patient deliberation. It made me happy to potter about double checking everything several times. It drove Mark nuts.

"We have four days to get there, we can shut down for four hours each night to get some good sleep and still make the delivery."

"If we keep rolling we'll be a day early."

"They don't want us a day early. And I'd like some food and a shower too."

"We don't need to stop for food, moi Gaiowe made me some stew."

"No-one made me stew and they don't want us early."

"We can ring and see. If we get a run back faster I can see moi Gaiowe before the weekend."

He'd called dispatch and asked them to check with the consignee whether we could deliver on the wrong day. They'd sighed. It's a pain. Just-in-time logistics don't work that way, the stuff has a window to meet so that it can be processed from the truck, not stored until required. But Mark's Gaiowe (Gail, I think) took precedence.

The fissures deepened with the weather. It was cold. That's cold for Canada, which starts at about -30. Winter had hardly started and we'd already had fog, blowing snow, slushy roads and a slight delay while the emergency services blocked the road digging a hapless tractor-trailer out of a ditch. I'd driven through enough Canadian winters by then to know that the weather this country throws at you brooks no compromise at times. Ice, snow, fog, freezing rain and the like control everyone's timetable. Canadians know that, delivery windows allow for the fact that people tend to die when they take on the elements. Delays for the winching of trucks out of ditches are a signal to take a little extra care.

"Perhaps we should find a place to stop overnight until the weather improves."

"When you're as experienced as me you won't need to stop."

"They're closing the roads, we can get stuck on the roadside or plan a proper break."

"We might make it through if we keep going."

The Brit mentality wasn't helping here either. The weather rarely controls your life in England and the correct response to a delay would always have been to speed up to make better time, so my tendency to respect the elements here drove Mark nuts. Of course the problem was exacerbated by our routine, starting at four in the morning I really did hit all the fog and fresh snow. Honestly. By the time he woke to find the roads nicely ploughed, all he could see was that we'd not got as far as he'd hoped. The accusations of mythical fog were never overtly stated but as his suspicions grew that I was lying, my attempts to educate him about Canadian weather grew ever more defensive. They fell on deaf ears. We'd both established on day one that the rookie knew nothing worth learning.

Mark was a whinger and I was a sulker. He didn't like the way I rested my feet when I drove, I didn't like his constant over-steering. I hated that he wouldn't stop for anything, he hated that I pulled into a truck stop for bathroom breaks. To begin with we discussed things.

"I know you like to get there as fast as you can but I really need sleep and food."

"When you've been driving as long as I have you'll cope better."

"I'm coping fine, I'm just sick of nuked noodles and there's no need to hurry."

"You can have a bit of moi Gaiowe's stew."

"That's nice of you but it's not the point, we'd be safer after some proper sleep."

"I think I'll ring moi Gaiowe and tell her how nice the stew was."

I would really have preferred to be out of earshot for the nightly calls to moi Gaiowe. Try as one might to pretend not to be there, there's only so much sound a cab curtain and earplugs can muffle but Mark would brook no delays, which meant our truck stop visits were few. Thus I rarely had the opportunity to remove myself from the nightly discussions of lovely stew, domestic hiccups and wedded bliss.

On the odd occasion when we did pull in for a break, it annoyed Mark that I would park close to the lights and buildings. It annoyed me that he would insist on parking as far from civilisation as possible. He would explain that parking right at the back of a truck stop meant that he didn't have to walk further than behind the trailer for a comfort break. I would moan that women had different toileting requirements and he was making me walk a bloody long way in the dark. I would add somewhat snottily that it was against company load security policies to park away from lit areas anyway. He would retort that loads were even safer backed up to a tree than they were under lights.

Mark nagged, I shut down. Passive-aggressive is my battle mode. My average speed dropped in inverse proportion to the whinge quotient. Just because. He would hare round icy bends on cruise, just because. The driver always won anyway so we were both perpetually irritated. The polite veneer ebbed away as we delivered our first load and turned east to head home.

***

I had been unfair to Saskatchewan. It doesn't just have Wossname Lake, it has the Saskatchewan Potash Interpretive Centre as well. How could I possibly have missed this gem on the way out when it was a major point of interest on the way back? And what is a Potash Interpretive Centre anyway? Well one has to Google, doesn't one? This little tourist attraction would appear to be an exhibition mine celebrating the province's modest claim to fame. Its website included the strap line *More to Saskatchewan than meets the eye*, which is clearly true, since nothing meets the eye.

People had told me relatively often of the boredom of driving across the Prairies, but only now did I get it. The only visual cue across two entire provinces is the horizon, there is nothing to ponder except the curvature of the earth.

This is why I was in a lather of excitement for driving through sunrise on the way home, despite the exhaustion. When the horizon is the only thing you can see, driving east at dawn has got to be almost mystical right? I braced myself for the longer western night and drove hopefully towards the sunrise, mentally composing a soppy romantic blog post entitled *Lovely girl, Dawn*, which would wax lyrical about sunrises past and present. But then, around Winnipeg, the fog descended. Freezing fog, blotting out the sky, settling on the mirrors and reducing visibility to a matter of feet. I would learn on future runs that it is always foggy around Winnipeg at dawn but this time it seemed particularly spiteful.

There comes a point when it's counterproductive to keep going. Once your speed drops to a walking pace you're always better off asleep and making up time when the visibility improves. Gregg said so, it must be true. I pulled into a closed weigh station in disgust and settled down for a snooze where dawn should have been. My disgruntlement at missing the sunrise was nothing to Mark's at finding me asleep instead of driving. Of course the fog had cleared by then, he almost accused me of inventing it, but not quite.

Our first real run was almost over when we blew a tyre. We had covered fifty-five hundred miles in five days and were a quarter of an hour from our destination in Toronto, just where two major highways met. Goodness, a disabled truck can cause some chaos on the ramp from the 400 to the 401 in rush hour. Differences forgotten we rallied, all teamy, to deal with the crisis. We leapt into action, positioning our reflective triangles at exactly the right distances behind us to alert the massive traffic jam that it was all our fault. We correctly assigned the relevant satellite message to the right department to get Challenger's breakdown service on the way. We congratulated ourselves on our teaminess. When Mark was nearly home with his wife and I didn't need a wee we could just about like each other. We concluded that our first run had been…ok. A relative triumph.

***

Mark and I settled into a routine for the next little while. We ran from Mississauga to Montreal, to Edmonton, and then to Calgary with mail and courier loads. We found a couple of coffee stops and some regular places to refuel. We tried new routes from time to time and bickered about the weather. I got used to walking too far in the cold when Mark parked us, he got used to me inventing fog. I ignored his jibes about being my trainer, he ignored my homilies about the elements. He cheered himself up while spotting my reversing by telling people he was my instructor. I'd have been really annoyed by this if I wasn't doing the same while spotting him.

I found another road sign to get excited about in

Saskatchewan. A road less travelled a little to the north of the Trans-Canada Highway introduced us, nay welcomed us, to Canada's Badlands. Now I love this country, you may have noticed, but occasionally the silliness gets overwhelming. What on earth happens in Canada's Badlands? Does the girl in Tim Horton's deliberately omit to say, *you're welcome* when you thank her for the coffee and doughnut?

There were things about the cross-Canada journey that delighted both of us, such as the bizarre border town of Lloydminster which lies partly in Saskatchewan and partly in Alberta. The provincial border is pointed out in a helpful but unassuming sort of way with a tiny sign at a set of traffic lights along the main drag. Since there is an hour's time difference between the two provinces, the helpful little sign denotes a time zone change as well. We whiled away a lot of kilometres wondering how they managed to get the school buses to run on time.

Being Brits, and townies, the wildlife was a novelty for both of us. Talking about deer and moose, smelling skunks and spotting eagles livened up our journeys as well as contributing to the bickering. It annoyed Mark that I used my high beams whenever we passed animal warning signs. It annoyed me that he refused to.

"I can see without high beams, I never used them in England."

"But here they help you see animals." I could quote Gregg 'til the moose came home, it made no difference. I didn't like that we were more likely to hit something while I was trying to sleep but it did provide another good reason to drive the dawn shift, I wanted to be at the wheel when we were most likely to encounter four-legged hazards. And it was just about at dawn that I finally met our first moose.

I'd developed the habit of selecting a different road sign to think about on each trip and it just so happened that I was having a ponder about wildlife signs at the time. Each province produced its own versions of the warnings and some of the little images of deer and moose were better than others. For example Alberta had a very strange sign that was probably supposed to represent a moose standing on a road, it juxtaposed a moose shape with white lines and looked for all the world like a moose on skis.

But this was northern Ontario and I saw a brilliant new sign. In my peripheral vision by the side of the road stood a perfect, life-sized, cut-out silhouette of a moose. I marvelled at the cleverness of the sign designer. You could almost imagine that this was a moose standing stock still on the grass verge. No silly moose-on-skis nonsense for Ontario. In the half-light it almost wasn't there and as I turned my head to see it better it seemed to absorb the light and disappear. I drew level with the clever silhouette warning sign as I contemplated its effectiveness. It turned to look at me in a lazy sort of way then kicked up its heels and skittered away into the trees, really quite nimbly for something the size of a moose. If it had run the other way I would have hit it. If it had been in front of me instead of on the verge, I would have hit it. Now I've seen the light-absorbing motionlessness for myself, I understand. Night vision is about movement and reflection. I heard Gregg's version of how-to-hit-a moose replaying. You don't want to be doing that. No you don't.

And then, finally, Mark learned something about Canadian weather. Leaving from the yard one day in the depths of January I popped the radio on scan. I wanted to catch the weather forecasts as we began the trek north from Toronto to North Bay because the internet search I had remembered to do before leaving was tracking a belt of freezing rain heading West across the Prairies fairly fast. It was entirely possible that it would pass Western Ontario before we got far enough north to meet it, but no. Every radio station was broadcasting watches, warnings, school and business closures, bus cancellations and the like.

Canadians are pretty hardy about trying to drive (slowly) through most winter stuff but everything shuts down for freezing rain. Well, apart from trucking, obviously. Freezing rain is not normal stuff, not ice or snow or hail. It happens when the weather system high up is warm enough to produce real, wet rain and the ground surface is cold enough to freeze said wetness on impact.

Everything gets covered in a layer of the slipperiest ice imaginable, trees, signs, roads, trucks. Imagine being able to ice-skate down the street in your wellies. You need a continent the size of North America to provide the conditions for such a phenomenon, I'd had to have it explained to me during my first winter here. I'd done the Brits-know-everything routine back then, scoffing at my friends for being stupidly cautious over some silly transatlantic version of hail and hurt myself quite badly hitting the deck as they explained that this was different.

I told Mark that we might hit freezing rain overnight and to expect slow progress. He sighed.

"When you're as experienced as I am you won't need to slow down for freezing rain."

"You don't actually know what it is, do you?"

"Of course I do, I've been skiing."

I channeled Gregg, set the demister to very hot, opened a window so I didn't suffocate, made sure the mirror heaters were on and proceeded gingerly. Fortunately the roads had been well gritted and stayed relatively ice-free but I had to make regular stops to chisel away the layers of ice which kept building up on all the lights.

By the time Mark awoke to take over the next driving shift, the entire truck (apart from the lights) was covered in a layer of ice half an inch thick. It began busily falling off in fascinating shapes as the temperature rose through the morning. As one huge ice replica of the driver's side mirror slid groundwards he produced the words that made my heart sing.

"What's that?"

"That's freezing rain."

OFF THE TRANS-CANADA

MAIL RUNS from Montreal to Edmonton, sheer tedium. The Trans-Canada Highway was boring and it had very few truck stops. Those that did exist were pretty basic. The one we tended to use the most smelled of unemptied septic tank, it wasn't easy to fancy eating or showering, regardless of hunger or grubbiness.

We did try a meal there once, I think moi Gaiowe had fallen short in the stew-making department that week. I was delighted to note that the little restaurant boasted perogies and cabbage rolls on the menu, a favourite of the Mennonite locals where I live in Ontario. They were very disappointing but that might have been the smell of septic tank rather than the actual food. I have rarely showered anywhere and felt dirtier afterwards than before.

I was getting more than a little efficient at managing my toileting requirements at the side of the road, under the trailer, hanging on to the landing gear for balance. I've never been much of a camper or rambler so the finer

CAROLYN STEELE

details of not soaking one's shoes had been new lessons, oddly enough not covered in school. It may have become second nature to check that I was facing uphill and upwind but I wasn't happy about having had to learn the hard way. I wanted to be exploring the countryside, driving the mountains, crossing the border and visiting a Flying J or two, like I had with Dave. I wanted buffet breakfasts and mints on my towels.

Mark liked the familiarity. He was happy to do the same run week after week, it meant no map reading. Occasionally we'd try a different road but the options were pretty limited. In Ontario you could either get from North Bay to Thunder Bay by Highway 11 or Highway 17. One had more coffee stops, the other had straighter roads. Crossing the prairies you could get to Saskatoon via Regina if you liked or you could miss it out for kicks and sheer devilment, turning north onto Highway 16 a bit sooner. There was nowhere nice to stop either way.

And then all of a sudden dispatch must have decided we'd earned our stripes, they started to send us to new places. Our first diversion off the Trans-Canada was to the aptly named Cold Lake. We didn't actually try the lake for aptness, just extrapolated from the wind-chill when we arrived. Cold Lake is about as far north as you can get in Alberta before the roads give up bothering to go anywhere. The only thing in town is an air force base, which is where we were due to collect something, from someone. The shipping address consisted of a mere three letters, CFB. We only knew this to be some sort of military establishment because we happened to have a cup of coffee with a helpful and friendly Challenger team in Edmonton.

We sent a satellite message to dispatch asking for a bit of help with finding our load. We assumed that the base would be easy enough to locate, signs and the like, but that there might be some sort of protocol attached to getting in and that it might include such security issues as knowing what you were supposed to be collecting and from whom. A name maybe, perhaps a rank of some description, or just a department. Driving a truck aimlessly about an airbase with no specific destination in mind seemed as though it might be behaviour designed to spark suspicion, for all they knew, we could be full of fertilizer and planning nefarious exploding activities. For once our joint Britishness worked in our favour, we'd both been around during the IRA's truck bomb years.

It was my driving shift but we had an agreement to stay up and about while problem solving, despite the bickering we managed enough team spirit to take pride in sorting things out without looking stupid if we could. I detailed Mark to explain the concept of a military base to the pen-pushers via the satellite while we headed north.

Dispatch were still mulling over the whole problem of whether it mattered what we were collecting from where when we arrived in Cold Lake. Quite why they couldn't just call the person who made the booking in the first place is beyond me but then I am just the grunt these days. We followed some remarkably pretty signs to the base and spotted a guardhouse and barrier in the distance.

"We'll just have to ask there, presumably they can call someone if we're not allowed in."

"It doesn't look as though it has a window at our height, maybe park back here and walk up?"

Please bear in mind that this is a team of two Brits

blundering their way around an unexpectedly alien culture. We parked a polite distance shy of the entrance and went to pay our respects. The guard house was empty, the barrier was up and a green light invited us in. I had a moment to wonder what might have happened if our truck really had been full of fertilizer but then this is Canada. Even the armed forces are friendly.

As expected, just like military bases the world over this one resembled a small town. Where does one park a bloody great truck in order to ask directions? We plumped for sticking to bigger roads while heading for the nearest available barrier that actually blocked the way to somewhere. That sort of thing might sport a person. A few tight corners later we approached just such an arrangement.

I considered pulling right up to the guardhouse but could see that, again, there wasn't a window at truck height and decided, again, to stop a few yards shy of it. We still didn't want any misunderstandings of a security nature. The girl in the hut spent several minutes piling on layers of winter clothing before ambling inquisitively towards us to see what we wanted. "I'm awfully sorry, didn't want to come right up to you in case we're not allowed through there but we have to collect a consignment from the base and don't know where to go." It sounded a bit lame.

She told us that where we had to go was back the way we had come and up a little street to the Military Police building. They would identify us, find our shipper for us and supply us with an escort. A small queue of jeeps and things was forming behind us.

"Um, could we come in and turn around?"

"There's nowhere to turn, unless you can use the

intersection here..." There was a small crossroads just beyond the gatehouse. "I can stop the traffic for you if you like."

Mark and I considered the space. It was tight but possible. Snow banks on all corners made the feat a little extra exciting but we had no choice. With a full audience of uniformed types, I executed a perfect U-turn and grinned my way off to be identified. Of course now we knew where to find it the MP building was the obvious place to stop and ask questions. It had truck parking and everything. Pity about it having no signage, we might have found it on the way past the first time.

An efficient administrator found our shipper and engaged an escort to take us into the relevant restricted area. He arrived in the form of a very red-faced squaddie who addressed himself entirely to Mark while explaining where we would be going. Mark just smiled politely, met my eye and said nothing. In the face of non-truckers we were still a team. Red-faced squaddie escorted us outside and managed not to look too confused when we headed for the wrong sides of our vehicle and it became horribly apparent that I was driving.

He led us through barriers, along lanes and finally through an apparently pointless narrow concrete chicane (which one could have driven around in better weather) to a large prefab which resembled a hangar in everything but contents. "Um, we need you to back up to that door there, sorry it's a bit tight." Tight was an understatement worthy of a Brit. It was a blind-side reverse with snow banks on all sides and an unhelpfully parked jeep, that you couldn't see from the cab, to avoid. A platoon of additional hefty personages appeared and waited silently to load our trailer by hand. My heart sank. There was me, determined to prove that women did this stuff, the worst of all possible manoeuvres to attempt…and an audience. Mark got it. Our differences evaporated even further in a joint determination to impress the crowd. He jumped out to guide me back, told the assembled chaps in no uncertain terms just how difficult this would be and muttered, "Just do as I tell you, it'll be fine." And after a fashion it was. Yay, put that in your pipe and smoke it squaddie-who-only-talks-to-men.

It took a couple of hours serious snoozing for the assembled company to load our trailer full of boxes of stuff and then we were ready to be escorted off the premises. I was a little cocky by then, I was going to show the Canadian Air Force just what women could do. It is therefore possible that I took the pointless concrete chicane just maybe half a kilometre per hour faster than before. And it was a tad tight anyway, designed for jeeps. ("We don't get many 18-wheelers up here.") There was barely enough space to swing the tractor around to avoid the next lump of concrete as the trailer wheels swivelled around the one you'd left behind. It was a bit like those puzzles where you have to get along a bendy piece of wire without making a buzzing noise, there was only one successful path through. Anyway, there's no getting away from the awful truth. We felt this 'orrible lurch as a front wheel dropped off the road through a snowdrift into a ditch.

The first thing that went through my head was, "Ah, this will be fun to write about." The second was, "Ohnoohnoohnoohno not here, please…" Gregg sat on one shoulder whispering in my ear, "You don't want to do that, no you don't." Jeff occupied the other shoulder... "And breathe…" and I can now report the amazing scientific finding that embarrassment can overcome physics. A spot of reverse, a smidge of forward, a bit more this-away and some jiggery-pokery over there and we were out of the ditch, through the chicane and off the base. Women drivers though. Useless.

***

They kept on sending us to more interesting places. We'd start the trip with Mark's favourite mail run and then branch out into map-reading mode. This was fine by Mark so long as I did the map reading. The next diversion sent us south, at last. After another cold, miserable, boring drive across the Prairies, fuelling up in the kind of wind-chills that generate frostbite on unwarily uncovered bits of person, dispatch asked us if we'd mind heading for Texas with a truckload of honey. Mark was apprehensive but I talked him into it. Here was an adventure, he could write home about it and be a hero. We could be warm for a day or two. We counted the Tupperwares, he had enough stew. I promised faithfully to do all the border paperwork, all the fuelling, all the map reading and he finally agreed to give the US a go.

Honey is heavy. A truckload of honey is pretty damned close to the maximum weight allowed on five axles and the shipper knew this. They had a scale on site for weighing laden trucks to check for legality before they left the premises. This was the first time I'd had to scale a truck so I was quite grateful to be doing it somewhere where the guy knew his stuff.

We'd had a quick lesson in how to use a public scale back in school when Jeff had taken us over a fancy scale at a local truck stop. That one had sported separate sections for each axle, merely driving on to it and stopping at a marked point meant that it could print out a tally of the unique loads on each of the steer, drive and rear axles. This scale was just one big truck-sized lump of concrete. Under instruction from 'the guy' we learned how to drive an axle off at a time so that he could do his sums, subtracting each weight from the one before to come up with all the weights we needed. The legal maximum total was 80,000 lbs, which we were just under, but it had to be distributed right to avoid being fined at a roadside weigh station, there were maximums for each axle as well.

The honey turned out to be just legal on all axles so we offered some thanks for the help and left to fuel up in the sort of blizzard that only the wind whistling across the flat prairies for thousands of miles, direct from the Arctic, can produce. I nearly lost a bit of finger on the frozen metal of a diesel pump due to a small gap in my fleecy work gloves. I also learned a new definition of cold. In the interest of ladylikeness I will continue to gloss over the athletics required to conduct an emergency comfort break under a trailer, suffice to say that there comes a temperature when the uphill and upwind stuff matters a bit less. The wee freezes as it hits the ground.

We headed back across the flatness to cross into the US at a small land border just south of Winnipeg. That leg of the trip took a full day during which I couldn't help but wonder why one sends truckloads of honey from Alberta to Texas. Do they not have bees? You'd have thought they might have even more bees, given the friendlier climate.

As the border approached I checked and rechecked the paperwork. This would be the first time I took anything across without someone else to make sure we were legal. It couldn't have been more correct than it was but they X-rayed the truck anyway. We had no idea why but stood where we were told and kept our traps shut as prettily as we could. After a mere hour's delay we were over the border because apparently everything was ok after all. Mark mentioned having overheard some truckers' chat that the little land borders X-rayed everything that came through because they were bored. We put our delay down to the idiocy of the system and headed south, still speaking to each other.

The following 24 hours saw us driving through North and South Dakota, Omaha, Missouri, Kansas, Oklahoma and Texas. It felt like a lot more progress driving south and passing all those state lines than it did spending two days plus just to get out of Ontario. It was almost like being on a small holiday.

Mark finally tired of his Gaiowe's stew and, while I swore an oath of secrecy, we stopped for a meal in South Dakota which, I can now report, is far enough south for biscuits and gravy but not far enough south for grits. I have yet to try grits, although when the chance finally does come I might chicken out, they just sound nasty. Try saying it out loud and then ask yourself whether you want to sample it (them?) for breakfast. I was almost tempted to risk the *biscuits and gravy elite* which included something odd to do with sausages but then got all conservative and went for my usual veggie omelette instead.

The server smiled a big, beaming South Dakota smile, and asked me, "Wheawhysurdohryroriscuit?" It took a moment. I had a flashback to the same question on a memorable trip from Victoria, BC to Port Angeles, Washington several years earlier. I really had been on holiday then. A pal and I went to America for the day, partly for shopping and partly to eat a breakfast of biscuits and gravy since I couldn't imagine what this might be like. Imagining digestives and Bisto hadn't helped but neither did the fact that the dish, when I finally saw it, did not look to contain either biscuits or gravy. It appeared to be a bowl of scones covered in chicken soup. Which is pretty much what it was.

Having observed the object of my interest from a respectable distance I'd opted for the veggie omelette on that occasion too and was asked this same incomprehensible question. My then escort and guide in all things American, Joe, had had to interpret for me. "She wants to know what sort of toast you'd like." I'd asked her to repeat it again slowly and we'd all had a jolly transcultural moment as she reiterated, "Wheat, white, sourdough, rye or biscuit?" So this time I was right on top of things after a moment's double-take and had the presence of mind to ask for rye, just in case my luck was in and it would turn out to be a marble rye establishment. Which it did. Marble rye was now officially my all time favourite bread. The new roving life involved getting excited about very small treats.

The stop in South Dakota was our only break. Otherwise we hammered all the way to Dallas driving ten hours at a time each, in order to arrive in time for a legal 36 hour break before logging driving hours again when we delivered the honey on Monday morning. We cheered up as the land became progressively less covered in snow. The drive became positively jolly as we crossed from Kansas to Oklahoma, I sang out, "I don't think we're in Kansas anymore, Toto!" just as Mark began the opening bar of *Oklahoma* with considerable gusto. Driving with another Brit did have its amusing side, we seemed to think of the same songs as we passed the names of places that ought only to exist on the telly.

We took our compulsory break swanning about a truck stop in Dallas, humming the theme tune a lot. The sun was out, the breeze was warm and we did that most un-American of things, we went for a walk. I wore a T-shirt and sawn-off trousers with pink baseball cap keeping the sun from my eyes. This was the sort of trucking I had imagined all those months ago.

To add to the joy, once honeyless they sent us further south to Houston. There were palm trees and the grass was green, properly green. Driving south in the winter, you could plot your progress by the grass. To start with there would just be snow, then gradually less snow until bits of grass would show through, but brown, dormant, winter grass. A state or two later you'd see brown grass and no snow at all. Then as time and distance passed there'd be a hint of green here and there, a tiny spot of a shoot under the dead stuff. The patches of green-under-brown might get a bit bigger in sheltered areas, but real, proper grass in winter was a first for me.

There was a slight, warm breeze under a clear, sunny sky. We were still in T-shirts and sawn-offs, sitting outside enjoying the fabulous heat while the forklift driver loaded our trailer with resin destined for Toronto. What is resin? I have no idea. I have a vague notion that people put it on violin bows but there can't be enough violins in the whole of Canada to need a truckload of the stuff, so presumably it must have some industrial application as well. And come to think of it, that's rosin.

Anyway, the pallets of resin-not-rosin were stacked outside the warehouse so our chappie had to drive out of the building and down a ramp to collect each pallet, then back up the ramp and into the building again to access the dock and our trailer. It was something to watch so we watched. Each time he had to pop outside he raised the furry-edged hood of his parka. We were bemused. Was it some sort of safety precaution? Not the slight breeze surely? Maybe this smidgeon of air movement passes for winter in Texas.

And what else can I tell you about Texas? Apart from the climate and an apparent inability of the locals to withstand balmy zephyrs. Texans have accents slightly easier to interpret than Georgians and seem to be even friendlier. In person that is. Unfailingly warm, open and chatty…we discussed accents, weather and food with all and sundry. Everyone made eye-contact, giving a sense that some real communication was going on, which eased the doing of business while asking stupid questions again and double-checking accent-related confusions on both sides. As we drove further into the state though another side of Texans began to emerge. There was a troubling touch of NASCAR wannabe behind the wheel.

The only discernible similarity between driving an ambulance and driving a truck relates to the behaviour of other road users when they see you coming. Most normal driving populations divide roughly equally into three categories. There are those who see you, observe a signal and opt to leave room for you do whatever-it-is. Then there are those who see the same and opt to have a little race instead, and most annoyingly, those who don't see you until they freeze, paralysed by the need to do something in a hurry.

The spread varies a little. England probably has a few more freezers, Canada, a few more polite people (except for Montreal). Most of the US appears to have a relatively normal spread but not those pesky Texans. Will they let a hapless 18-wheeler make a lane change? No they will not. The moment that indicator goes on everyone on the road puts pedal to metal. The road becomes a metaphor for life and no Texan ever gets left behind.

We emerged from the tangle of racetrack ring roads with our resin on the Monday afternoon. I drove until my legal (in the US) work shift ended, then Mark took over and drove through the night. This consignment was due to cross the border with a newfangled sort of customs clearance which neither of us had attempted before. It required a driver with a FAST card. I had mine but Mark's was still in the mail, so it was imperative that I be in the driving seat when we attempted to bring the truck back into Canada.

Back to the Hours of Service maths test. I'll let you off the test from Chapter Two and mention, just in case the finer points got lost, that in order to be able to drive legally in the US one needs to have had ten consecutive hours off duty. In Canada however, one can split those ten hours into two periods of rest so long as one of them is eight hours or longer consecutively.

So what with one thing and another we calculated that although Mark had to have ten hours off before driving again, I could get away with eight so long as I took over again at the duty-free shop before the bridge to Canada in Detroit, because then we weren't legally in the US any more. This would only work if we timed the stop for midnight, because in Canada your rest time has to be in the same 24 hour period although in the US it doesn't. (Aargh.) Calculations checked and rechecked for legality, we kept the truck rolling round the clock and planned to arrive at the border at midnight on Tuesday. Even I could see the sense in not stopping on this run.

Mark seemed a little crestfallen as we did the sums to arrange for me to be driving at the witching hour when our log books would stay legal. "It's ok, I'll tell them you're my trainer."

He drove as far as Memphis and I took us on through Nashville to Indianapolis. I scanned the radio channels excitedly, hoping for some traditional country music stations and songs with lyrics you can laugh about but, despite the road signs for attractions with the names of local music stars, all I found to tune into were religious stations. And they were more sermons than music. I could have maybe tolerated a bit of rousing gospel music but bible exposition wasn't going to keep me awake. I do want to visit the Loretta Lynn Dude Ranch though, if only to find out what a dude ranch is. I thought I knew what a ranch was, and what a dude was, but if you can have a thing called a dude ranch then the things in my head don't quite fit. Why all the sermons though? If the locals were so devout, who needed saving? Truckers like me presumably.

The snow began somewhere around Indianapolis, as did the radio stations with weather warnings. We were definitely heading back north and it was Mark's turn to negotiate Detroit in the obligatory blizzard. At the entrance to the Ambassador Bridge from Detroit to Windsor we pulled into the truck park by the duty-free shop and swapped seats. We checked and rechecked the paperwork, cards, barcodes and rules for electronic pre-clearance of goods into Canada. The helpful flowchart supplied by Challenger managed to make this system look very simple, give the customs officer three cards with barcodes on. That's it. We were sceptical, no faxing bills of lading to brokers? No sending of satellite messages to customs experts? No scribbling of massively long numbers on bits of paper? Not even any bonds to fail at the last moment? It sounded too good to be true.

I lined up all the available bits of paper ready for when things went wrong, fixed on the polite face that answers all pointless questions without a trace of irritation and proceeded to the window. There are rules for approaching the border. Remove your hat and sunglasses while waiting for your lane to clear. Switch on your interior lights, tidy up the dash. Wait until the previous truck has completely cleared your lane before daring to move, pull up slowly and make eye contact with the guard if you can. This is all to make you look honest, open and suitably 'umble. As you drive up to the booth, match your window to the guard's window exactly, they do not like being expected to stretch. Switch off your engine, do not set your brakes. Prepare politely for humiliation.

I'd learned with the fabulous Dave how to react to being asked stuff that they know that you know that they already know. He taught me that when they ask, "Where do you live?" the correct answer is, "Kitchener, sir," not, "It tells you on my FAST card, you pillock."

I'd also learned how to handle the daftest question of

all back then. The sheer stupidity of, "How do you two know each other?" never ceased to annoy me and I'd tried answering it different ways to produce an affectation of the suitable demeanour. It remained difficult to keep any trace of sarcasm out of my voice while replying, "We work for the same company, ma'am," but I'd had a lot of success with, "I'm a trainee and this is my instructor." Most guards softened a bit and let up on the nonsense. It didn't have to be true of course and I'd wondered back then how long I could get away with the rookie routine.

I was planning to try it again to save Mark's blushes but on this occasion I merely presented the three cards with barcodes on and that was that. It really was that simple. We were cleared to go. The easiest border crossing yet. I will happily move resin about the world again, I may not know quite what it is but it's so much less trouble than beer or honey.

WHITEOUT

CANADIAN WINTERS go on forever. The weather tends to worsen as January becomes February and there are more blizzards to the pound, especially once you are out of the protected little corner of Ontario that houses most of the nation's population. And I learned an even newer new definition of cold. When it matters even less which way you aim because the wee appears to be freezing before it hits the ground, that's beyond 'brisk' even for a Canadian.

It was late February, when everyone has had enough. Somewhere around the end of Manitoba and the beginning of Saskatchewan it began to snow properly. There had been a partial thaw the previous day and the sudden drop in temperature had turned anywhere previously ploughed into an ice rink. Ice under thick snow is lethal. We started to receive satellite messages of impassable roads and iced-up truck stops. Saskatchewan was sort of closed.

It was my turn to sleep but we made a plan first. With

the truck stops closing we might have nowhere legal to stop, so unless we came to a roadblock we'd have to keep going. If our usual stop was closed due to ice we'd switch shifts at the next accessible haven. If Mark drove for longer and I got extra sleep, I'd take a longer shift the following day. He promised to take it easy.

I was getting better at dozing off in a moving truck and had quite taken to the cave-like qualities of the safety-netted hidey-hole. A pair of earplugs to muffle the engine noise completed my cocoon and I drifted off nicely. Then a dream began which seemed to involve someone calling my name from a great distance. It carried on, the name calling seemed to get nearer and louder. It managed to be insistent and apologetic at the same time. Eventually I surfaced, realising that it was Mark calling my name. Loudly to bypass the earplugs but apologetically because, well, we were stuck on the ice in a truck stop and the shovel was under the bunk I was sleeping in.

Up I got and surveyed the problem. Mark had cleverly found an open truck stop, one which had managed to grit the area around its fuel pumps before the flash freeze. Then he had opted to park in his usual manner, as far from the buildings as possible. Where the ice was. We tried using our shovel to break up the ice, we used clever stuff like inter-axle differential locks to get more traction but the truck was going nowhere. I recalled planning to stow a container of cat litter for shovelling under the drive wheels at a time like this, I also recalled not getting around to bothering so I kept my mouth shut on topics involving the word 'stupid'.

The last thing either of us wanted was the embarrassment of calling for a tow, so I toddled into the truck stop to do my pathetic-waif-in-the-night-who-shouldn't-be-driving-trucks routine and see if they had any grit or sand about. A splendid chap took pity on me, piled on several layers of outer clothing, and skidded with me back across the ice with a wheelbarrow full of sand and a second shovel.

"What's the point of that?"

"We'll put it under the wheels."

"That won't work, you're supposed to grit before you get stuck."

"Do you have any other suggestions?"

"We could use a mat."

The chappie looked at me. I shrugged and told him we'd return the barrow later. Mark collected both rubber mats from the cab floor and tucked them carefully under two of the drive wheels, then he swung back into the cab to drive us out of trouble. I stood well back as both mats flew into the wild blue yonder, waited for the drive axles to stop spinning and began to shovel sand under each wheel. There was enough sand in the barrow to put a little under the rear axles as well and I worked on in silence, glad of the walk to the back of the trailer. It gave me the opportunity to tell myself to keep my mouth shut a few times.

I risked, "Let's try the diff lock again and first gear," and received silent assent. The truck shifted slowly off the ice and Mark's demeanour shifted with it, maybe there was stuff to learn about winter after all. He had the decency to return the wheelbarrow while I went back to bed and off we drove into the snowy gloom.

Later the same night I had the same dream. And we were stuck in deep ruts of snow at the very back of another truck stop. Another truck stop that had gritted and ploughed…the bit where the pumps and buildings were. This one didn't have wheelbarrows of sand. I was too tired and cold for the conversation that began, "Why the hell?" and as we fretted and shivered a helpful driver ambled over to assist us with the vital task of standing about, looking helpless and discussing how embarrassing it would be to call for a tow.

"Have you tried chains?" he asked. No we hadn't. What a brilliant idea, we had our legal complement of chains, we could lay them out in front of the wheels, push them under a bit and see if that gave us some traction. I was on it, but helpful driver had a better idea. We should put them on the wheels and half-attach them and this would be better. Mark seemed keen but I had my doubts. Somewhere in the back of my sleep-befuddled brain there was a bit of an issue with doing things this way but I couldn't for the life of me remember what it was. However, it would be impolite to look a gift idea in the mouth so we helped out with handing things to our hero until he declared the drive wheels chained-ish enough to have a go at moving the truck.

Mark got in to attempt to get us rolling, therefore I got a grandstand view of the moment that the drives began to spin and the chains wrapped themselves neatly around the axles between each set of dual wheels. And it was then that I remembered my issue…that bit of the chaining-up lecture. If you don't fit them exactly square on and tighten them the same each side they have a tendency to fly off and tie themselves around your axle. Hero driver melted into the night. We called for a tow.

Oddly enough, once we were over the embarrassment

asking the night crew at the Challenger repair shop to find us a tow truck during the worst road conditions of the winter turned out to be a blessing in disguise. We were in the middle of nowhere and it took most of the night to find a chap to call out, who then had to drive a long way to find us. Slowly. That meant some lovely non-moving-truck sleep, a rare treat which set us up with a bit more energy for the next thing, which was just as well since the next thing was going to require some energy. From one of us, anyway.

When the tow truck finally arrived the driver solved our first problem by pulling us out of the ever-deepening ruts of snow we'd created with our wacky attempts to get moving. Eventually we were deposited safely in the ploughed part of the truck stop but we still had a bit of a chains-round-axles issue to contend with. Clearly somebody was going to lie on their back in the snow, slither under the truck and check each section of chain methodically for the bits that hooked together. In the dark. Who should that somebody be? Consensus among the chaps seemed to be that it was a job for the smallest person.

At least I found out that my new trucking parka was snow proof. I had asked the shop assistant when I bought it what the difference was between water-resistant and waterproof, they had both sorts and they looked identical but water-resistant was cheaper. She hadn't been sure. "Do you think I could lie in the snow in it?" I'd enquired, thinking about chaining wheels at the time. She seemed to think I could but didn't ask why. I should go back and tell her she was right, it kept me relatively dry during what felt like forever.

I found one connecting hook quite quickly but we were no nearer being freed, there were another two lurking somewhere. I remembered that bit from the lecture. My arms were tired, the chains were heavy, greasy and cold and I was losing the feeling in my fingers. By dint of getting the chaps to hold the bits of chain they could reach and take some of the weight off, I finally found the recalcitrant hooks and we were out of trouble.

"Thank you." Mark muttered after the tow truck chappie had left. "I don't know a lot about chains really." Something shifted a little closer to equality in our bickering that night. Maybe keeping my mouth shut had paid off.

***

It got a bit windy on the Alberta side of Lloydminster. Snow began to drift from the fields onto the road. As dusk fell the wind got worse and so much snow blew from the fields that it became a tad troublesome finding the road at all. Darker and windier, now the snow was blowing across my field of vision as well, almost a whiteout. Not so total a whiteout that you couldn't see the cars in ditches all over the place or the trucks on the hard shoulder, having clearly given up trying to drive for the night, but nearly there. Stopping on the hard shoulder for anything other than a breakdown is a bit of a major no-no, dangerous and frowned-upon in all circumstances so I wasn't minded to join them. I decided to keep driving slowly until I reached one of Alberta's famous roadside turnout lay-bys to stop for the night. Only in Canada would these natty little places exist, sort of drive-through recycling centres where you can pop your accumulated picnic rubbish into a series of car-window height bins angled for your convenience. They are also handily truck-sized for taking a break. I probably passed several, couldn't see them of course.

It got windier. Now blooming great snowdrifts were being lifted from the fields and blown onto the road so that every time I drove through one and scattered it behind me it totally obscured my view of the car behind. Presumably I was blinding its driver. Whenever anyone passed anyone, kicking up that little bit more snow as they went, the whiteout was total. I plodded, white-knuckled and awaiting the sickening lurch into a ditch for 400 kilometres. As we reached Edmonton and buildings began to block the wind a bit, it was clear enough to be able to find the road again. And all that ice spread over it. Mark popped his head out from the bunk, nicely timed to help me find the Canada Post facility (I always got lost in Edmonton) and asked how the drive had been. "I'll tell you in a minute, I just have to find a washroom and throw up first."

We delivered our trailer full of mail and waited for the next destination. The satellite message asked us politely whether we felt like driving The Rockies. We looked at each other for moral support. "Got to do it sometime." We accepted the load. It was for a little town in British Columbia called Castlegar, way off the beaten track in the middle of said mountains. There was no obvious way to get there, it was a long way south of the main Trans-Canada highway, so we asked dispatch for some routing advice. They sent us instructions with the friendly little tip, "Be careful on Highway 3, it has a lot of very sharp bends."

Mark drove down to Calgary and across to Banff, then

took us down our first terrifying grade as we turned off the main drag. It was narrow and steep and we both forgot to breathe. I had been playing on my new found role as expert in all things Canadian and telling Mark what to expect from the mountains. I'd got my information from Dave while driving the Smokies before Christmas, I had asked him about the sort of grades I'd end up driving in the Rockies. "Not much more than this," he had said, we were on an 8% downhill at the time. "The runs are longer, and the drop at the side of you gives an optical illusion that it's steeper but if you can drive this you can do the Rockies." It was with supreme confidence therefore, that I assured Mark we'd not be driving anything much steeper than 8%.

This was going to prove to be true for the Trans-Canada to the north of us, which we drove on the way home but Castlegar is not where the main drag cuts through natural passes, it's in the middle of a mountain. Mark's first downhill grade was 10%. The next was 11% but he missed out on that. He headed to bed with a jolly, "That's the hard bit over with, you can drive the rest," and snoozed as I tackled the remainder of the way to Castlegar. I think he was thinking of something the size of Snowdon, one climb and you're done. The Rockies, however, are 1,000 blooming kilometres across. There's more than one hill.

The grades are short to begin with, which helps a bit but not much. Going up is ok, you just slow down as the weight of the trailer drags you back down the hill. The trick is not to stop, which involves knowing which gear you need before you are going too slowly to engage it. Going down is a different kettle of fish since the weight of the trailer is now pushing you down ever faster.

Gregg was sitting on my shoulder again, reminding me how to 'snub' the brakes…using them intermittently instead of constantly to avoid overheating. We were in runaway ramp territory.

Now I could see them I understood Gregg's stories. I'd had the principle in my head at the time, a sort of siding that carried you up instead of down to head for if your brakes failed, but I'd failed to grasp the reason why you and the truck would be lucky to survive one. I got the point as soon as the first one appeared though, narrow gaps facing steeply up the mountain side with huge raised earthworks running across them to stop you rolling back. Hit one of those at speed and you and the vehicle would be shaken to pieces. You'd not kill anyone else though, which was, of course, the point.

Before each steep downward grade is a lay-by, a brake check point. It is compulsory for trucks to stop here and actually check their braking system for problems before setting off again. It was too dark to do any fancy measuring but listening for leaks and checking that none of the wheel hubs had heated up was deemed sufficient, and that was easy stuff so I did it religiously. Every time.

Stopping at the top of a hill also serves the useful purpose of enabling you to pick a nice low gear to stick with for some noisy engine braking to help with holding you back on the way down. There is also a handy gadget known colloquially as a Jake brake which uses engine compression to slow you down on hills but it's only safe to use on dry roads, a hint of slush or ice and it's out of the repertoire of things to use. I looked wistfully at the button. I discovered I'd been taught well, using gears and the right kind of braking I managed ok. It was stressful and tiring though. The final 17 kilometre stretch of 10% grade all on one huge bend down into Castlegar itself nearly killed me with frustration and the sort of back-of-the-neck pain you get with total concentration, but I did it. And I now know that Castlegar is the second highest town in North America

That stretch from Banff to Castlegar had been driven mainly in the dark. When Mark surfaced we chatted about what a shame it was that driving at night meant we hadn't seen the view. We felt sure the landscape we'd been driving through must have been spectacular and were sorry to have missed it. But as Mark took over driving for the trip from Castlegar on to Vancouver to collect the next load and bring it back to Toronto, via the main drag this time, we both learned two very important lessons about the mountains. Firstly that the 1,000 kilometres of mountain between the prairies and the coast takes a long time to drive, if you miss a bit it's ok, there will be plenty more. Secondly, driving at night is infinitely less terrifying. There's only the road to be frightened of, not the sickening drop just next to it.

I began the drive from Vancouver. The coastal mountain range begins almost as soon as the city limits end. The road is a well-made, four-lane highway, there is nothing narrow or scary about it at all. It climbs steeply and steadily on a gentle curve, it's not a difficult drive but as Dave rightly predicted the sheer scale of the upness on one side and the downness on the other make you feel like you are walking a tightrope over Niagara Falls. The only way I could think of to refrain from fainting or vomiting at the wheel was to switch off my peripheral vision completely, but scanning your surroundings as widely as possible is good trucking, that wasn't a very safe option. I needed a coping mechanism fast, it was either that or stop in the middle of the road and lie down until the world stopped turning. The trick I plumped for, rightly or wrongly, was to keep my eyes fixated on the mirrors when they weren't on the road. It was a bit like night driving without the darkness. I'd not have seen moose or pedestrians as early as normal, but then the Rockies aren't noted for their population of either.

The ranges blended into one another. Up one mountainside, brake check stop, down a grade (back to Dave's not much more than 8%, piece of cake) up another, it became routine. Gradually I risked looking about a bit. When the upness is on your side of the road it's exhilarating and brilliant. When the downness is on your side of the road the knuckles get a little white. When the road reduces to one lane in each direction chewing gum becomes a vital accessory. This upset me a little. I loathe gum. I hate people who chew gum. I can't bear that little squelchy noise you can hear them making. I have maintained stoutly for many years that under no circumstances would I ever become one of those people. I did secrete a packet in my trucking bag though, just in case I ever needed a coping mechanism of last resort. Distressingly, I now chew gum but only, and I wish to make this abundantly clear in case you are already resolving never to sit next to me at a party, only when driving down a mountain on a single carriageway in daylight.

The weather held for us, a few slushy, foggy bits but nothing that required chaining up. We both managed some pretty scary ravines and saw some spectacular scenery.

We'd driven the Mountains in winter, nothing would ever be that hard again. Or it wouldn't have been if we hadn't made an elementary mistake when choosing our route home. We survived the prairies with no more than the usual foul weather and then plumped for Highway 17 through Northern Ontario, without checking the weather forecast. It had slightly nicer stops you see and we reckoned we deserved treats but it also tended to suffer more during blizzards. The parts which hugged the coast of Lake Superior were particularly prone to closure during the dreaded Lake Effect winter storms and we ran smack into a prime example of the species.

It was Mark's turn to drive through the crappy weather. I went to bed while it was snowing and blowing and settling. Visibility wasn't good. You could see the yellow line from time to time, occasionally a bit of tarmac, but keeping to the road involved a good amount of guesswork. I half awoke at one point in the night under the impression we were reversing, put it down to a wacky dream, turned over and went back to sleep.

At about one in the morning I felt the truck stop and popped my head out of the bunk to see where we were. "Police roadblock," advised Mark. It had all got a teensy bit worse. He had been directed to pull into the car park of a little motel adjacent to where the police had closed the road...and it wasn't a dream, we had been going backwards. Shortly before being forced to stop anyway Mark had been contemplating the same after losing traction completely going up a hill. As the truck ground to a worrying halt he observed that the tarmac on the other side of the road was slightly better ploughed, so he had reversed all the way back down the hill to try going up again on the wrong side of the road. We were somewhere near Marathon, Ontario.

Mark went to sleep and I promised to check out any road-opening progress when my shift began at four. I duly arose at before dawn and looked out of the window, the police car was still blocking the road. In need of a wee, I hopped out to investigate the facilities and landed in a knee-high snowdrift. The loos were closed. You will now understand what happened next if I tell you it was cold. I was thoroughly chilled and miserable by then anyway, so decided to nose about a bit in search of practical ways out of the car park ready for whenever we got moving again.

There was another truck parked close in front of us. I would need to take a bit of a sharp turn to get round him, which would bring my wheels directly into some nasty snowdrifts. Sharp turns are fatal for maintaining traction so I decided to wait for him to move off ahead of us when the road finally opened. Taking the drifts at a more oblique angle would give us a better chance of escape.

I snoozed for an hour or so, looked out of window, road still closed. Snoozed for a bit longer, looked out of window, road still closed. At about eightish I spotted a trucker striding purposefully towards the motel with travel mug in hand. Naturally I followed. A real loo trip and a coffee later I was all perked up and ready to drive. Road still closed. I wandered around the truck checking tyres and brushing snow off lights and reflective strips, we would be ready for the off as soon as they let us through.

Eventually the road opened. All the trucks arriving after us had been lined up on the hard shoulder, presumably the police had realised after the first two that corralling trucks in a snowdrift-filled car park was a daft idea. The roadside trucks set off in a cloud of freezing exhaust fumes but the truck in front of us in the car park remained stationary. I went and hammered on the door. Several times. A sleepy face appeared and grimaced at me as I pointed out that the road was open and we could move but he was in my way. "Ok, ok," and he disappeared inside again.

We sat, we waited, we watched. As I drummed my fingers impatiently on the steering wheel and the truck in front of us didn't move, normal people began to emerge from the motel and dig themselves out of the snowdrifts they were now parked in. The first to leave was a little U-Haul van. He made a desperate attempt to run the snowdrift that now filled the entrance to the car park but failed miserably.

We were still going nowhere but at least now there was something to watch. People came and went with shovels and cups of salt. A little snowplough arrived to shovel the car park and tried to push the van forwards into the road. Then he tried to push it backwards into the car park. He gave up and began ploughing the bits he could get at, bearing in mind the two dirty great tractor-trailers and the lodged van in his way.

An hour or so later a tow truck arrived and finally pulled the little van into the street and on his way. The snow plough driver hastened to clear a bit more of the exit but he went inside for a cup of coffee and a warm-up half way through the task.

People took advantage of his absence and while I yelled, 'Noooo!' somewhat pointlessly, another car attempted the impossible, getting itself stuck between the truck and the exit.

People, shovels, cups of salt, little plough trying to get round them and clear piles of snow away. By the time this car had been shifted the car park was a mass of ridges of packed snow. "If he's got any sense," I said to Mark, referring to the truck in front of us, "he'll wait for the plough to do that bit over there before he tries to get out." As I said this, the truck in front of us gave me a cheery wave and headed off out of the car park…to get his trailer wheels well and truly stuck in the snowdrift he'd not avoided by trying to avoid the bit that wasn't ploughed yet.

People, shovels, ploughs etc. The combined nuisance value of a truck stuck in the car park and a motel full of delayed residents alerted the local police, who sent a little patrol along. He helpfully dug out another car or two while commandeering a couple of highway snowploughs to come and help sort out the mess. He detailed one to widen the exit from the car park and the other to tow the truck out of the snow bank. We sat and watched. Another hour passed. I took a few photos.

Eventually there was nothing between us and the exit and therefore the road home, except for a great deal of mangled snow.

"I think I'm going to go and tell the little plough that I'd like to sit here for another five minutes while he finishes off the middle there," I told Mark. "We're so late now it won't make any difference and it'll be easier to make the turn."

"I'll go, I've still got my boots on." So Mark trudged over to the poor man who'd been trying to do his job all morning, in between digging people out, and told him we'd wait for a bit. He was ridiculously appreciative. Five minutes later we were out and on the road.

And this is the trip from Marathon to Wawa, famous for having a truck stop, where we narrowly missed the 17-truck pileup. On our return to civilisation, while Mark entertained the drivers' cafeteria with tales of how he'd driven the real mountain and let me do the easy bits, I looked back on our survival as having a lot more to do with luck than any sort of judgment and reconsidered my career options.

WOMEN DRIVERS

IT WASN'T really the snow, the work or the exhaustion, I just wanted to drive alone. The pressure cooker of 24/7 in the same cab, sleeping badly, being different people, having different opinions, refraining from murder, it didn't ease the stress. You'd think that having another person along for the ride would make things easier but this was stress squared.

There was little prospect of a solo run at Challenger, I'd committed to teaming as part of the employ-a-rookie deal. So, I quit. And looked around for another freight company to work for, it had been dead easy to walk into my first job, how hard could it be to find another? I had a bit of experience under my belt…mountains, customs, winter, keeping of temper under severe provocation, even chaining up. Well, unchaining at least. I was damned good and I knew it. I was about to learn however that total rookies were more employable than the semi-experienced, a lot of doors slammed in my face. The recession hadn't helped, many highly experienced drivers had been laid off while I was safely employed by an outfit large enough to withstand the downturn. Companies and agencies who would usually test drive anyone with seven-to-nine months experience had moved their goal posts. Now they could pick and choose and they wanted at least two years.

Being a woman didn't seem to be helping either. Trucking had been much more welcoming than I'd expected in many ways but when the chips were down, when supply exceeded demand, an old idea here and there clearly helped with sifting applications. I had a few snotty conversations with recruiters who were adamant that any woman who'd been a team driver had actually just occasionally held the steering wheel for a husband or boyfriend. That meant never doing any of the real work, so they weren't proper truckers.

I protested my credentials in vain. I realised I was contacting the dinosaurs because the dinosaurs were recruiting, the young-thinking, forward-looking, rookie-employing outfits were all full. I'd been an idiot to leave Challenger and I knew it but the whole experience did enable me to have a bit of a ponder over attitudes to women drivers over the years.

I'd been twenty-five when, seeking a little more excitement out of life, I'd ditched postgrad research to become an ambulance driver. That was 1980ish. Feminism had gone a long way towards ensuring that women had equal opportunities in male-dominated professions but those opportunities still only really existed at recruitment level. We were entitled to be interviewed and aptitude-tested. We were entitled to be trained and examined. Instructors were quite rightly tasked with making zero allowances for our stature and limited upper body strength but if we could do it, we were entitled to the job. On the other hand, if the training wasn't quite gruelling enough and some of us ended up employed, no legalities or political niceties ensured acceptance on the job.

The attitudes had been predictable enough, easy to counter, but there all the same. They ranged from the irritatingly predictable such as *women can't drive* to the endearingly personal, as in *my wife won't like it*. And from the fake solicitous, *there's only one toilet, women don't like that*, to the downright silly…*women keep going sick with PMT!* We'd had fun with this one. Even if it were true which it wasn't it would mean a paltry one day off a month, as opposed to the day off every week a chap was expected to take due to hangovers. Referring to these as PMT days at any and every opportunity saw that excuse off relatively efficiently.

The only attitude I had any time for was that women weren't necessarily as good at defending themselves, which might mean we'd need other crews to help us out of trouble. This was at least reasonable and I didn't want to cause anyone any extra work but the good news was that women generally didn't need to. Defend themselves that is.

The same chaps who were so solicitous of our welfare when they thought it might keep us out of their working lives became amusingly fond of sending the all-female crew to sort out pub brawls, *because you're less threatening*. And we were. An all-male ambulance crew wading into Kilburn's Biddy Mulligan's on a Saturday night risked a smack or two. Inebriated egos wishing to demonstrate their prowess to lady friends would hit out at anything in uniform. On the other hand my crewmate Rachael and I merely had to opine, "Dear oh dear, what a mess," to each other on entry to have a pub full of bruised and bloodied gentlemen falling over each other to settle down nicely. After a general chorus of, "No swearing now, ladies present," the protagonists would burst into tears in the back of our ambulance because we reminded them of their mothers. Or sometimes their sisters.

Their ultimate weapon, the tactic of choice for upsetting the laydeez so much that they'd cry and leave the job was to run a series of blue movies in the mess room on night shifts. Rachael and I retaliated by settling down with our knitting and criticising the acting, it was fun. The movies stopped. Eventually we all fell into an uneasy truce which gradually grew through grudging acceptance to mutual respect and honorary chapship. You knew you'd arrived when nobody saw anything amiss with inviting you to a stag do.

This may be sounding as though I don't respect the male of the species but those years taught me some fundamental workplace rules that I value to this day. Say what you mean, deal with conflict up front and watch the other person's back regardless of personality defects. Have a row, have a beer, forget it. I can't work any other way these days and find myself in frequent hot water when office politics require a defter touch…a little more subterfuge, deceit and grudge-remembering.

Maybe this was another reason why I had drifted back to the guy stuff. There was the freedom of driving for a living, the romance of the open road, getting paid to see America and all that but just as importantly it was a world with rules I could understand. My work gloves were fur-lined and covered in diesel instead of latex and covered in blood, I might have been be permanently terrified (and not really *that* good yet) but the satisfaction of real getting-your-hands-dirty work in which safety trumped personality, that was familiar and comforting.

What about this 'women drivers' thing though? It was thirty years on, give or take. Had anything really changed since the trail-blazing days? Recruiting in a recession aside, I was minded to say yes. A few old timers looked down their noses, occasional insults flew via the CB radio, but I was discovering that women could be positively popular with some freight transport companies. The absence of testosterone made for caution and therefore safety. We were allegedly easier on clutches and brakes and saved on maintenance. We were polite to border guards which minimised delays. I was reliably informed by several trainers that although we had a tendency to take longer to get the hang of reversing a 53 foot articulated trailer (tell me about it) we were invariably more accurate in the end. Bluntly, we bent less stuff.

On the road the respect felt less grudging these days but maybe the difference was me. Back then I'd had a trail to blaze, a gender to defend and plenty to prove, somewhat angrily. I was in my fifties now and a tad less energetic. Any gentlemanly soul who offered to help me with a recalcitrant landing-gear winch could be thanked with a smile and the offer of coffee, not growled at to bugger off and leave me alone. Both sides appeared to have mellowed. At this rate, maybe one day I would even be able to field a 'women drivers' joke with a wry grin instead of a snarl.

***

It took a while, but I was finally offered a job. On the face of it the offer from Schneider National was great news. They pretty much hired me over the phone on the strength of the fact that Challenger only employs decent drivers and then trains them well. So, no initial test drive, a solo run into the US and a pay rate that reflected my experience. Hoorah. But then came an odd thing called 'pre-employment screening' and I thought I had found another subtle way to keep women at bay.

All the paperwork was standard enough—medical, police check, driving abstracts, both private and commercial, sight of your passport and FAST card—all normal. But then, a fitness test. No-one else did that. The recruiter helpfully handed me a list of all the exercises complete with little diagrams. The routine was supposed to be designed to mimic the day-to-day tasks one carried out around the truck. Said recruiter then suggested that I have a chat with their in-house physio about ways to prepare for this part of their screening system.

Of course the intrinsic contradiction of requiring a physiotherapist to help you prepare to demonstrate things you were supposed to be doing all the time seemed to be passing these people by. And I have to tell you that these exercises were not easy. Neither were they in any way related to the opening of truck doors or bonnets, the pulling of pins or the winding of landing gear. And here is where I thought I had spotted rampant sexism at work.

Some of the exercises were about bending and stepping, these made some kind of sense since you do have to clamber about a bit, up and under things and some truckers can be, putting it politely, less than agile. There was some pushing and pulling, yes, fair enough. But there was a lot of pointless lifting and carrying, stuff we just don't do.

The rationale went that you might have to unload your own trailer one day but nobody does. I'd just had a conversation with the same recruiter about company compensation for out-of-pocket expenses, one of which would be the paying of 'lumpers' who unload your trailer for you if necessary. The worst one could expect would be to use a hydraulic hand cart once in ten years. So why, pray, would you want me to demonstrate that I can lift to my waist and carry for 30 feet a basket weighing 60lbs? Why would I need to be able to lift 40lbs from my waist to my shoulders three times? Why on earth would I ever want to raise 30lbs from the floor to above my head weightlifter-style?

The excuse for this one took the biscuit. You might have to load a heavy duffle bag of your own belongings onto the top bunk so the physio really needed to see you wave that basket of weights over your head and take your pulse after each exercise to make sure you weren't going to have a heart attack every time you stowed your luggage.

It's all nonsense, obviously. Apart from the fact that a 30lb duffel bag on the top bunk would fly off and kill you while braking for the first set of red traffic lights you came to, the choice to pack smaller bags doesn't make you a crap trucker. Just a clever one.

I was sensing misogyny. Pointless exercises targeting upper body strength for the hell of it, mimicking tasks nobody needs to do—and making tasks that do exist harder than they need to be—this was clearly designed to keep women out of the company. But then, why offer me the job in the first place? Were they all just stupid?

I had my chat with the physio. I tried to be nice, not spiky and suspicious at all, just interested. How long had the company been running these tests? Who devised them? How often did their drivers have to redo the screen? How difficult did the physio find doing them? (That last, put in for a little polite devilment. Half my height and twice my width, he looked as though he had never lifted anything much heavier than a pie.) My feigned avid interest paid off though, with answers partly interesting and partly peculiar. I mentally filed them away for further contemplation at home.

I had to listen to some seriously self-important crap as well, all about how much more the physio knew about the right way to lift things than I did. I doubted this. I've carried all shapes and sizes of people—on stretchers and in wheelchairs, off building sites, out of attics, in and out of vehicles and up and down stairs—for enough years as a paramedic. I know exactly how to use my legs and bodyweight instead of my arms and back which is precisely why so many of these exercises were pointless, there were easier ways to open bonnets and pull pins than the assumptions made on my little page of diagrams. I did learn something immediately useful out of the exchange, the physio really liked the sound of his own voice. This meant that I could ask innocent questions between one exercise and the next and he would answer at length. That might give my over-fifty-year-old pulse a bit of extra time to recover.

The oddest answer he gave me was that no-one ever had to retake the screen once employed. The most amusing, that the physio didn't have to do them at all. I enjoyed the sheepish face, ("Oh I can't do any of that,") and tried to look earnest as he demonstrated correct lifting techniques to me using an empty box. He clearly wanted me to understand that one should bend one's knees instead of using one's back so he bent his knees to pick the box up from a table and put it down again. If he'd been my height this might have made sense but he wasn't, so he ended up resembling a crab as he had to compensate for the pointless knee-bend with an equally pointless elbow-tweak.

I also learned that the pre-screen was only about three years old and had been devised by an 'ergonomics' company in the US. Since the fitness screening was mandatory for the US terminals in the company, Canada's branches had to do it as well. I Googled the source of my irritation and hey presto, all became clear. It was really all about US medical insurance. Here's a telling quote from *ATLAS Ergonomics'* website in a section entitled Protecting Your Borders:

If you are in an industry or community where you share an employment pool with other companies, you also need to consider what those companies are doing. If they are conducting pre-employment screens, their rejected employees will seek employment elsewhere. As more companies implement screens and reject employees, the risk of the employment pool increases. Eventually, those companies who do not conduct screens will absorb the risk avoided by others.

I was vindicated in that the tests were indeed a load of nonsense but they weren't sexist, they were personist. They were fattist, cardio-vascularist and under-the-weatherist. The idea appeared to be to push each candidate to their physical limits any which way to weed out anyone who might become ill later on during their working career. So, if you were perfectly fit to do the job (the normal Ministry medical sees to that) but might have a heart attack, stroke or back injury down the line, they'd push you there now and ensure that you couldn't work at all. No wonder no-one had to redo the routine, if it was all about insurance the last thing you'd want once you'd hired someone would be to risk pushing them to their limits again. Despite all the bleating about how beneficial it was for us to have this screening to help us work better.

With US healthcare in the news, and people who lived in saner countries learning with disbelief how those medical insurance companies behaved, I was still a little shocked that people could be treated in this way. And heartily glad I lived in Canada. We have sensible universal health care, most Canadian firms wouldn't need to take up such nonsense. If I failed this damned test for Schneider there would be other jobs but in the meantime I had some serious working out to do.

I filled a big plastic recycling box with 10 and 20 kilo bags of salt left over from the winter. I carried it about the kitchen, picked it up from the floor, (bending my knees, natch) raised it to my shoulders and occasionally waved it perilously over my head as the cat ran for cover. I ran, stepped, crouched and took my pulse. I'd been a runner in previous years but all that time on the road had played havoc with the pre-existing fitness routines. I was aching and knackered and my pulse was erratic. I jogged a bit to get my resting pulse down as far as it would go but five days wasn't long enough to get terribly fit. I practised every test I could mimic at home and hoped for the best with the one that couldn't be replicated with a recycle box full of salt.

I failed of course. Yes, the test I couldn't rehearse,

pushing a bar on a string until a digital scale read 100lbs. This was supposed to mimic closing a trailer door. Now I have occasionally struggled with bits of this, that and the other on the road, finding whimsical ways to deal with my build—up to and sometimes including bribery—but I've never not been able to close a door. At least I knew to blame US insurance companies rather than misogynists.

***

The answer to my problem presented itself by way of a tiny ad in the local paper. Linamar Transport was holding a job fair open day, you just turned up with a CV, did a test drive and got an answer on the spot. No phone calls, no doubtful recruiters to convince, just a chance to drive a truck before any awkward questions started. I knew that was all I needed, nobody could resist my fabulously polished commentaries. The job was as good as mine.

"What are you looking for in an employer?"

"Just the expectation that I'll run a legal log book, sir."

"We work a lot of less-than-load, how do you feel about that?"

"I've only worked pin-to-pin so far, it would give me the opportunity to learn more about the industry." I can bullshit for Britain when I feel like it.

A test drive later I was employed. Take that Mr Physio. Solo driving, mid-haul, mainly American mid-west. A couple of weeks of learning the ropes with another driver and I would finally get my very own truck. I danced home. Well, as much as one can in steel-toed trainers.

But first, another company, another orientation day. Odd how the work can be so much the same and yet so different. I resented the implication that I needed orienting all over again but apparently some things had changed in the few weeks I'd been trying to get re-employed. Added to which some things had been, well, to be brutally honest, sort of forgotten.

It took a full day to learn Linamar ways. They were not Challenger ways but that was fine, a lot of the work would be simpler. Challenger was a freight company with a wide portfolio of different clients. We were hauling chicken soup one day, sofas the next, followed by beer and then auto parts...but mainly mail. Linamar was a manufacturing corporation with a freight transport wing, mostly shifting its own products. This made the paperwork a great deal simpler. No FDA documents, meat certificates, alcohol clearances, in-transit bonds, just a bill of lading that usually said 'auto parts' going one way and 'dunnage', the fancy word for empty bins, going the other.

Simpler paperwork was good but some things had become more complex. We all know the US discovered terrorism in 2001 but it had taken a few years for the discovery to transmogrify into new regulations. Time was when the only thing anyone smuggled from Canada to the US was cannabis and the only thing that US travellers smuggled into Canada was themselves. It was probably still the same but CNN, Fox News *et al* had convinced Americans that Canada was a breeding ground for terrorists therefore Homeland Security must be seen to act.

There was a brand new 17-point anti-terrorist check that had to be performed, and recorded, every time you left the rig unattended on its way to the border. That would be every pop-in for a coffee then, and every re-pop-in half an hour later for a wee. In my case the combination of caffeine addiction and aging bladder would be necessitating a good few terrorist hunts, although in practice it wouldn't make a huge amount of difference. I'd learned from Gregg to jog round the rig whenever I got out, checking for strange occurrences...damaged tyres, duff clearance lights, packages strapped to the underside and, of course, every lady's Lot Lizard defence, spotting a sneakily pulled 'pin'. I was a fanatical checker-around anyway, the main difference would merely be remembering to write it down.

Next in the orientation whirligig came a day or two with a local driver learning where places were, getting my hands dirty again and severely upsetting the left knee. All Linamar's local plants, 20 or so, were located within a couple of miles of each other in the north end of Guelph, Ontario. My allotted guide and companion, Luis, shepherded me around in ever decreasing circles to get to know the idiosyncrasies of each location. Since the plants were all part of the same company everyone knew everyone else and there were names and faces to learn as well.

The faces smiled and the atmosphere was positively friendly, unlike the frostiness I'd got used to at Challenger pick-ups where truck drivers were clearly the lowest form of life. But running bits of this and that here and there all day within a claustrophobically tiny radius was hard work. Much traffic, a lot of tight turns, way too much reversing for my liking and a whole lot of climbing up and down and in and out. Highway driving is a lot easier on elderly knees. That double declutching a heavy pedal is all very well at the start and end of a trip but an unrelenting day of it can remind an over-fifty-year-old left knee that it stopped carrying people up and down stairs for a living years ago due to a touch of joint wear and tear.

There were things I had forgotten, like the difference between driving a light and a heavy load, and things I'd never known, like how to handle a day cab. Linamar's local drivers used smaller tractors than I'd been used to. There was no accommodation unit to extend the wheelbase, the space that the bunks and living area took up at the back of a highway tractor added several feet to the overall length of the truck. Without a bunk section the two pivot points of steering axle and fifth wheel were closer together, things happened differently.

My first reverse in a Linamar truck was an utter disaster. Luis saw the frustrated horror on my face, "It's ok, if that had been a highway cab you'd have nailed it first time." My confidence plummeted anyway and I spent the rest of the afternoon giving anyone who cared to observe the local traffic an object lesson in falling to bits. Luis was nice about it. "You don't have to impress me, you've already got the job, just drive, you'll be fine."

The smaller wheelbase on the day cab, once I'd learned to allow for it, turned out to be perfect for learning a bit about the tight spaces we had to manoeuvre in at all of the local plants. The downside to this of course was that once I was back in a highway cab the manoeuvres would have to be learned all over again.

There was the plant where the docks were through a car park and you could only get to them without swiping a fancy car with your trailer by going *that* way. There was the one where the docks were on an angle to the building and a different angle to the roadway and you couldn't actually work out if you were straight or not unless you got out to spot a sightline through the trees first. There was everybody's favourite, the single dock where you had to reverse in off the road from one direction only, down a narrow slope with propane storage on your blind side. Then there was the plant where shipping was on one side of the building and receiving on the other and you needed to use a different entrance for each, otherwise much driving round in circles ensued and everyone could see that you'd forgotten what you were doing.

My particular nemesis turned out to be the plant where an untidy gaggle of dumpsters insisted on inhabiting all the available turning space. (Brits, think cross between a skip and a wheelie bin.)

I mastered the day cab in my allotted couple of days. My reversing improved by default. The failing memory was battered into submission and after serving my time knackering the knees I was duly declared sufficiently familiar with Linamar ways to hit the highway. I treated myself to yet another pink baseball cap.

THE LESS-THAN-LOAD LIFE

I SAT nonchalantly in the drivers' lounge with a cup of coffee, chatting to my new pal Newfie as I waited to meet my 'experienced driver' for the next phase. I was a trucker now, almost in possession of my own cross-border home and I was really something. Newfie and I had started on the same day last week and we were both being teased about our accents. Everyone from Newfoundland is a newfie, and just as obviously I was 'English', I relished having a nickname already.

"We've found a lady driver who's prepared to take you out," said the guy who hired me as he popped his head round the door. "I know you said you didn't mind either way but it's nicer when you're away overnight." I thanked him for the consideration. "Name's Hazel, she'll be here to collect you in a minute." He disappeared remarkably fast.

A few days a bit like driving with Dave in the company of someone a bit like Janice and then I'd be free. It might be annoying, it might be ok but mostly it would soon be over. Newfie and I continued our chat, comparing backgrounds, trucks, trucking companies and exotic destinations. Then a tiny personage bundled beneath a huge baseball cap barrelled into the room and started barking at me.

"What are you doing sitting about, we need to get going, on your feet girl come on, this way." I jumped to my feet in a panic, scattering coffee, papers and bits of stuff over the floor. "Get on with it woman, what the hell are you doing?" Newfie shot me a sympathetic look and muttered, "Go on, I'll clean this up." Was there a trace of knowing grin under the comradely smile? Did everyone in the building know what I was in for except me? I trotted after the barking whirlwind feeling oddly bedraggled for a dry day.

"I have to get some stuff from my car."

"Well don't be long, we've work to do. And don't bring much, you're not here to gad about looking pretty." She looked me up and down in disgust as though I were dressed for the catwalk. Was it the absence of baseball cap that upset her?

"Um, no, I'll be quick." She disappeared towards the lines of parked tractors muttering and grumbling. Her words were lost in the wind. I was grateful. As I retrieved my bag of stuff and pile of maps I surveyed the growing collection of available baseball caps. Maybe not the new pink one today.

"I've done the vehicle check, you'll do it tomorrow."

"Ok," I'm scared to say much more.

"I'll drive this morning, you can take over this afternoon."

"Ok."

"We're local for a couple of days, I want to make sure you can drive before we leave town."

"Ok."

Hazel ranted as she drove. She has been trucking for thirty years, she learned her trade in the days when women didn't do that sort of thing and she can't abide the sort of women who join up only to let the side down. She has been a flatbedder and a tanker driver and is ten times as good as any man. She put me in mind of the ambulance version of me. Except that she had stayed angry down the years. During a pause for breath I risked mentioning that I might be a rookie trucker but I wasn't a rookie woman in a man's world, I'd been fighting for recognition in ambulances at about the same time she'd entered trucking. We'd had to be ten times as good too, in a different game on a different continent.

She softened slightly. We conversed a little more like people and a fraction less like barker and barkee. The intimidation level was marginally lower by the time I took the wheel. I risked asking if it would be ok to engage commentary mode for the first few hours, adding that it helped me concentrate in new situations, although to be honest it was more of a defence mechanism. I wanted to be in charge of the noise level in the cab while I was trying to think. The risk paid off, this was apparently an impressive thing to want to do. I had a brownie point and the day picked up.

Hazel tells you exactly what she is thinking. If you are wrong, stupid, muddle-headed, misinformed or dangerous, you will hear about it. Loudly. She will, however, take careful note if you listen, sort it out and won't want to be doing that again, no you won't...and she will make the follow-up observation out loud as well. This training style leads to a tiringly emotional rollercoaster of a day but at least when she issues a compliment it's genuine. I appreciate that. Especially as I am receiving slightly more compliments than bollockings. Mostly. Unless tired.

We spend a frustrating day or two revisiting all that reversing. Much though I am sick of the sight of all those wacky docks there's no avoiding them, it's vital for getting the job done. Most commercial warehouses have a line of docks for loading and unloading with varying amounts of space to manoeuvre in and varying visibility of the natty yellow lines supposedly painted on the ground to help guide you in. Even at unchallenging destinations the reverse has to be spot on, the bays are exactly trailer-sized with just enough room from one to the next for someone to walk between the docked trailers to mess about with stuff. A few feet at most. If the trailer can't be wiggled onto the dock between two other parked trailers offering minimal wiggle room, inch-perfect and straight, the forklift won't be driving into it to shift stuff about.

Most warehouses also have a system involving the designation of a specific dock they wish you to park at. Even at destinations more accommodating than Linamar's bizarrely located single docks, angled up hills, down roadways and round dumpsters and propane tanks, my old talent for parking in the bay adjacent to the one I'm aiming for won't pass muster. Linamar are fully aware that their plants are, well, challenging. I must repeat the Guelph circuit in Hazel's highway cab to relearn all the setups.

We picked up and delivered at every local plant until I could manage each dock without incident. More or less. With a little advice and gesticulating from Hazel. My setups weren't always perfect (and the secret is in the setup, put 75 feet of stuff that only bends in one place in the wrong position to start with and you are stuffed) but I'd learned to notice a problem early enough and fix it fast enough that there was less chance of me smacking anything 75 feet behind me when left to my own devices.

By the end of that first week it was official, we were ready for the border. It couldn't have come soon enough for me, I didn't mind hard work but 12 hours of manoeuvring round in circles in an Ontario humid summer had me more than a little exhausted and bored. Hammering down an Interstate with the air conditioning on and the radio playing had to be an easy day in comparison.

***

Except that it wasn't, there was worse to come. Admittedly there was some beetling down Interstates with the a/c on and the radio playing, there was plenty of wearing the baseball cap (not pink) and feeling like a real trucker, but mostly there was Too Much Information.

More places to find, new procedures, a trainer who yelled about stupid little details until I froze in terror and then said she was only being tough on me because I was good enough to take it. The more pleased she was with my progress—the closer I got to being ready to go solo—the more persnickety the barking. I was glad she was pleased with me, I really was, mainly because I was desperate to be rid of her as soon as possible but the yelling led to stress and the stress led to confusion. In the world in my head I was failing to shine. I should not still be getting confused.

Having driven across the Ambassador Bridge from Windsor, Ontario to Detroit, Michigan more than once, how come I still got lost trying to weave around the bollards which marked out temporary truck lanes during what appeared to be permanent construction work? How come when the customs officer asked me a question the simplest answer escaped me?

I had taken to writing my destination, weight and contents on the windscreen with a dry-wipe marker so that I could crib the details in any and all circumstances, that was just sensible, but I really ought to be able to remember where I live without scribbling that on the windscreen as well. It wasn't as though I hadn't crossed the border before with Challenger but something had changed and I didn't know if it was the bridge or my head.

Perhaps the road works were new. The Ambassador now seemed to be an ever-evolving Spaghetti Junction with no signage but that was no excuse for forgetting where I lived. Life with Hazel wasn't doing my confidence much good, I'd spent months whinging about wanting to drive alone and now the prospect loomed I was terrified.

There was significant good news in the stamina department though, I could still drive for eleven hours straight without collapsing. Since this was still the US legal maximum and I knew that the more familiar things became the less befuddled by anxiety and tired I would be I was minded to declare myself fit for purpose. I celebrated surviving trip one of Hazel's unique brand of highway training by going shopping.

Cheering purchase the first, a big cooler-fridge for all the snacks and drinks required to keep one amused at the wheel. It had been on sale, half price, at Canadian Tire. My own fridge would represent my freedom from other people's trucks more than anything else could. Everyone's cooler had been full of their stuff. There had been no room for an appliance of mine in any truck to date and little space for my kind of food and drink in other people's coldness. Buying the 12 volt plug-in cooler, big enough to sit on, had been seriously exciting. I'd had to inform everyone working in Canadian Tire that day, "I need it for my truck you know." Now there would be my drinks, my snacks and my healthy options for days on the road. With a generous supply of soda water, muesli bars, and fruit I should be able to justify one big truck stop feed per day without gaining too much weight. Snacking how I pleased would be a sign of new-found freedom and I would stow carrots if I chose.

The cooler savings made me feel a bit better about cheering purchase the second, an expensive but professional-sounding truckers' GPS. The sort that knows which roads you are and aren't allowed on and where the low bridges are. I felt sure it would pay for itself over and over in not-getting-lost time, I'd learned the disadvantages of a normal GPS in Montreal with Mark, but actually sending off for it before earning any significant wages still felt like a slightly risky investment.

When on our next trip out Hazel and I were sent to a company we'd delivered to the previous week, I realised that some of it was sinking in. Auburn, Indiana will remain a favourite place, it was the first actual real bit of memory and thus seriously special. I'd made a few notes about this customer's location in The Notes, a grubby little diesel-covered book of scribbles that never left my person. When I re-read them I could both remember the way and picture the building. I read recently that recalling routes, directions and locations is a workout for one's hippocampus, apparently London cabbies have huge hippocampuses (hippocampi?) and mine was finally responding to exercise.

I ran through it in the shower the morning before we set off…'I94 to I69, exit 129 for Indiana Road 8, turn left from the ramp, third lights after the rest of the 94, turn right. Entrance on the left, just past a big blind bend, wind round the building on lanes with huge boulders to stop you driving on the grass. Relatively easy set-up for a straight reverse on the dock.'

If I could recall everywhere I went after one visit (with notes) even while being barked at then maybe, with my trusty GPS as well, I could do this after all. I just had to whip the old hippocampus into shape with regard to navigating the impossible and ever changing Ambassador Bridge.

***

It took two weeks of hard knocks and difficult lessons. Driving for the automotive industry after a spot of experience with a general freight company was totally different to delivering sealed trailers full of mail.

A lot of Linamar's work is 'less-than-load', rounding up several shipments from a few suppliers in one region to bring back to different local plants. There is much checking that everything is loaded in the right order and learning to secure stuff down so that it doesn't shift about and get damaged on the way. There is learning to move the rear wheels of the trailer to and fro and charging and dumping the trailer's air suspension to account for the requirements of different shippers and their loading bays. In other words a lot more actual physical graft. Clambering about, messing with straps, metal bars and complex ratchets, getting grazed, bruised and dirty and ending the day looking faintly reminiscent of Pigpen; all this was a lifestyle I associated with the flatbed work I'd left behind with Barry. But it was back with a vengeance.

Add in the strange places we have been required to find and I can see why even seasoned drivers have to be oriented with a trainer for a while. Challenger tended to deliver sealed loads to large distribution warehouses on industrial estates on the edges of towns. Linamar drivers collect and deliver at small manufacturing facilities down obscure turnings in city centres. With very tiny shipping and receiving areas. In car parks. Full of people's cars, that they like unbent by passing freight.

The sorts of foundries we visited were no easier to manoeuvre around than Linamar's own plants in Guelph. Driving a long way in a straight line was the easy bit. Finding badly signposted factories in crowded side streets, working out how to get in and out of them, how to wiggle onto the docks, how to correct someone's paperwork so that there are no issues at the border and how to tell the forklift driver to arrange things in your trailer…these were all new headaches.

I learned this the hard way at a tiny foundry in Windsor, Ontario. They'd asked us to visit two plants on the way to the border that day, both in Windsor. We had to deliver one empty thing called a broach to *Colonial Tool* and collect a truckload of dunnage from *ExCor* to go to Coleman, Michigan. There had been a lot of debate about which company to visit first since the broach delivery was a lot closer to the bridge than the load collection was. So, we could either do the two stops in logical geographic order and hope that *ExCor's* shippers would kindly unload *Colonial's* broach for us and then reload it behind their freight when they were done, or we could get rid of the broach first and then double back for the shipping, driving unnecessary miles. I'd had no idea what a broach was and didn't know how big or heavy it might be so I'd just nodded sagely and refrained from opening my mouth while Hazel weighed the options.

The thing called a broach turned out to be a very small wooden pallet, when we saw it we reckoned we could probably shift it ourselves if required so option one became the plan. As we pulled into the first stop, many and various signs told us that we would have to shift the trailer wheels as far to the rear as they would go before docking. For safety reasons. I was a bit hazy about the point and, truth to tell, about the details as well. We'd heard about this extra chore in the classroom back at Tri County, sliding the rear axle to and fro to distribute weight in the trailer evenly on all the wheels, but we'd not had to do it at Challenger so I'd fondly assumed it was another of those Ministry things that no-one did these days.

"Do you know how to slide the bogies?" I looked blank. Not only did I not know how to move the rear axle about, I didn't know that this was what Hazel was asking me either. Bogies? She produced that almost imperceptible tilt of the baseball cap that I now knew heralded barking. "We're already in the way, we'll have to do this fast. Do as you're told." And, in a flurry of barks and sweat and misery we slid our bogies. There were buttons and knobs at the back of the trailer and there was, "Red button out, forward now, stop!" And eventually, after docking, when we weren't in the way any longer and I'd mopped myself down Hazel pointed out all the new things to know. It was a lesson that might have come in really handy down the line in another more fortunate universe.

Sweat notwithstanding, the bogie sliding did make for significantly less bouncing around of the trailer while the forklifts were buzzing in and out. I finally twigged the safety angle and the common sense of it stuck in my mind. I was one thing wiser even if the day hadn't begun too well. It was already verging on the piriform when leaving *ExCor* became a nightmare that left me dripping and miserable for the second time before the day had properly begun…a right turn into a load of coned off road works, followed immediately by a dog-leg through more cones and an easy-to-miss ramp onto the highway. Not demolishing any cones had actually been a triumph of trailer dancing although it was hard to notice what with all the yelling and hooting and such.

When we located stop two, the place awaiting our little palletty thing, the premises looked small and there wasn't an obvious way in. Hazel recommended parking up on the main road in the turning lane between the two yellow lines, sticking the hazards on and phoning for instructions.

"But those yellow lines are for a turning lane…"

"It's only paint girl, they can get round you."

I would remember *it's only paint* with relief whenever I had to pull up somewhere inconvenient. It may be illegal to park a truck on the side of the road but there are no specific rules about turning lanes in the middle. I might end up turning, mightn't I?

The receptionist who answered the phone told us all

about how to drive round the building and enter the car park from Seneca Street, and that the dock was on the right. It emerged later that she had misunderstood the bit about us being in an 18-wheeler but for the time being I dutifully drove round the building and into Seneca Street. I looked doubtfully at the car park and the dock.

"I don't think I can turn around in there," I ventured, already in preparatory meltdown.

"I'll direct you," quoth Hazel, "it's tight but you can do it."

I turned into the car park at just the same moment as a little food and coffee wagon entered from the other end. He parked right in front of the space I needed to use for turning. We sat and waited politely, noting as we did so that the dock was actually just a big door, there was nothing to reverse up to for a forklift to mess about on. As we sat, people began to emerge and shout

. Apparently it was time for them to go home and we were in the way.

One particularly obnoxious individual demanded that we get out of his way. Hazel, who does a good line in sweetness and light with menacing undertones if she chooses, told him that we would be doing so just as soon as the coffee wagon got out of our way. This wasn't good enough. She asked him where he thought we should move to, and he told her. Things were getting a little ugly by the time the forklift driver arrived to say, "Oh, you're in here, usually tractor-trailers park in the street and we drive out and unload them from there."

"Why did you drive in?" another member of the happily expanding audience enquired.

"The receptionist told us to…" I was embarrassed,

Hazel was furious, the guy who wanted to go home was apoplectic and what with one thing and another I learned a big lesson about the wisdom of driving onto unknown premises. You can't go far wrong assuming that there be dragons.

The *ExCor* forklift people had kindly removed and replaced our little wooden thing on the back of the trailer just as we'd requested, so that when we finally emerged from the whole being in the wrong place crisis it was removed quite effortlessly by the chap who normally drove his forklift out into the road. I went back there on my own a week or so later and was very pleased with myself for remembering where to park. I forgot something else equally vital, but that's another tale.

*****

There were a couple of occasions when Hazel took over the manoeuvring. Places so tiny that only one setup would work, docks so awkward that screwing it up would be a disaster. It made sense for me to watch and draw the setup so that I stood a chance next time around when I was alone. The first of these was a tiny medical supplies company. Hazel grew suspicious as we arrived, the entrance looked small. She advised the turning lane trick again while we called for instructions.

"Do you have room for us to pull in and turn around?"
"Oh yes."
"Are you sure, we're in a tractor-trailer."
"Everyone pulls in and turns round."
"Thank you."
The docks were opposite a brick wall, on the wrong

side of an enclosed yard. Getting in, parked and out again had to involve some sort of u-turn but there wasn't enough space. The trucks that the receptionist said had space to turn must have sported 48 foot trailers, not our 53 feet. But we'd driven in by then. Hazel paced out the space, deep in thought. "We'll slide the bogies as far forward as they'll go to shorten the turning circle." I nodded dumbly. "I'll do this one, it'll behave very differently. Watch carefully though, next time you'll be on your own." More dumb nodding. We moved the trailer's double axles and I stood in awe as she tweaked the monster around about an inch from the wall on each side.

Once she was facing out of the yard again the trailer had to be backed onto the dock but there was no space to set it up, the brick wall sat where the cab needed to go. She wiggled and wobbled the trailer around while I fretted about the day it would be my turn and I'd get stuck and have to be rescued by a man and it would all be awful.

Eventually the truck came to rest with the cab at an angle which clearly dissatisfied her but it wasn't going to get any straighter, the wall was in the way. At least we were pointed out towards the road. The trailer was almost square onto the dock and we asked the shippers if it was close enough.

"As close as anyone gets, we have an extra wide docking plate because nobody can get it square on, although backing in from the street can help a bit."

"Has anyone told your receptionist?"

Hazel watched my face as we moved the sliders back to a legal wheelbase for driving. "Now you know the secret. You'll be fine. You won't do anything harder than that."

And on we went to our next pick-up. Which was

harder than that. A single dock between two buildings, a blind-side reverse with no room for any sort of set-up at all. I drew a diagram of it as Hazel mulled over the best way to attack it. The notes included such helpful comments as *this wall not square* and *don't use for sightline*. She completed the manoeuvre—which involved setting the cab on the wrong side of a small roadway while cars whizzed past in both directions and getting out to look at where the bum had got to at least a dozen times—in about ten minutes.

The shipper was mightily impressed. "Women always get onto the dock eventually," she observed. "It can take them twenty minutes but the men just give up and get someone else to do it for them." A moment of pride and relief. If I ever did have to give up and get someone else to do it for me I'd still be as good as any bloke.

Life with Hazel, stress notwithstanding, has been quite an education and I have learned a great deal more about being a woman on the road, as well as some mighty fine reversing. It's summer now you see. Back in the winter when all truckers were bundled up in layers of fleece and woolly hats, no-one could tell from the outside who was driving. When I'd finally found out what my sartorial faux pas had been on day one, I'd received a sound ticking off. The issue had been a v-necked stretchy T shirt, donned for comfort and ease of movement clambering in and out of the backs of trailers. In Hazel's book one is required to look as androgynous as possible behind the wheel. This is, I now know, an important safety precaution in a truck such as hers. Whether it will matter when I get my own truck only time will tell, however the reasoning has to do with those pesky speed limiters and unravels thus…

The engine limiters demanded by Ontario, and much of the rest of Canada, cut in at varying speeds and although that should be around 100 kph some trucks, including Hazel's, end up limited to a little over the average. This can both a blessing and a curse. That extra two to five kph can make the difference between getting clear of truck traffic on the highways and sitting for hours behind someone slightly slower than you without the acceleration to get past them. That's the blessing bit, unfortunately a chap in a slower truck does not like to be overtaken by a woman and some of them can get quite snippy about it. We may be talking an accident of mechanics here but that doesn't ease the ego, hence the wearing of baseball caps. With a cap over my eyes (so long as it isn't pink) hair tucked up into it, large sunglasses and a golf-shirt I can just about pass for anybody.

I did think Hazel was being a little OTT about the whole androgyny thing until I left the cap off one day due to being so hot that even my hair was sweating. Overtook a truck just south of Toledo and he tried extremely hard to run us off the road.

***

Hazel declared me trained and ready for the final pre-solo road test. I wasn't terribly confident. The benchmark Linamar required for freedom from baby-sitting was set at 'experienced driver' level and our time together had had a depressing sense of one-step-forward-and-two-steps-back about it. In my defence, this was mainly due to a dirty trick that dispatch chose to play on us during our last run together. I hadn't minded the aggravation and trickery too much, smiling and doing as I was told helped with the stress levels somewhat, but once the other person in our confined space was fuming long and loud to a crescendo it did get difficult to concentrate.

Cincinnati was the problem. They asked on Thursday if we would like to go to Ohio, it would make a change from Michigan for us. The run sounded ideal, head south with enough time to get close to the customer before dark, take a legal ten hours off and deliver at ten in the morning. Plenty of time and daylight for a return load that should get us home by early afternoon on Friday. Hazel had family plans for the weekend.

Dispatch knew all about the return load that couldn't be picked up until seven o'clock on Friday evening, they just didn't tell us until we were over the border. Now this was a bit naughty but if they'd told us we'd not get home until five on Saturday morning we wouldn't have said yes to the run, would we? And I understand that everyone else in the company is wise to this stunt now, so naturally they have to foist it on the newcomers whenever possible.

Things were not improved much by the unwelcome discovery that Cincinnati has no truck stops. None. Somewhere to while away the day, mayhap a shower, a meal, some gentle shopping might not have been so bad. As it was, we were stuck having to camp out in the shipper's driveway in the heat and humidity and bad-temperedness of a day gone horribly wrong. Hazel was not happy. Her weekend was ruined and she took the deceit personally. She vented at the shipper who pointed out, remarkably placidly, that it was Linamar who requested the seven o'clock pickup, nothing to do with her at all. They could try to bring our load forward slightly but the just-in-time business meant that it hadn't actually been manufactured or packaged yet, it really wasn't a case of her being awkward.

She sighed wearily as she told us that every Linamar driver, twice a week, went through the same litany of fury, questions, abuse and moodiness and she, personally, was getting a bit tired of it too. I offered her a sympathetic glance, she was as trapped a target for the barking as I was. The sympathy went both ways as Hazel's ire transferred itself to the other available soft object, the trainee who could suddenly get nothing right. I tried to use the delay to get some sleep.

We loaded up after dark and drove angrily home, already exhausted. I was in bits before we set off. The familiar spiral of yelling, confusion and memory loss had ramped my anxiety levels to traumatic proportions and I had barely a day to recover my wits before the final road test. A Hazelless open road beckoned, I knew that all I had to do was hold it together for half an hour and I could be free but I wasn't sure if the prospect of not being yelled at any more, by anyone, would pull me through in the apparent absence of a brain. Still, taming Hazel had taught me that my main party trick sometimes worked.

"Um, where shall we go? I know, drive me to the 401, choose any route you like."

Crank up the commentary girl, this is it.

I have been issued with a whole heap of plastic cards. Cards for tollbooths, bridge crossings, diesel purchases and phone calls. I have been issued with another heap of paperwork and a third heap of, well, stuff. Bolt cutters, logistics straps, trailer seals…but most importantly I have been handed the keys to my very own truck. Whaddaya know? I'm an experienced driver. It's a bit elderly, newcomers get the crappiest stuff, but it is mine and I am moving in. It may be a bit noisy and bouncy and cramped but it has one overwhelmingly endearing feature. There's only one idiot in the cab.

PART 3: FLYING SOLO

AVOIDING CHICAGO

MY FIRST solo run would be to Wisconsin and back, a three day trip. I had been out to buy more golf shirts. And a tyre buddy, a ball-end hammer, a rubber mallet and a massive clamp which Hazel had taught me how to convert into a brake check device. All these were vital pieces of equipment to have stowed around the truck and I wouldn't be borrowing anyone else's any more. I also treated myself to a squeegee on a telescopic handle for mirror cleaning and some shop towels for polishing lights and trailer reflectors. My truck was going to gleam. I added some new work gloves to the basket. I was kinda proud that my old pair had worn through, nothing said 'experienced driver' quite like holes in your work gloves.

I moved in. This took hours. You could move house in the time it took to inhabit that cab. The combination of wanting to try and be a bit organised about where everything went, not really knowing where to start, and the long-awaited chance to import as much as I bloody well wanted to made for a busy morning of box and bag Tetris. Pigpen was replaced temporarily with one of those smug organiser types from the telly. And Schneider's physio would have been proud, I did actually chuck a few heavy items on the top bunk, but only to get them out of the way while I considered my storage options.

It's an old ambulance habit, organising a small space to perfection. The need to know exactly how to put my hands on every single item blindfolded had less to do with safety these days and more to do with mild obsessive-compulsive disorder but the occupying of other people's vehicles had driven me nuts. All that living out of a chaos of bags and boxes on the end of my bed because their stuff was stowed in all their available storage areas, horrible. So, I settled in with a vengeance on the first day of my glittering solo career. Clothes here, dedicated showering equipment bag easily accessible, food there, tools in handy places, torches, books, maps, chargers, pens, spare windscreen wash, my dizzying array of happy new things to hit the tyres with...all neatly assembled in logical locations. It would all change around of course as I discovered just how impractical the initial system was, but it was a system.

There had been mutterings in dispatch about sending me out on a run as soon as I'd stowed my stuff. I would have preferred a night's sleep first, given the several hours of messing about and getting my act together that they didn't know about but I wasn't planning to argue. Then the elderly tractor played into my hands by requiring some servicing. I was fond of it already. Whoever had abused it before me clearly hadn't checked their brake adjustments or emptied their air tanks for an extremely long time, necessitating a spot of tinkering to make things safe and legal.

A round trip to the mechanics' shop a few miles away for this and that took up the afternoon nicely, while my run was given to someone else. This also offered the bonus of an opportunity to 'bobtail' around for a while getting used to the gearbox before I had to haul anything anywhere. These shenanigans also turned me into a star rookie. I'd not only thought about checking the brake adjustments, I'd had the right piece of kit to actually do it and had located a major infraction before hitting the highway. My Challenger days of sitting in the cab while a grease monkey ran about in a pit yelling *BRAKE* might have been over but the addition to my shopping list of Hazel's clever clamp had saved me a hefty fine on day one. I was thankful for Tri-County's obsession with brake adjustment checks. And fonder of Hazel, now she was history.

I arrived in the yard the following morning an hour and a half before collecting my paperwork, another hour before dispatch had suggested that I leave. They'd given me the destination and timings by phone the previous night so I'd already had a chance to work on a rough route but I was leaving nothing to chance. The vehicle would be checked within an inch of its life, the paperwork proofread and treble checked for errors, everything customs could possibly ask me would be scribbled on the windscreen in dry wipe marker and Betsy, my friendly truckers' GPS, would be set up with watertight instructions. I filled the new cooler with glee. Yes, there were carrots.

I took everything one step at a time. The load of empty

metal storage bins—known from here on as 'dunnage', as befits the writing of a pukka freight transport professional, unless they misbehave in some way and require individual identification—was waiting for me in a loaded trailer. This was a help and a kindness from dispatch, I could just hook up and go instead of driving somewhere complex to be loaded and wasting half the morning messing about. I remembered to clamber in and check that the right stuff was in the trailer before setting off with it. I remembered to strap the load down, I even remembered how to work the straps, things were looking good. I remembered to add where I lived to the scribble on the windscreen ready for when I forgot at the border. I remembered how to find the Flying J on the way out for fuelling-up purposes, found the truck entrance on my own and negotiated the complexities of entering my card and PIN at the diesel pump, all exactly like a grown-up who knows her job. I was on a roll.

I had worked out a brilliantly sneaky ploy for coping with that spot of disorientation at the bridge. Just before all the baffling bollards and U-turns required to divert trucks into their correct lanes sat a well-signposted filter lane for truck parking at the Duty-Free shop. The parking spots were easy to pull through and the shop had nice clean toilets. Best of all, you could follow another truck out and sit behind him the rest of the way out of the country. It all went swimmingly until a slight greengrocery-related bollocking at the booth itself.

When Canadian border guards ask you, "Anything to declare?" they would like to know if you are importing any alcohol, tobacco or firearms. The US counterpart asks the same question but he wants to know whether you are packing any fruit or vegetables. I declared the on-board vegetation; my apple, peach and small bag of peeled baby carrots. He demanded that they be produced for inspection. This took a few moments ferreting about in the cooler, which was suddenly a lot bigger than is practical. He waved my apple aloft with an indignant air.

"These don't have decals on!"

"I'm sorry, should they?"

"All imported fruit must have a label detailing country of origin."

"I didn't know that sir, I do apologise."

"Next time it'll be confiscated. Goodbye." And I was through, duly chastised for my fruit faux-pas and left wondering whether it was Canadian or US produce that was allowable and whether I should stick to crisps and chocolate from now on. Maybe customs was the real reason truckers got pudgy.

It was 5:50 PM. The traffic through Detroit was hellish but I remembered to breathe, which helped. Once outside the city I stopped at the first available rest area to consult Betsy and the maps, I needed to choose a good place to sleep and finally have a proper look at where I was actually going. Taking one thing at a time had meant leaving this bit until now, which had seemed a sensible policy when I dreamed it up. Oh look, round the bottom of Lake Michigan and up again. And, um, through Chicago.

Looking at Betsy's etas, I was on target to stop either just before Chicago at nineish that night or just after Chicago at elevenish. There was a handy Flying J in Benton Harbour, Michigan, which would do for the 'just before' bit. I could stop there anyway, ask myself how I felt, and either sleep or keep going when the time came. This step by step business was working out fine.

***

I took my time, found the aforementioned J, had a coffee, a wee and a think. I reckoned that I had another couple of hours driving left in me. I pondered Chicago. I could tackle it now, in the dark while tired, or start early in the morning and deal with it in daylight. My previous experience of cities led me to conclude that the first option was a clear winner. Chicago would best be tackled for the first time at night, there would be less traffic and Betsy would guide me through anyway.

Happy with an intelligent decision I had a quick meal and pinpointed another truck stop that appeared to be two or three hours further on. A fine plan. That sleeping point would leave me a mere three hours from my consignee, I could knock those hours out mid-morning and be in good time for my delivery slot. There was no point in being too early…the reload wasn't scheduled until seven in the evening and I had to get some decent mileage back under my belt after that before my daily hours ran out.

It was all a bit complicated, this route-and-hours planning, and I was doing it solo for the first time. I'd not previously thought of truckers as mathematicians but blimey there's a lot to consider. Not just the best way to get somewhere and how long it will take but how you will fit it into a 14 hour workday, making sure you drive for no more than 11 hours and that a 10 hour rest can be fitted in before you start again. Oh, and arriving on time as well.

My plan had two significantly fatal flaws. Firstly, Chicago is not quieter at night. It is a permanent traffic jam in all directions and at all hours including wee small ones. Secondly, I had rather taken against the plethora of toll roads which seemed to criss-cross Chicago at all angles and had set Betsy to avoid tolls. It looked as though a perfectly serviceable non-toll highway ploughed straight through Chicago and that would do me for now. Challenger had provided transponders for US tollbooths, Linamar did not. I didn't fancy fumbling with bits of change and filing receipts in the dead of night on my first outing. I would learn about tolls another day.

I sat in interminable traffic jams for at least two hours longer than I had allowed for the negotiating of Chicago. This brought me perilously close to 11 hours actual driving and instant illegality. It was late and dark and I was exhausted. I needed to stop but Betsy had kindly done as she was told and routed me around all the toll roads. Emerging from Chicago to the north, the non-toll Highway 94 suddenly became a horribly non-actual-highway-road 41. I couldn't make my chosen truck stop legally, and there would be no rest areas along here, they happen on Interstates.

Searching desperately for somewhere, anywhere, that looked as though trucks might be allowed to park I finally found a small laneway into a patch of gravel that already sported a couple of trucks. I swung in a little too fast and realised I had taken the wrong entrance, I would not be able to tuck in neatly beside them. Having broken the golden rule of never driving into a space that you have not scoped out first, I surveyed my options. I could just about get myself out of everybody's way if I pulled up into an area that looked as though it was probably for turning round in. I made a rough job of straightening the truck, decided it would have to do and settled down for the night.

***

I'd like to be able to tell you that the first night in my very own truck was cozy, fun and contemplative, an occasion to pat myself on the back for being brave and clever and Making It Happen, but actually it was a tad stressful. I had no idea where I was or whether parking there was legal. I spent most of the night waiting for someone to hammer on the door yelling, "You can't park here!" I slept in my clothes just in case of early-hours encounters and berated myself hourly for not going to sleep.

When dawn broke I risked a look out of the window. Amazingly, I was in the parking lot of a tiny truckers' breakfast stop. Rigs had been arriving and leaving all night, presumably without much inconvenience from me. If I had been in the way they appeared to be coping. I finally dozed off for a couple of hours.

Up again about ten and the place was buzzing. Everybody gave me a cheery wave as I ambled by to locate some coffee and loos. The coffee was nice, the loos clean and the people friendly. Nobody pointed at the sign I had missed in the night…"Truckers welcome but please don't sleep here." I suppose I'm not the first unwise soul to have been caught out.

Of course, I was in a horrendous position for getting out again. My trailer was angled towards the road with ditches and bollards on all sides and a truck directly behind me. I would like to think I provided a spot of free breakfast entertainment as I wiggled and fretted about, to and fro, up and down, trying to inch the trailer into a position where I could back it round the other truck, in the right direction, and far enough into the car park to turn back out onto the road. But, I made it.

While recovering from the exertion at the truck stop I had planned to overnight in a few miles up the road, all parked up prettily and availing myself of more coffee, pleasant facilities and shopping, I contemplated day one of the great solo career. Fruit and Chicago related crises aside, I had survived. I was in Wisconsin, a mere couple or three hours from the people expecting my dunnage. All I had to do now was find the place, get onto the dock without incident, unstrap one load, strap up another, sort out the customs paperwork, find somewhere to refuel and get home. Possibly bypassing Chicago.

Things went a little better on day two. Wisconsin was quite pretty in the daylight, not exactly hilly but undulating enough to make a change from flatness, and dozens of different shades of green. It reminded me a little of Ireland. Betsy seemed to know where we were going and I was on time. I knew by now that if I had the moral fibre to look around and take in the scenery the terror was receding into the background, so I popped the radio on, found a station I could sing along to and declared this to be, at last, Real Trucking.

The foundry my load was destined for was visible from the end of the street. This made a significant change from all the tiny Linamar plants in Guelph which were barely identifiable from a crappy little smudged and photocopied diagram. It had a well-marked one-way system and a place to park and go make enquiries. Deliveries were back out to the road, left and left again. Then round the block and back down here to load the pickup.

I repeated the directions out loud, which confused the gatekeeper a little. I'd come to the conclusion that this technique helped to hammer things into my head for a while but I was still expecting to get lost. Maybe the forgetting had been a stress thing though, or a being-assessed thing, or possibly a being-barked-at thing because it all stuck in my mind this time. Round the block I went. I found the delivery dock, waved at the receiver and waited where directed.

It took a minute or two to wiggle onto the dock, mainly because I'd been told to wait in a stupid place and had to pretty much drive out of the yard again to line up for it. But, I got there. Nobody shouted. The bins were unstrapped and unloaded and nobody shouted. The paperwork was signed and exchanged with zero yelling and it all seemed to be going according to plan.

The reload was timed for seven o'clock and I found myself driving back round the foundry, having remembered the way, at six-thirty. I had already scoped out the loading dock and realised it would be an easy set-up and a straight reverse so all of a sudden, shortly after seven, I had fulfilled the first part of this assignment. I had all the border paperwork sorted out and was ready to head home. Despite a horrible night and a couple of hard lessons it had been a great deal less terrifying and trouble-filled than I had expected and my confidence was on the up.

***

I was determined not to get caught out for somewhere to sleep again so I had spent some of my waiting time mulling over the route home. I pondered the toll road question. One of the reasons I'd set Betsy to avoid them was because I'd noticed huge queues of traffic at the tollbooths, they clearly didn't offer a lot of gridlock avoidance. Looking at the map quite carefully I realised that all the toll roads took you to the same spot in central Chicago where the congestion had been at its worst last night, it didn't look as though that had been the cause of my traffic problem even though it had contributed to an awful night's sleep.

There was a workaround to the whole issue though, Interstate 39 South would take me to Interstate 80 East, bypassing Chicago completely to the west and the south. It looked a little further but not far enough to take an extra couple of hours. An added bonus would be the choice of a couple of rest areas to stop and overnight in. I could do what I did yesterday and pull into the first for a snack, decide if I was tired or not and drive on to the next to sleep if I felt like it. This would put me either eight or ten hours' drive from home which would be both manageable and legal the following day. I could stop between eleven and midnight, start again between nine and ten and be home by seven. Since the delivery could be any time up until nine tomorrow evening I would be on time, possibly even early.

All this went to plan. The diversion added about 30 kilometres to the total distance but that took 20 minutes, not several hours, and I pulled into the second rest area to sleep at 11.30 feeling just utterly brilliant. I was getting to like rest areas. The US has them on all its Interstate highways and they are a marvellous thing. They are easy to pull into, easy to park in and easy to get out of. Some of them have toilet facilities and a few vending machines. I had decided, on the strength of half a trip with me in charge, that I preferred overnighting in rest areas anyway.

You didn't get the facilities of a truck stop but could always pull into the next one down the road for a coffee and shower as the first break of the day. What you did get from a rest area was total anonymity, since they were less social places. Lots of trucks parked up overnight, nobody getting out to go anywhere, no-one to know that this truck had a lone female in it. I felt safe and I slept like a baby.

Day three went to plan as well. I returned to the J I'd found on the way down to refuel, topped up on coffee as well as diesel, had a shower, breezed through customs with everything correct and nothing to declare (I'd eaten the apple) and headed for home on target to arrive at seven. I sent my eta to dispatch via the truck satellite with not a little smugness. My adventure was rapidly turning into a triumph and I was pretty damned pleased with myself. The only crisis on the way back was a soggy emergency peanut butter sandwich, owing to some cooler condensation and careless wrapping. It wasn't really nice enough to eat and I didn't want to stop again just to buy food so I made do with nibbling trail mix and baby carrots. After all, I'd be home in time for a decent and very well-deserved dinner.

I found the plant waiting for my truckload of metal castings. My dumpster nemesis. I'd remembered which one it was though, where it was, where to wait, how to find the receiver and how to set up to back onto the dock. The place was empty, hooray, no-one to rush for. I was tired by then and wanted a no-stress reverse. Unfortunately while I was getting the papers signed another truck pulled in behind me causing instant anxiety. Now I was both holding someone else up and being watched. The dumpsters were in their usual spot, ie where you wanted your nose to go. It was a 90 degree manoeuvre with a trailer to get past in one of the other docks.

Of course I screwed it up. The faster I tried to work the wronger it went. The more I tried to correct being too close to the trailer in the next dock, the closer to it I got. Of course I hit it. The scratches weren't too bad, I might have been tempted to pretend nothing had happened and someone else must have done it, but when I pulled off the dock to close my trailer doors I realised I had also bent the hinge on my own trailer door. It wouldn't close. That would be a bit of a giveaway.

Tired, miserable and defeated I drove back to the yard with one trailer door pinned back. There was an easy reverse to park it but I messed that up anyway just for good measure and spent about half an hour trying to get it straight enough to walk away from. Forcing back the tears I took all my piles of perfect paperwork to dispatch. "Do you want the good news or the bad news first?"

They grinned and sent me home. Apparently it happens. Two loads had been successfully moved across an international border to meet just-in-time delivery windows and somebody would sort out the minor problem of a bent hinge with a crowbar during the night. I appeared to have kept my job.

IF IN DOUBT, EXPLOIT THE ACCENT

I WAS a little concerned about fallout from my small trailer-door-related incident but there appeared to be a conspiracy of silence. Somebody really must have quietly taken a crowbar to the hinge during the night because nothing else was ever said. I have added a crowbar to my pile of neatly stowed tools. Not that that particular crisis will ever happen again, I have made a fierce pact with myself to make each stupid mistake a mere once only. I have observed the usefulness of crowbars however and you never know, I might be able to get another hapless rookie out of trouble one day, being so experienced and all. So, on to the next thing. An easyish jaunt across Michigan to deliver more dunnage and pick up new bins filled with something autopartish.

This uncomplicated trip was another kindness from dispatch, they clearly put some effort into spoon-feeding their rookies with easy work to begin with. I did wonder at what point they would decide the training wheels could come off but for the time being I was grateful. I'd been to this shipper before with Hazel, it was in The Notes. It was easy to find and had a helpful guard at the gate. I knew that because The Notes said, *guard called Lonny, knows everything.* Well, they might have said Lennie, there was a grease smudge on that bit, but the principle remained.

The only unsettling issue was the timing. I was due to start at four in the afternoon, pick up the bins at five and deliver at eight the following morning. Now there was no way to do this legally because of the ten hours off after fourteen on duty thing, so a little massaging of the books would be required.

Dispatch, whose spoon was clearly getting a bit bigger, reminded me that you only had to be 'on duty' on paper if you were driving from one town to another. Pootling about within the same conurbation didn't count. Specifically, pootling about within a radius of 160 kilometres didn't count as real driving so long as you didn't hit a highway. Because of this legal loophole the Linamar convention went that you didn't have to start your log book until after having collected your load and brought it back to the office for them to process the customs clearance. That was all officially pootling, being within a radius of a mere mile or so. I would therefore be going 'on duty' two hours or so after actually climbing behind the wheel. Then you could get to the destination, mark your log book off-duty and complete the delivery sometime during your ten hours off. Because it's in the same place and therefore completely legal.

This did of course require that you shouldn't expect to spend your ten hours off actually sleeping and I wasn't sure how I felt about that, apart from tired. I was learning the hard way that the industry makes a lot of noise about ensuring that you get plenty of rest but actually turns a blind eye to the details.

Anyway, I picked up my paperwork and checked the vehicle over at four, duly appeared at the plant round the corner at five and backed onto a dock. It took a couple of minutes but I managed it without hitting anything. I waited for the shipper to finish loading the trailer next to mine. Half an hour later I caught his attention. "Empty dunnage gets loaded at the other end of the building."

I dutifully drove round the block and backed into the new dock, next to a friendly container driver I'd seen pull in ahead of me. I remembered him because he'd waved a greeting and I'd felt all professional and quite the real thing so I knew that parking in the wrong place hadn't delayed me as such, he was still sitting there waiting. An hour later we were both still waiting. I ambled into the warehouse on both our behalves, found a forklift driver and made polite enquiries. We were definitely next but he had to have the paperwork sorted out first and I could help speed things up by taking it to the office. Great, where should I do that? The office I'd first thought of at the other end of the building. I walked, it was quicker.

I finally got out of that plant at seven, whereupon all the paperwork had to go back to our office for clearance. The border crossing would be electronically pre-approved but the people who do that bit still required a fax to get the ball rolling, for that, one needed a fax machine.

I got rolling for real about seven-thirty, having been on duty since four. Since my log didn't begin until I left the yard for the second time I could 'work' until nine-thirty in the morning if necessary. I fully intended to sleep for a goodly part of the night somehow but it would make my delivery time appear legal if my log happened to be inspected on the way.

Road works on the 401, a queue at the diesel pumps, a huge bottleneck at the border, it was dark and late and I was already knackered by the time I'd crossed into the US. Too tired to fully appreciate how much nicer and easier it was to negotiate the Blue Water Bridge border crossing at Sarnia and Port Huron when you are used to fighting the Ambassador from Windsor to Detroit. A straight road on and off, no wheeling around sharp bends to avoid badly marked construction and pretty as well.

I had very carefully bought US apples this time and ensured that they all had little labels on. I'd Googled the fruit thing and it appeared that one merely had to prove all fruit was North American in origin but I thought maybe US produce would make the guards happy. I'd pondered the wisdom of sticking an emergency US apple sticker to the dash in case of sudden inexplicable label-loss in transit but this guard didn't ask about fruit. He quizzed me for a while on my citizenship, what was in the trailer and where I was going but no produce-related enquiries at all.

Betsy showed that I'd get to Muskegon, Michigan about two-thirty AM but I was in no shape to drive there in one hit, even though my newly acquired pile of audio books from the library helped with the monotony of night driving. That was another definitive *this is my truck and I'll do what I please* statement, eschewing other people's music. I thoroughly enjoyed the early parts of Going Postal, read by Stephen Briggs, complete with voices, but knew when I'd had enough. I stopped at about half past one in the morning in a rest stop an hour or so out of town. It made sense to sleep for a few hours then get up at six and find the place in daylight. I could sleep again after I'd been loaded, rewrite (for 'rewrite', read 'forge') my log to represent having been there all the time and be ready to leave after a putative ten hours off at about one in the afternoon.

Lonny was helpful as ever. It may have been Lenny of course but my accent made the issue fairly moot anyway. This foundry put all its visiting trucks on a weigh scale on the way in and on the way out. It had clear, logical paperwork and fixed procedures which had to be explained to every driver every time, no matter how frequently they visited. Lonny/Lenny remembered the accent and congratulated me on being instructor-free. He apologised for telling me everything over again but I was delighted not to have to remember it all or ask any stupid questions. He pointed out where I could park to sleep and told me not to come back to the scale until I was completely ready to leave, that way his paperwork would match my log. Things were looking good as I backed my trailer full of empty bins onto the dock as directed. The receiver looked at the packing slip I handed him.

"You've got a mix, metal and plastic."

"Yes," I smiled. I knew my dunnage.

"We'll unload the metal here, then you have to drive round the building to the other docks for the plastic. Then back here for the reload." My smile evaporated as I realised just how much longer it would be before I could lie down again for the second half of my night's sleep. At least two more reverses. And the reload took over an hour. By the time I had parked up (out of the way, under some trees) any thoughts of setting an alarm to time the start of my trip home were thoroughly silenced. I was snoozing until I stopped.

I slept until one, had a brisk rub down with a flurry of wet wipes and talc, changed a few clothes and felt ready for anything. A seven hour drive back would mean that I would just get to Linamar's plant in daylight, I didn't much fancy docking in the dark just yet. A coffee would have gone down well but I've not got around to buying a portable kettle. That was ok, I'd be on the road soon so coffee wouldn't be long.

Back to the gate and onto the scale. They'd loaded 44,000 lbs, which is pretty close to the maximum legal load for a truck with the usual complement of axles. Lonnie and I agreed that it would be sensible to weigh each axle separately. The regulations governing how much weight each axle should carry hadn't changed and the inspection weigh scales along the interstates seemed to be open more than ever.

He did the sums as I drove each axle off the solid scale. I hadn't had to do this since Mark and the honey but at least it was an intuitively sensible routine, that made things easier to remember. It's just as well we bothered because one axle came out overweight, I had 1800 lbs too much on the drive wheels and not enough on the rear. I sighed. I was going to have to slide the bogies. There was no Hazel to bark orders this time, which meant digging out a text book to make sure I got it right. Lonny/Lenny grinned sympathetically, I must have looked as crestfallen as I felt.

"You can pull up over there to do that, just make sure we can get another truck on the scale behind you."

I checked the books and waved my hands around drawing diagrams in the air to make sure I was going to slide the rear wheels of the trailer the right way. The axles had to go forward under the trailer to shift the weight of the load towards the back and away from the overloaded drive wheels on the tractor. If the back wheels were going forwards then the tractor had to go back, I calculated that it had to move two and a half feet to shift the right proportion of weight.

I'd learned a clever trick for measuring this. You pace out the distance from a point you can see from the cab, the diesel tank cap say, then drop a grubby glove on the ground where you want your marker to end up. I unlocked the slider bolts, paced my distance, dropped the grubby glove with the aplomb of a maiden starting a joust, set the trailer brake and attempted the shift. Nothing. The bugger wouldn't budge.

I checked the bolts. They were clear but the section of trailer designed to slide was rusted together and seized. I tried pulling forwards and backwards again to see if I could jolt it loose. Nothing. Lonny/Lenny's afternoon shift replacement came out to help. He helped by observing, "This happens a lot." Bogie sliding (I don't have any idea where the slang comes from) doesn't get routinely checked, unlike so many other bits of truck. The afternoon chap asked about my accent as we stood around looking knowledgably at the seized sliders.

Trucking seems to involve a lot of standing around looking knowledgably at bits of truck and nodding your head sagely. Afternoon chap seemed minded to hang around and help and he transitioned from unhelpful helping to suggesting a remedy they had tried before...sticking a bloody great lump of timber behind the wheels. It was a friendly gesture and I appreciated the moral support as much as I appreciated the lump of wood. I seemed to be unaccountably close to tears again and they're harder to hide when your face is filthy.

It didn't work but I'd made a friend, who gave me free rein in his little office. I called dispatch to tell them I was delayed by an equipment failure. They put me on to a trainer. "Have you tried dumping the suspension?" I hadn't. I felt a fool, there was a detail I'd forgotten and I was just being a stupid, troublesome rookie. I dumped the suspension and tried again but it really was the trailer and not me, it was seized and that was that.

By this time I was pouring sweat from everywhere, which helped to clean the teary streaks. The afternoon guard who liked my accent and I came to the same conclusion, I'd have to go round the block, back onto the dock and get them to reload the trailer with more weight at the back. I watched my daylight arrival back in Guelph disappear as the time slipped by, if I ever got out of there carrying a legal weight I would be docking in the dark.

He called the shippers, explained the problem and told them I was coming back. He showed me the quickest way to turn around and said they'd reweigh the axles when I came back. Muskegon, Michigan seems to breed angels in human form.

The forklift driver was grumpy.

"I always load that way."

"I know. It's my trailer, the wheels won't slide."

"I wish someone would tell my boss that, he thinks I did it wrong."

"I'm so sorry about that, I'll tell him, where is he?"

"It's ok." He seemed mollified by my contrition. Or maybe the accent. I decided to capitalise…

"Thank you so much for your time, I know you're busy, but it will get me out of here…" He smiled. He got on with it. Maybe people aren't usually nice to forklift drivers.

I finally hit the road at about half past two. I was tired, hungry and fed up. Going Postal helped a bit but not much. I opted to 'hammer down' and get home as fast as I could instead of stopping for coffee and food. My stomach had been playing up anyway. It might have been the unusual routine or the combination of anxiety and fear but I didn't seem to be able to eat much at all. I was surviving mainly on trail mix and soggy peanut butter sandwiches. And American apples.

I breezed through the border for once, no stupid questions at all, treated myself to a coffee while fuelling up an hour from home and arrived back at the Guelph plant just after sunset. Yip, I was reversing in the dark. Only one dock open, squeezed between two parked trailers. My heart sank as I surveyed it and I mentally added another hour to my day. In order to achieve the inch-perfect impossible and refrain from smacking anything I'd have to get out and recheck the trailer angle every couple of feet.

Unbelievably, it took about ten minutes. A rookie reverse but verging on competent, things were looking up. The load was docked, safe, correct and on time, the paperwork in order and I finally handed a complete envelope full of stuff back to dispatch at about ten. I'd been away for two days but it felt like a fortnight.

***

Surviving a trip or two seemed to ease the anxiety. As the list of things I wasn't sure I could cope with decreased, I seemed to turn back into the (relatively) intelligent adult I had been before this mad enterprise started. Now that there was room in my head for things other than blind panic, I managed to learn small lessons from each mistake.

Solo trip three threatened to go pear-shaped when the directions on my trip plan didn't coincide with either the road signs or what Betsy wanted me to do, but what went through my head was, *Ah, the directions must be from Northbound, not South which is why the trip plan is wrong.* Followed by, *Betsy's trying to route me via a divided highway because I told her to.* Which was a much more helpful collection of thoughts than *OMG, OMG, OMG, I'm going to get lost,* followed by *OMG, OMG, OMG, I'm lost!*

The truck and I were in Virginia at the time. I was sufficiently perked by the prospect of coping with a whole run without a meltdown to eschew the distraction of audio books for a while and pop the radio on. I wanted and see what Virginia had to offer by way of weird radio stations and thus get back to that folksy travel writing which had, somewhere way back, been part of the point. I'd had enough of writing blogs for those who followed my adventures that began, "Arrgh, I'm tired and stressed." And presumably, so had they.

I've mentioned the dearth of interesting radio stations in the US before. Even around Memphis there had been no country music to laugh at, just tiny local religious stations apparently wishing to convert passing truckers. I'd heard hymns and sermons but nothing that I thought of as properly 'country' enough for a sense of local auditory amusement. But I struck lucky in Virginia, I really did. I found a station of such startling countryness that I began to memorise a list of song titles to repeat over to myself for fun. Now there would be some real US flair in the travel writing.

I was charmed by *Redneck Romeo*, tickled by *Everything's Good in the Trailerhood* and then utterly horrified by something nasty about three crosses by the road. I didn't catch all the words but it was about a road accident and some preacher waving a blood-stained bible at people. It made the hair stand up on the back of my neck and I went right off Virginia on the spot, abandoning the radio and going back to my audio books from the library. Enough local character already.

I looked the lyrics up later just in case I had imagined it in some sort of sleep-and-starvation-induced waking nightmare. Here they are for your edification and delight:

A farmer and a teacher, a hooker and a preacher,
Ridin' on a midnight bus bound for Mexico.
One's headed for vacation, one for higher education,
An' two of them were searchin' for lost souls.
That driver never ever saw the stop sign.
An' eighteen wheelers can't stop on a dime.

There are three wooden crosses on the right side of the highway,
Why there's not four of them, Heaven only knows.
I guess it's not what you take when you leave this world behind you,
It's what you leave behind you when you go.
That farmer left a harvest, a home and eighty acres,
The faith an' love for growin' things in his young son's heart.
An' that teacher left her wisdom in the minds of lots of children:
Did her best to give 'em all a better start.

An' that preacher whispered: "Can't you see the Promised Land?"
As he laid his blood-stained bible in that hooker's hand.

There are three wooden crosses on the right side of the highway,
Why there's not four of them, Heaven only knows.
I guess it's not what you take when you leave this world behind you,
It's what you leave behind you when you go.

That's the story that our preacher told last Sunday.
As he held that blood-stained bible up,
For all of us to see.
He said: "Bless the farmer, and the teacher, an' the preacher;
Who gave this Bible to my mamma,
Who read it to me."

There are three wooden crosses on the right side of the highway,
Why there's not four of them, now I guess we know.
It's not what you take when you leave this world behind you,
It's what you leave behind you when you go.

Now, I've read this though a few times and pondered it for ages while driving through regions with no radio stations and I still don't get the point. Is he saying the hooker should have died too? Surely not, she was his Mum. Maybe she had to live to get to give him the bible, is it a redemption tale? Should we assume that she changed her ways? And what's wrong with the oldest profession anyway? Civilised societies criminalise the customers these days don't they? Is he getting at one of the drivers? In which case, which one? Truckers don't miss stop signs.

And—a big worry for me, this one—what about the poor old bus driver? Didn't he deserve a cross by the road?

With hours of solitude to worry about something even more perplexing and possibly more trivial than Interpretive Potash Centres, I have opted to be offended on behalf of everyone in this horrible ditty. It's by Randy Travis. I won't be dashing out to buy the album. Even though 18-wheelers can't stop on a dime.

***

This trip was going well. Dispatch had routed me back via a pickup in Ohio. I found the shipper in record time, was early, got onto the dock relatively untroubled and was loaded and ready to leave in good time to get home before dark. Famous last words. I called dispatch to let them know I was leaving.

"How much room do you have left in the trailer?"

"Lots, they only loaded seven bins, about forty feet."

"We'll find you something else to load on the way back, call in when you get to Michigan."

This would be the first time I would have to find somewhere without printing off an emergency Google map as a backup for getting lost. I was trusting Betsy by then but belt'nbraces felt better. I dutifully set off with Jeff on my shoulder telling me to breathe to quell the rising panic-about-nothing and calculating how long my detour could take before I'd be parking in the dark again.

But dispatch were being kinder than I realised. My detour was on the way home, along the route back into Detroit. The nerves set in as I programmed Betsy to find it but she was a star and got me right there in record time, I still might make it home in daylight. Then I saw the dock. In a car park rather than through one and the arrangement of cars meant that the only option was a blind-side reverse. I never did get time to practise those with Hazel, she kept saying we'd work on it but then we rushed off somewhere else. And here dear readers, just in case you still think I'm a tad intrepid, is where I let the distaff side down on a massive scale.

A gallant young gentleman overheard my conversation with the shipper. "I love your accent," he schmoozed. "What are you driving?" He surveyed my highway cab, which was clearly too big to negotiate the car park with ease. "How's your blind-side backing?" Remembering that I had one asset which could be a handy way to win friends and influence people, I put on my best *Mary Poppins meets Maggie Thatcher* voice, and simpered disgustingly.

"Not terribly good I'm afraid, I'm very new at this."

"I'll direct you in and show you how it's done."

"How lovely of you, thank you sir, you're an angel." He smiled delightedly, I appeared to have made his day.

He directed me perfectly onto the dock. Years ago I would have sent him off with a flea in his ear for daring to imagine that just because I was a girly my blind-side reversing might be a bit suspect. Even if it was. Which it is. But these days I'm just flattered that anyone would feel good about helping me out and relieved that one more assignment might work out ok. I'll have to reverse blind-sided on my own soon enough, maybe I'll have learned something today. Apart from how to exploit an accent.

I left on time but torrential rain slowed me down and for the third time in a week an accident had closed off Highway 401 from Windsor. Yet again I found myself being diverted off the only road between the border and home. The emergency detour route takes one on a startlingly pretty meander along tiny lanes and around farms, taking right-angle bends between corn fields and through calendar-perfect little Ontario towns. The houses have wrap-around porches, the children have healthy glows and people chat on street corners. There are dogs and horses, horses and buggies, this is Mennonite country. On a nice day when you are not exhausted and desperate to get home and/or in a truck it is probably lovely. In the rain however, at the end of a day when you have done nothing but sweat and worry and as the light is fading, bearing in mind that all the picturesqueness is actually just more stuff to go under your wheels if you aren't psychic, it is pure torture.

I got back to Guelph about nine. It was still raining. I was delivering to the dock built at an annoying angle to the building. After dark you can't see the trees you need for a sightline and I expected to mess up the reverse but things were changing. Way back in school Gregg had told us, "You'll struggle and struggle and think you'll never get it and then one day it'll just click and feel like an instinct." Everyone had said the same, that you get better by doing it. I'd been doing it and I was getting better. Yet again, who'd have thought?

DETROIT

WHY SHOULD Detroit warrant a chapter of its own? A city is a city, right? Traffic, attitude, road signs, construction, I grew up in London, I should be used to it. I drove an ambulance in London, I should be extra used to it.

Maybe Detroit just had it in for me. I hadn't liked Chicago much, driving through Dallas is no fun and I really hate Montreal but Detroit made it personal. With the turn of the seasons it had exchanged blizzards for construction and the sort of signage that just invited you to get lost, in both senses. The first time I'd crossed the border with Hazel I'd still been reeling from the peculiarities of the bridge itself when her instructions for dealing with the lack of road signs began.

We were sitting on a weigh scale at the time, just past the border itself, at yet another truck-height booth with a jobsworth in it. I'd had to tell said person what we weighed. Hazel had calculated it roughly in her head as we'd waited in the queue and told me to scribble it on the windscreen. I'd made an idiot of myself by not knowing that the US side toll had a weight component and then again by wanting to know why, if we were sitting on a scale, we had to tell them what we weighed.

"Is it another way to see if we're lying?"

"No, the scales just don't work."

"I don't remember this from before, is it new?" There was yelling next.

It worried me that this whole scale thing was a surprise, I'd crossed at Detroit with Dave and with Mark and we'd never driven onto a scale. Or had we? Was I stupid or mad?

It would be another two or three trips before I twigged that the scales were an American thing, you only encountered them going out. The couple of times I'd crossed here with Challenger we'd been coming home which was a simpler process. In the meantime it was another thing-to-fret-about that was taking me too long to process as Hazel pointed out the signs up ahead. You could only turn left or right from the bridge itself and the signs listed each Interstate out of town. "Those are the last signs you'll see, the rest you just have to learn."

We'd wanted Interstate 96 West. That meant turning left. This turn took us to an apparent dead end in a defunct industrial area where a hidden 90 degree left turn took us to a stop sign on an otherwise deserted narrow street.

"Lock your door."

"Why?"

"Just do it right now."

So I'd locked my door. As we drew up to the stop sign the panhandlers appeared and I twigged that having to stop made us a sitting duck. I'd lived in Tottenham for long enough to know that there are some places where it's advisable to lock your doors in a car but who in their right minds would climb all the way up to the cab of a truck?

"You'd be surprised," Hazel added, "these people are desperate." Now Hazel is terrifying and she doesn't scare easily. I looked around at the grim cityscape, derelict and deserted. The shops and businesses were boarded up, their windows either broken and jagged with threats or dusty and dead…as though the buildings were regarding you with blind eyes.

The lonely building sites might have bustled in more prosperous times but now they lay low, abandoned to wait for half-erected scaffolds to rust and decay. The streets were devoid of anything except panhandlers and I began to get it. Trucks were the only traffic in this part of town. And they had to stop.

At the stop sign we turned right. There were no signs to highways. At the next lights we turned left. No signs. The highway signage reappeared just after the turn, precisely at the point when you'd either gone the right way with a lucky guess or missed the road completely.

"If we were going east we'd take that right lane over there." Hazel pointed. I looked for signs. Now she drew attention to it, there was a tiny one on the ramp that you would have had to be in the right lane for already to be able to see it. "The ramp we want today is just past the next lights but it's only signed when you get there, when you see it you'll be too late to change lanes."

Going west involved keeping in the left lane and just knowing where the ramp was because the only sign for Interstate 94 appeared when the ramp did and anyway we wanted Interstate 96 which wasn't signposted at all because it left the I94 a mile or two further on. Which you just had to know.

My head was still spinning with all the roads and lanes I'd have to learn before I'd be able to negotiate this route alone when I learned the next thing about Detroit. The access ramps to its highways were round extremely tight bends and horribly short. You couldn't see the traffic you would merge into until you were fully on the ramp and then you only had a few feet in which to react. "Just signal and go," fumed Hazel, "they're used to it." Unfortunately I had become a courteous trucker. There was shouting.

The traffic dodged and weaved around us, nobody signalled, I sweated. Hazel opined that the best way to negotiate the inner city highways was to get into the centre lane as soon as possible and stay there. That way the dodging and weaving would be up to everyone else and we would lose the need to react to other traffic merging and leaving. It made sense.

I managed the lane change eventually and we headed out of the city. Finally we crossed a bridge with startlingly bright blue girders which seemed to be some sort of demarcation point for the city limits. As soon as we left it behind the traffic suddenly settled down to more normal levels of insanity.

"That's pretty impressive," Hazel observed.

"What is?" I was ready for a compliment of some sort, I bloody well deserved one.

"I've never seen anyone hold their breath that long before."

***

I began to view Detroit's tangle of Interstates with nothing much between them except road works, diversions and panhandlers as a depressing introduction to a country that makes you jump through such arcane hoops merely to assist its international commerce by bringing it freight.

As a freight vehicle, when you descend the US side of the massive Ambassador Bridge over Lake Erie and worm your way correctly round the spaghetti, you pull into one of seven or eight truck lanes leading to the border proper. The seven or eight lanes are generally full of trucks waiting their turn to approach the border guards' booths. At busy times or at jobsworth shift-change the tailback extends up and over the bridge. It is very high. You can sit up there for an hour or more contemplating the icy depths and getting a little dizzy. I am developing a morbid fear of dying by drowning in a vehicle.

Once at the booth, everyone must be quizzed. The questions vary but the intent is the same. Not only do they want to make sure you are who you say you are, going where you say you are going and carrying what you say you are carrying, but—as Dave had explained way back in another lifetime—yes, they really do want to piss you off as well. With electronic pre-approval by customs brokers who know their stuff (tractors notwithstanding) mostly they know the answers to all the questions they ask. They have on a screen in front of them who you are, what's in the back, where you are headed and where you blooming well live. You have to tell them anyway though because, allegedly, your demeanour while doing so will display suspicious signs if you are up to no good.

Now that I was sitting alone in my cab awaiting my turn with no-one to distract my attention with wise tutelage, conversation, bickering, barking or bollocking, I had time to observe the routine.

Every so often the slow progression of trucks through the booths comes to a stop. A green light above the lane containing the offending vehicle turns to red and the body language dance begins at the rear of the hapless truck. Someone is being inspected. The trailer must be unsealed and opened. The driver must do this, observed by as many guards as can be spared to make sure he knows exactly how much trouble he is in.

The uniforms don't need the aggressive stance, the one person not in uniform may or may not have been displaying the wrong sort of demeanour from the comfort of the driving seat but is now moving in as non-aggressive a manner as can possibly be demonstrated. The hands still rest on the gun holsters. Just so you know.

Sometimes the truck under scrutiny is sent on its way after a satisfactory search, sometimes it will be sent for X-ray, sometimes (and this is what everyone dreads) it is turned back to its country of origin to start the customs paper trail all over again. Then someone's freight will be very late and jobs are lost.

That worry overlays the border preparations every time. I am getting better at the 'how to be ready' routine...hat off, sunglasses off, light on in the cab, bunk curtains open, window down, papers and FAST card ready. Turn off engine, don't set brakes. Have answers scribbled on windscreen. Have apple sticker handy. Make eye contact. I have even managed to remember where I am going and where I have been the last couple of times. I have been declaring my apples religiously but no-one else has wanted to see them. They just look for new and ever sillier ways to be annoying.

My accent seems to upset some, they demand to know my citizenship. The first time this happened I told the truth, "British and Canadian, sir." This did not go down well. "You can only have one." These are Yanks of course, it's true for them. I go for the easy option now and tell them I am Canadian. This seems to satisfy, although of course my dual citizenship is flagged on my FAST card so they know I'm lying.

**

When dispatch called to ask if I'd go out on Friday night it was by way of asking a favour, Linamar's drivers appear to expect to have their weekends off. I needed the Brownie points though and it didn't sound too bad a run, drive over to some suburb of Detroit, sleep, deliver in the morning, collect a new load at lunchtime and be home before dark. So I said yes. Then of course I thought it over. Detroit has no truck stops. Or rest areas. Even if it did, I don't think anyone in their right minds would avail themselves of the facilities. I called the company and asked whether they had anywhere I could park overnight. "Oh yes," the lady in the office told me, "just ask the guard, he's very good, he'll show you where to park." This sounded promising although as I think I may have mentioned it has been known for ladies in offices to not quite know how big you are and how much space you need.

I was beginning to realise that most of the anxiety around finding new places had less to do with getting lost and/or manoeuvring onto strange docks than it did with not knowing where you would be able to sleep. Betsy would always find your address eventually and there was usually someone around to help out with docking, that was just about time and embarrassment, but I'd learned in Chicago what it felt like to be out of hours with nowhere to stop. Without significant planning, and sometimes even with it, you could be running illegally and exhausted with no immediate solution, the experience was one I never wanted to repeat. Each trip to somewhere new made for one more place that you were familiar with though and there was only one way to learn. I would get to know another bit of Detroit this weekend and thus be a little more seasoned.

I found this company after a minor panic trying to read unlit road signs on a small trading estate in the dark. Betsy had delivered me to the relevant turning but had been no help finding the building among a bewildering range of factories and warehouses which all seemed to share the same address. Once I found my building however it transpired that the office lady had been right for once, the guard at the gate was splendid. He directed me to a big 'holding pen' that was easy to get into, easy to park in and easy to get out of. He showed me where the ladies' loo was. Luxury.

"What are you delivering?"

"Empty cartons, they're due in at eight."

"They get in at five, they might take you then."

"Tell them not to bother, I'd rather sleep until eight."

It was about one in the morning by then. I settled in for the night. I was starting to sleep quite well in the cab once I knew I was safe and legal. At five AM there was a hammering on the door. I toppled off the bunk, fell over my cooler, couldn't find my glasses and attempted to peer out of the driver's door window. Half expecting this occurrence I'd had the presence of mind to sleep decently dressed.

"What are you delivering?"

"Empty cartons."

"They won't be unloaded until eight."

"I know."

Apart from that minor annoyance it was a doddle to deliver to. By way of a treat almost as nice as the holding pen, the docks turned out to be widely spaced with masses of turning room and yellow lines on the ground that were freshly painted and easy to see. Most warehouse docks have these, they are supposed to make it easier to line your wheels up before the dock edge markers heave into view but too often they are so faded and old they may as well not be there at all. I was offloaded by nine and had been given permission to spend the next few hours snoozing back in the holding pen before setting off for my lunchtime pickup down the road. This was turning into a good day. I was beginning to almost like Detroit.

Things took a downward turn at the next customer, a small foundry in a more cluttered part of town. I arrived carefully early, assuming that most people who work on Saturdays want to get home as soon as they can. I parked across the road and scoped out the dock. Oh dear, blind-side reversing off the road, this was going to be fun. The shipping office was empty so I ambled about a bit looking for someone to wave at. Eventually I found a forklift driver who said he knew nothing about any shipments going out, he told me to back onto the dock and he'd see what he could find out.

I was going to have to do it and there was no-one around to laugh. I was early so I could take my time. I took a deep breath, examined the available space, pulled round and into a driveway on the opposite side of the road and somehow, bit by bit, with much getting out to check and plenty of toing and froing, managed to blind-side the trailer into an approximation of the right position.

I was about a foot from perfectly docked when jobsworth of the day appeared.

"What are you doing?"

"I'm taking my time getting onto your dock sir, I'm very sorry if I'm in anyone's way."

"No, I mean why are you here?"

"I'm collecting a delivery for *Hastech* in Ontario."

"Those docks are round the back. And you're early. I'm not ready yet, I haven't even started to sort it out. Why are you early? You should be here at one-thirty, I've got to have my lunch."

"I'm very sorry to be early sir, I didn't mean to cause you any problems, I'm just new and I didn't want to get lost and be late. I have no wish to rush you sir, I can wait." Grovelling was getting easier. He seemed slightly mollified by the contrition and the body language settled down somewhat, he subsided from furious to, well, antsy.

He showed me a small map of the building detailing where I needed to go. Which was not only 'round the back' but down a narrow alley between two buildings, past a load of cars, around in a junkyard behind the foundry and into a tiny dock down a slope between two small walls too low to be visible in the mirrors. My time-consuming but beautiful blind-side manoeuvre had been pointless, and a deal easier than the next one was going to be.

I continued to grovel. I told him it would take me ages to get onto the dock so I would most definitely not be early by then and that there was no need to alter his (clearly vital) schedule for the day. I was beginning to wonder how long I could keep up the hapless rookie routine, it seemed to work wonders with inspiring assistance and cooperation from all and sundry. Jobsworth became positively helpful on the surface although I suspect he took an extra long lunch anyway, just to make sure I knew who was in charge.

I took my time to wiggle past the cars, make an inch-perfect turn on the only path which would avoid the junk on the way in to the yard, miss the little walls as I swung around and set up for the reverse with my nose in another pile of junk. There would be zero opportunity to put right a bad setup in the space available so I spent a bit of time walking around my chosen starting point before attempting the reverse down the slope.

A couple of lunching warehouse chappies loped out for a smoke as I surveyed my positioning. They did the standing around looking at stuff knowledgably thing, as they surveyed my positioning. Presumably they'd observed many a doomed setup in their impossible yard. When they'd established their knowlegeableness to each other sufficiently well they nodded approvingly at my truck. Thus encouraged I shimmied onto the dock, almost making that trailer dance, and was so gobsmacked when I got there that I took a photo.

I waited about an hour for jobsworth to load the trailer as slowly as he could, using the time to calculate just how late I could leave and still be home before dark. I'd scoped out the exit by then, that was going to take some time too, possibly longer than it took to get in.

Home-before-dark was still just about possible when I'd fought my way out of the foundry from hell, parked up to mop away the sweat and called the customs broker to see how fast they could expedite my border paperwork.

"Our computer's down, we're going to have to walk it over physically, could you lose about an hour before you get here?"

I promised to try and lose an hour, thinking that maybe I'd pop into Duty Free for a coffee and a browse, mayhap a spot of imported chocolate, I deserved a treat. I programmed the border crossing into Betsy and set off but Detroit had other ideas for my lost hour. The entire city was being dug up that weekend and every highway Betsy tried to make me drive onto had the on-ramp closed and a diversion signposted. I spent a lot more than my allotted hour driving round in circles trying to follow ever tinier diversion signs in rapidly diminishing visibility due to torrential rain.

I knew I was approaching the right part of town at least twice as I drove under, rather than across, the Breathe-Out Bridge…once in each direction. Still, at least, by the time I arrived at the border my paperwork had had time to be walked to customs, copied by hand in triplicate and illustrated by monks.

Mentioning to dispatch on my return that sending a Londoner to Detroit on a weekend when they closed all the highways was a foolhardy decision, might, with hindsight, have been a mistake.

***

Detroit's road works were responsible for my first ever sixteen-hour day and for that alone I will not forgive the city. Montreal can consider itself positively rehabilitated.

Sixteen hours are sort of legal in Canada under some circumstances. This had gone over my head in school. I'd rather assumed it would never happen but dispatch enjoyed reminding me that although your fourteen-hour day is sacrosanct in the US, the Canadian rules let you extend your work shift to sixteen so long as you take two hours off for rest sometime during the day. Or pretend to, if put under enough pressure.

I got back to dispatch one Thursday at about four in the afternoon. I was quietly hoping there would be no more work for me, quite often there wasn't on a Friday. I'd been up since four that morning, just the twelve hour shift, and wanted a decent night's sleep.

"There's a load for you leaving at two in the morning."

"What? I can't do that, I need to sleep."

"There's no-one else, and you've been here over an hour, your log can finish at three, so you can drive from one, you'll have had your ten hours."

"Legally, but not really. I'll not get home 'til five, I need to do laundry, sort out the cats, buy food…"

"That's trucking." My dispatcher says that a lot, now the be-nice-to-the-rookie routine has worn off. It makes him feel clever, as does sending me into Detroit on a weekend.

I whinged. They called the customer and got a delay on the delivery time so that I could start two hours later, which they presented as the sort of huge favour you have to be grateful for. I dashed home, showered, made an omelette I didn't really want, ate half of it and headed for bed about seven to try and get some sleep before getting up at three in the morning to start driving again at four.

Exhaustion aside, it wasn't actually too bad a start to the day. By making a fuss I'd pushed the timing round to miss the dreaded three-in-the-morning physical dip and there would only be a couple of hours or so to drive in the dark. I'd learned to like a 4 a.m. start with Mark, perking up at dawn really helped the day along. It turned into a happy enough drive to the now-familiar suburb of Detroit with the nice guards, handy loos, pen for sleeping in and easy docks.

I called dispatch when I was unloaded and they sent me my return run via the satellite. An easy drive round Detroit to a more northerly suburb to collect a load to bring home. Excellent. Half an hour to the next customer, an hour to load, on the way home by eleven, an early finish for once. I looked the new place up on the map, plugged it into Betsy, decided I liked the route she plumped for and set off.

Some familiarity with Detroit would have helped. Betsy's route looked ok to a grockle but it took us around a stupid ring road which wasn't quite a highway. It had lots of lights, lots of traffic and lots of construction. Lanes were coned off and shifted about every few yards, cars and bikes were weaving in and out around me and the drive got more than a little stressful.

All of a sudden the satellite messaging machine went off, making its annoying beeping noise. We're not supposed to read messages while driving so I left it. Then my mobile started nagging as well, someone clearly wanted me urgently but it was illegal to answer either horrible beep whatever the crisis and I'd been warned that Michigan police were vultures. I picked up the message at a set of red lights (yes, still illegal but at least I was stopped). Dispatch had changed their minds. Someone else was going to the customer they'd sent me to and could I pull in and call for a new assignment?

The short answer was no. I couldn't pull in, I was in the middle of Detroit in road works. You can't just park a truck in the middle of a city, it's illegal and dangerous. They know that. The only way I could stop would be to find the nearest highway, head out of town until the traffic thinned a little and pull onto the shoulder of an off-ramp. Illegal again but relatively safe, I wouldn't be able to stop for long but it might be enough.

Driving out of Detroit in heaven knows what direction on goodness knows what highway, it was just the first one I found, I lucked out. I passed someone broken down on the shoulder with a patrol car in attendance. With a dazzling display of presence of mind I pulled onto the next ramp along hoping that the patrol's attention would be held by the 'bear bait' for at least another minute. It looked like there had been paperwork and that takes ages. I had no idea where my new destination was and no time to look it up properly so I punched it into Betsy and hoped for the best.

I'd got over the lack of printed map by this time. I still felt better if I had one but at least I could still breathe if I didn't. She might not always take me the best way round but she'd get me there somehow. Of course, first I had to turn round and go back the way I'd come. Since I'd driven quite a long way in the wrong direction before finding my stopping point I was looking at another hour at least before I made the pickup. I don't think I took the optimal route, judging by the number of 'Michigan turnarounds' I ended up performing but perhaps it was just a classic case of *if I were you I wouldn't start from here.*

The Michigan turnaround is an evil invention designed to frighten the baseball cap off a rookie trucker by over-complicating turning left. It involves driving past the junction you want to turn at, taking a filter lane on the left of the road you didn't want to drive along into a small u-turn crossing in the median, coming back the way you came, crossing three lanes of traffic in a few feet…then turning right instead. It's probably not so challenging in a car. Most of the little u-bends are built so that trucks can just about make it round but you have to attack them spot on, while remembering to take up a lane and a half to start with and 'bend the traffic' as you complete the turn. All very well when you know where you're going but lost, late, sweating and trying to quell the panic they are no fun at all.

I found the new shipper just as the warehouse staff went to lunch. There were two trucks in front of me waiting to be loaded. The drivers of the trucks in front of me had their noses in books and newspapers. This was not going to be quick, although in a way that helped me with backing into the only spare dock. These docks were under cover, inside the building. Another new form of torture which I'd discovered meant that although the reflective marks delineating the dock edges were there, you couldn't actually see them until you were under the roof. By which time it was too late to use them. I called dispatch.

"I'm waiting for them to finish lunch and load two trucks in front of me, it'll be at least an hour."

"That's ok, we don't need the load back until nine tonight."

"But if I don't leave by one I'll be out of hours, I

started at four."

"You gain two hours when you cross the border, cross at Sarnia, you're only an hour away, then you can drive two hours longer."

"I can drive for longer but my shift won't extend unless I take two hours off."

"That's trucking."

In the end I left at one-thirty. They were right about Sarnia, I was still officially in Detroit but in a suburb so far to the north it would take longer to fight back through all the diversions to the Ambassador. I could just make it if I made no stops and had no delays at the border but Detroit had other plans. Betsy directed me, via another half-dozen Michigan turnarounds, to the freeway that would take me to I94 North and Port Huron for the Blue Water Bridge border crossing.

Road works had closed the ramp from one road to the other yet again, and the tiny orange detour signs funnelled everybody off onto a small local road to pick up the Interstate about ten miles further north. It took an hour and a half, by which time the Friday afternoon tourist traffic had piled up heading for weekends of walking, camping and fishing in Ontario. I finally crossed into Canada at four in the afternoon with at least two and a half hours driving to get home, then a delivery to make, and only two hours left in my shift. I wouldn't be back within the Guelph pootling radius in time and anyone examining my logbook on the way would know this.

Fortunately I'd wasted so much time driving round in circles in Detroit that I could spend my time in the border crossing queue rewriting my log to pretend that I'd had two hours off in the middle of the day. Matching miles to hours it would look perfectly fine, thus suddenly a sixteen-hour shift became legal because I'd crossed the border. It was all legal anyway of course, because I'd driven round in circles within the magic 160 kilometres. The letter of the law might be knackering but nobody did anything naughty. Not really.

I delivered the load at half past six, waited for it to be offloaded, drove back to the yard, dropped the empty trailer, parked the tractor, finished off my paperwork and delivered it all to dispatch at eight in the evening, having started work at four that morning.

Maybe I'd have felt better if that mythical two hour snooze had been real. I held Detroit personally responsible.

RETURN TO CINCINNATI

FAMILIARITY was beginning to help. Occasionally I was returning to places I actually remembered and that felt good, there was more breathing. It had started with Lenny/Lonny and the bogie sliding incident. I may have been in bits but people who dealt with truckers all the time knew who I was.

The memorable accent and incongruous appearance were beginning to create a touch of the mascot about little English. I was too old to be cute but at least I could be entertaining. Knowing how to find customers, how to set up for their docks, where to sleep, how full the local rest areas and truck stops might be, all this helped to ease some of the crippling anxiety. Sometimes. And the mascotness meant that everyone grinned when they saw me. Laughing at rather than with they may have been but I still brightened their day and that made them mostly helpful.

I was even learning when to bother to switch the CB on for traffic reports and diversion advice. I'd developed a bit of a loathing for the CB to be honest. When I'd first mooted this mad idea, as well as buying me enchanting little gifts of Yorkie Bars everyone had sung *Convoy* and called me 'rubber duck' but now I was trucking for real I hardly used the dratted thing. I absolutely didn't want a 'handle' despite Dave's endearing attempts to think up something suitable. He'd suggested 'Lady Penelope' which, come to think of it, might have helped to put me off.

Not only had I struggled to think straight when all my driving partners had insisted on having both the CB and the normal radio at maximum volume (plus mobile phone conversations at top of voice to be heard over all the noise) it just wasn't very entertaining. The romanticism of *Convoy* had been well and truly knocked out of my head, I'd even stopped humming the tune although that took a bit longer.

Time was when the CB was the only way for truckers to pass the hours and ease the boredom but now, everyone had Bluetooth etc therefore anyone who wanted a pleasant chat would be talking to family and friends, not other truckers. Radio traffic seemed to be restricted to people saying hello to each other, discussing who'd died, slagging off one another's driving and moaning about stuff. I fondly hoped that the miseries who had nothing better to do than bitch at someone who was taking their time to get out of the middle lane were an unlovable minority who had no-one else to talk to, I wasn't meeting these dinosaurs face to face anywhere.

The CB airwaves seemed to be the only place left where racism and sexism were alive and well. Mostly I kept it off, I could live without the ill-tempered entertainment and I certainly wasn't going to use it to talk to anyone. I'd heard the reactions when Janice and Hazel had been unwise enough to broadcast our gender, my voice and (even worse) my accent would be bound to set off a whole load of grief. There was little point in the baseball cap and sunglasses and all that sleeping in anonymous rest areas if I was going to start telling everyone within earshot that I was a daft, lone, English female. Mascot status notwithstanding, I still had a limiter that overtook people.

Occasionally the CB did come into its own as a useful tool, when there was trouble on the road the camaraderie returned and knights of the road shared their wisdom with each other for no other reason than a generous instinct to help out. If I'd kept it on all the time I would have heard about such matters as bear traps, chicken coops etc and local tips for the avoiding thereof, but I opted to run the gauntlet of speed checks and open weigh stations. I was obsessive about my vehicle checks anyway, I had little to fear and I preferred the silence.

I quickly learned which cities and highways had regular accidents and diversions though and when to switch on for helpful truckerly information. As soon as a traffic snarl up developed everyone would start asking everyone else what was going on and someone out there would know. Often it would be a truck driving in the opposite direction to the trouble. He had just passed whatever was holding you up and could tell you what had happened, how many lanes were closed and how many miles the traffic jam covered. Then someone local would join in with whether it was worth taking another route or not and if so where to turn off the highway. Eventually you could work out whether to sit tight or which truck to follow.

Here's a tip for you, next time you are held up on the

road watch the trucks. If they all start to head for one lane or another follow them, they are being coached by someone who knows.

The other new form of support was The Little Black Book. I'd begun The Notes of course under Hazel's tutelage, when they had made themselves useful while I was so generally freaked out and terrified that nothing stuck in my head at all. I kept it up when I realised that every time dispatch said, "You went there last week," I would stand there looking gormless, uselessly searching the synapses for any kind of recognition until they offered a small detail by way of a hint to bring the place back to mind.

The Notes had grown and were now the LBB, slightly less dog eared and dieselly and a bit easier to read. Sometimes the LBB made sense. For example, since the bogie sliding incident The Notes regarding Muskegon, Michigan had been transcribed and had grown from *Guard called Lonny, knows everything* to *Lonny might be Lenny the scale guy, under rlwy bridge, Michigan turnaround, scale on rt, must weigh in and out, metal bins 2nd dock, plastic and loading 1st dock, sleep under trees, CHECK BOGIES*.

Sometimes the LBB was of more limited use. *Muhashi, Battle Creek. Brown bldn to L of ball diamond, use intercom, mad car park.* Effectively pointless. Once I found the ball park the memory kicked in but I'd not noted down quite how much it looked like the road had fizzled out before you got to it. Or quite how to negotiate the mad car park.

Sometimes the LBB was just plain wrong. It wasn't always my fault. When I wrote *Detroit, bridge from I94, exit 213B, DON'T MISS IT, signs for Toledo, not bridge*, I didn't know that Detroit kept moving its routes around road works all the time. I should have written *look for stupidly tiny orange signs* instead.

Occasionally I had just been an idiot. Remember the car park we were not supposed to drive into? The one with the coffee wagon and the people trying to go home? Just after the bogie-sliding and all the road works? You could be forgiven for not quite recalling the details, it was a few chapters ago but I really should have paid more attention.

What with all the delays and the whole memorable series of debacles that day I'd allowed myself to put off making The Notes until the end of the run. Thus, when I later wrote, *Colonial Tool, Windsor. Must shift duals to back, air pressure knob retracts pins, dog-leg through road works* and *ExCor, Windsor. Park on Seneca St, forklift will come out, turn L past bldn and go round it*, I had recalled each location perfectly. I really had. I was impressed with my powers of recall all over again when I transcribed them into the LBB. I just didn't realise I'd got them back-to-front until I had to return to one on my own.

***

The plan was to turn up at the yard at noon, collect a preloaded trailer of empty bins and take them to Cincinnati. Even without the LBB I remembered Cincinnati; Hazel's Friday meltdown, the sympathetic shipper and the driveway you could park in. I'd had the presence of mind to ask whether my reload would have to wait until seven in the evening again and the answer had been no, I'd have a reload right away. Recalling that Cincinnati had no truck stops was another personal coup, I knew I could sleep in the company's drive but also looked up which highway might boast the region's nearest facilities. I found a truck stop about an hour out of town to the south, not on my way but I'd have to fuel somewhere. It was a Pilot, not a J, but they accepted our fuel cards so I could justify the extra mileage. Depending on the time I had two options for overnight safety.

This was going to be a nice run, not only starting in daylight but a preload. That meant the border paperwork would be all ready and I could hit the road right away. Cincinnati was about an eight hour drive, if I got moving smartish I could not only get to my chosen truck stop in daylight, I'd be just an hour from delivery in the morning. I was really beginning to enjoy having been somewhere before.

I arrived in the yard a few minutes before noon, I wanted to get all my checks completed and be on the road nice and early. "We have an extra stop for you." The dispatcher displayed body language which implied he knew I'd be pissed off. That is to say he kept his eyes on his computer screen and threw the information over his shoulder. They only do eye contact when they are going to make you happy. "It's on your way. You just have to collect a couple of broaches first and deliver them to Windsor." That wasn't so bad, at least I wouldn't have to hang around waiting for border faxes.

I headed round the corner to load the extra thingumies. There weren't many bins pre-loaded, only the first ten feet or so of the trailer were occupied so I could see why they wanted to take advantage of my spare space. Once the second load was in the trailer I hopped in to think about strapping. Now I was in a hurry, I wanted to make the most of the daylight but there really was no excuse for rank stupidity. The bins were stacked floor to ceiling at the front of the trailer. Two small but perfectly formed pieces of expensive-looking, beautifully turned machinery (I couldn't tell you what they were but they were shiny, round and complicated) were strapped to the small wooden pallets called broaches and sitting right at the back of the trailer, by the doors.

About thirty feet of empty space stood between the bins and the shinies and I sort of knew that I should probably strap something somewhere to prevent stuff crashing about on the way. From where I stood it looked as though the main problem would be bins falling over from the height they were stacked and damaging the nice shiny things. I strapped the bins securely in place at the front of the trailer, making sure the top strap was as high as I could reach. Then I headed for Windsor.

I'd checked the LBB for *Colonial Tool*, it was the place where you had to slide the bogies. I'd proudly made that part of my vehicle check, the sliders on this trailer weren't rusted together. I'd even moved them an experimental notch, I was ready for today.

I remembered where the place was, I could picture the road works and the shenanigans required to turn onto the highway and everything. I punched the address into Betsy though just to be extra careful, I didn't want any more delays and it made more sense to rely on the GPS than my memory, even if I did have a kickass hippocampus these days. That was the only thing I did right.

Betsy took me a strange way into Windsor. I got a bit rattled as we headed further west and less north than I'd recalled for the bogie-sliding establishment. Of course if I'd been in less of a hurry to set off the broaches might have been my clue. As I headed further into downtown Windsor than I wanted to, a car cut me up and I had to brake sharply. I heard—and felt—a couple of heavy, sliding sort of thuds behind me. Things in the trailer were on the move. I visualised the layout. I'd strapped the stuff at the front to stop it falling over. But braking sends things forwards, why hadn't I strapped behind the broaches to stop them moving as well? Because I'm stupid, that's why.

Betsy took me to *Colonial Tool*. As she told me I had arrived at my destination I recognised it as the place where you had to drive round the block and park in the street. The one without the loading dock. The implications of this minor hippocampal hiccup didn't hit me at the time, I was just rather proud of myself for remembering where to park despite having got the notes reversed. I sauntered in to find someone.

It was gone five in the evening by now and there weren't many people around. There was no-one in the shipping office, just a couple of young lads who appeared to be watching machines with the sort concentration generally required to nod knowledgably at trucks. One of them abandoned his machine, which appeared to function fine without being watched, and jumped into a forklift to come and offload my broaches for me. As I opened the back we both registered and then slowly digested the horribly obvious problem. The two shinythings had skittered to the very front of the trailer and away from the doors. The plant had no raised loading dock from which to drive in. Their forklift was the sort that lifted things off the backs of trailers. Between us we had no way to get the pallets from the front to the back.

"Do you have a pump dolly?"

"Um, no. Do you?"

"No."

"Oh."

"Maybe we can push them."

"I'm sorry."

I was visualising how simple it would have been to have popped a strap behind the shinies to hold them in place. I also twigged that the people loading the trailer knew they were sending their handiwork to a place without a dock, even if I didn't. That was why they'd loaded them right at the back in the first place.

"Not to worry, we'll sort something out. We're paid by the hour." The lads grinned at each other. "You weren't to know we didn't have a dock, nobody expects that the first time they come here." These nice kids were on my side, they weren't cross or anything so why did I then say, "Actually I have been here before, I should have remembered"? Because I'm an idiot, that's why.

They tried pushing. They tried pulling. But the momentum of my little emergency stop had pulled some anchor ties loose, the shinythings were now a bit wobbly on their broaches. The lads twinkled at me and then disappeared for a few minutes, returning with several massive lengths of chain with hooks on the ends. They hooked one chain around a broach, linked all the others together and hooked the other end round the forklift. One lad manoeuvred the forklift slowly and carefully away from the truck while the other one stood inside the trailer yelling instructions. Every so often they regarded the stupid driver with the defeated and miserable demeanour and offered supportive smiles. They were having fun, this was more interesting than watching machines, but I was watching the daylight and thus my night in a truck stop disappear. Arrive any time after ten and the only truck stop for miles in any direction would be full. I think maybe I'd have felt better if someone had shouted.

When the time came to sign the paperwork declaring that the consignment had been delivered in good order the taller kid, the one who fancied himself a bit, twinkled at me one last time.

"You do know that if you'd delivered these to Ford or somewhere they'd have refused to accept them don't you?"

"Yes, I've learned a few things today, thank you very much for being so nice." I'm actually getting sick of doing humble rookie, I want to do brash old-hand but I'll have to beat the stupidity first.

***

Having given up any hope of a meal and a shower that night I hammered down and headed straight to the next customer. I parked and slept in their driveway and appeared bleary-eyed and in need of coffee in the shipping office at eight o'clock in the morning. I'd not had my ten hours off but that was nothing new.

"Hello!" The shipper seemed delighted to see me, "Are you on your own now?"

"Yes, I don't need a babysitter anymore."

"Did she bully you all the way home?" I offered a wry grin. "It's nice to see you again." I asked about available docks. "That guy is ahead of you really." She indicated a fancily tricked-out Pete, all pointless chrome and macho appendages, parked up behind me in the drive. "But he's still asleep so we'll get you loaded first, put it in dock two. Do you remember where the coffee machine is?" I didn't but she found someone to guide me there. The day was looking up.

I was docked, unloaded, reloaded and sorted out with paperwork in record time. The faxes were sent, the phone calls made. Despite my stupid mistake which no-one need ever know about (unless I do something really daft like write about it in a book or something) I had survived Cincinnati with time to spare and was minded to celebrate.

Cincinnati straddles the border between Ohio and Kentucky. I had delivered on the Ohio side of the state line, but in need of fuel and deserving of shower and food I decided I could definitely justify the extra mileage to finally check out that truck stop. Kentucky felt sort of further away and therefore more adventurous.

Showered and happy, I went in search of a meal. There was a small restaurant advertising country-style, all-day breakfasts. I hadn't eaten anything more substantial than half a peanut butter sandwich (soggy) an apple (American) or a handful of trail mix (the cab floor resembled a birdcage) for several days and I fancied breakfast so I headed on in. They bring you coffee pdq in a truck stop, they know how much you need it. I was on the outside of my first cup since the well-meant but nasty machine dishwater of early morning before the menu arrived with a welcome caffeine refill. I ordered a veggie omelette and sat back to enjoy the conversation about what I would like to have served with it. Fries, hash browns or home fries? I asked for home fries because they're part of the fun.

Breakfast potato accompaniments, just like toast options, vary by state and home fries vary more than most.

In some places they resemble sauté potatoes, all crispy with onions, sometimes they'll be shredded more like a rosti, occasionally they are closer to an oven-wedge sort of thing. It was a minor amusement to add to the litany of breads…the *whewhysordhryoriscit*. I knew by now that there would always be wheat, white, sourdough and rye (marble if you're lucky) but it depended how far south you were what came last. *Or biscuit* was very southern and Washington State and South Dakota aside seemed to start in the Carolinas.

In Florence, Kentucky I can now report that they offer *or Texas toast*. I was tempted because I wasn't quite sure what Texas toast was but settled for rye, the need for comfort food overtaking my customary culinary curiosity. I clearly hadn't been paying proper attention last time I ordered breakfast in Texas because I set to wondering whether you got biscuits and Texas toast there or whether it was only Texas toast outside of Texas. Like English muffins.

My omelette arrived with shredded rosti-like home fries and marble rye. It looked good, loaded with fresh veg, no slimy tinned mushrooms or plastic cheese.

"Would you like Hot Sauce?" the waitress asked. That's another location thing, this was far enough south for the offer but a bit further south and the green and red Tabasco bottles would already have been on the tables alongside the ketchup.

"No thank you," I replied, "but I wonder if you have any vinegar?" She looked confused, they always do. I had my emergency vinegar stowed in the truck but I was having fun. "It's a Brit thing," I added, as though that might actually be helpful for her.

She thought for a moment and brightened, "Yes we do, I'll bring it for you." And she did. She brought me the little oil and vinegar condiment set from the salad bar and beamed from ear to ear as she set it down. Americans love being able to cater to your every whim no matter how weird they may find it. I'd not had raspberry vinegar on potatoes before but it wasn't too bad, much nicer than the previous time I asked for vinegar in the US and received low-cal Italian salad dressing. The emergency vinegar had been retrieved from the cab that day but it remained stowed away in Cincinnati.

I had nibbled about a quarter of my brekkie when the waitress returned.

"Would you like another omelette?" I thought that she thought I wasn't enjoying it and wanted something different, since I was making a very untruckerly job of ploughing through it slowly.

"No thank you, it's lovely, I just wasn't as hungry as I thought."

"Well, it's all-you-can-eat, so let me know if you want another one when you're done." I let this piece of information sink in. She was offering me a second omelette after my first one because the restaurant advertised 'all you can eat'. I'd not come across that before. All-you-can-eat buffets and salad bars, yes, and I've been offered extra toast, salad, garlic bread and the like when they are sides to an entrée, but no-one has ever before offered to recook my entire meal. I double-checked that I'd understood her right and we had one of those conversations that began with, "I love your accent," and ended with, "You come back and see us again now," and I wished I could have finished my first omelette and made an attempt at a second, just to make her happy.

I bought another coffee in the little shop on my way back out to the truck. Wandering around the displays to see what else could be had (I was constantly amazed by the range of travel-sized things you could buy for a truck) I happened upon a natty little dustpan and brush set. I remembered the disastrous day Mark had tried out a travel Hoover, back in the team driving lifetime. Not reading the manual because, well, nobody does, he'd managed to fill the air with recycled dust and we'd coughed for days. I decided the dustpan and brush might be a better investment and took it to the counter with glee.

The girl asked me how I was today and when I replied we had another of those conversations that began with, "I love your accent," and ended with, "You come back and see us again now," and I was minded to declare Kentucky the friendliest state I had visited so far. Yes, there had been a couple of dodgy moments in Berea back with Dave, but even then I had ended up with a free coffee. Kentucky people definitely liked to give you extra comestibles. All in all, my return to Cincinnati appeared to have been relatively triumphant. An eight hour yomp across the border and I'd be home in daylight. I had this business beaten.

ALL TOGETHER NOW

I WAS looking forward to a nice little run down to Virginia. It sounded as though it was going to be a happy trip, starting early enough in the day to get a good distance covered in daylight. Virginia is pretty so long as you refrain from putting the radio on. There isn't an obvious way to get there though, what with the mountains and stuff, so I spent a bit of time mulling over the best possible route while I waited to be loaded.

There was time for plenty of mulling, I'd had to drive an hour west with a trailer full of empty bins and the shipper was going to unload those and then put more stuff on before I could head for the border. Since the best crossing for Virginia is at Buffalo, not Detroit, I would be redriving the hour east to Guelph before making any real progress. Those lakes get in your way something terrible.

This was going to be a full 44,000 lb shipment of metal bins full of heavy clutch plates. They would be loaded half at the front of the trailer and half over the rear axle to spread the weight as legally as possible. I asked dispatch about the bogie sliding issue, I was wary of maximum weight these days.

"These people are pretty good, they get it right, you shouldn't have a problem."

"But have they got their own scale?"

"Don't think so, but you'll be near the J, scale it if you want to, but really, they're good, we've never had a problem." I made a mental note to scale the load anyway.

"You'll need four load bars though, they should already be in the trailer from the last trip, check before you leave."

I hopped into the back of the trailer to check for bars but it was full of empty bins, floor to ceiling, front to back. I went back to dispatch.

"I can't see any bars, the trailer's full, will they be up the front?"

"They should be but we ought to check. I'll come and help you." I couldn't see quite why the nice young man thought it would be helpful for two people to stand at the back of the trailer saying, "You can't see to the front, it's too full," but when he lit up a cigarette the second he escaped the building I realised that the 'help' wasn't entirely for my benefit.

"Better throw some more in, do you know where we keep them?"

"No."

"I'll show you, then I can smoke another."

This was my first foray into the world of load bars. I'd become relatively adept at strapping loads and could manipulate the straps quite quickly since working out how not to get my work gloves caught up in the ratchets, but the bars were heavier. They were also unwieldy and prone to expanding and contracting at will if you didn't carry them exactly horizontally. My progress towards the back of the trailer resembled a Laurel and Hardy routine and my helpful smoker hid a smirk as he threw three bars on the back of the trailer while I tried to keep my balance under the ever-shifting weight of the one I had bravely picked up at the wrong point to have my hands anywhere near its centre of gravity.

"Do you know how to fit them?"

"Do I look like I know how to fit them?" The smirk morphed into a proper grin, I had another new pal.

"Hop in, I'll show you." He had a cigarette to finish after all.

I appreciated the lesson more than I allowed myself to let on, since I now knew not only how to fit the bars but exactly where they needed to be placed to secure the gap between each pile of bins. And it hadn't really taken that long. I hustled a bit to get moving after the load bar delay and was only quarter of an hour late for my three-thirty appointment for the unloading of dunnage.

I needn't have hustled of course, the dock I was destined for still had a truck in it. I waited for an hour. Back to the maps. Culpeper, Virginia lies half way between Interstate 81, which runs between the Blue Ridge Mountains and the Appalachians, and Interstate 95, which runs through the Baltimore and Washington conurbation. Given that no-one voluntarily drives round either city, it would be the mountain route for me...but there are two alternatives there too. Highway 15, which follows the path of the Susquehanna River through the top end of the Appalachians, or Interstate 79 through some foothills of the Alleghenies to Pittsburgh and then the Pennsylvania

Turnpike across the Appalachians further south.

Highway 15 would be bendier, the Turnpike would be uppier and downier, I thought. Possibly. Looking at mountain ranges on a map and translating them into driving conditions was a relatively new skill, the burgeoning of which made the Londoner in me pretty damned proud when I was talking a good drive, but the details were still a little hazy. I asked Betsy and she wanted to go via Pittsburgh, but then I'd told her to prefer Interstate roads so she would, wouldn't she?

I remembered Highway 15, I'd driven it with Dave. Following the valley cut by the river it winds and curls around offering you a grand new vista round each bend. From time to time it crosses over a bridge and the road follows the opposite bank, so that the water and the rise of the land change places in your peripheral vision. It would be a lovely drive in daylight but, not being an Interstate, a bit short on rest stops. Since I had no idea what time I'd be where for sleeping purposes I decided to let Betsy rule. Bigger roads would be better roads after all and the Turnpike, being a toll road, would naturally be better kept and easier to drive.

The truck in front of me left and they said I was welcome to back onto the dock but it might be another hour before they got to me. This was a bit of a blessing, it was another of those indoor arrangements where you can't see what you're aiming for until you've missed it. Plenty of time to mess about in reverse suited me fine but plenty of time is finite and after I'd been waiting three hours I began to fret. I had until three-thirty the following afternoon to get to Culpeper.

Whichever way I went it was going to be a slow drive and I had to try and fit in a legal sleep break somewhere, so I needed to be heading for the border right now.

The unloading finally began but the forklift chappie must have been being paid by the hour, I've never seen a trailer emptied so slowly. He found the errant load bars though, which meant I'd not needed to collect up the extras. I fitted the spares anyway here and there along the trailer, it seemed more sensible to have them fixed to the walls than flying about loose. And it was something to do.

I finally drove out of there four and a half hours after arriving. The sun was going down. If there was one thing that put me in a grump it was sitting about watching the light fade, knowing that I could have driven in daylight but now I will drive in the dark instead.

Three hours to the border took me to after ten. I decided to get as far as I could on the other side by midnight, stop while the roads were still flat, get a good sleep and tackle the difficult stuff in daylight tomorrow. It looked as though I could get through New York State and into Pennsylvania in the available time, stopping just before the road turned South at Erie. There was a rest area on the map, it would do.

Of course, the first time you drive a road there's no way to assess what the rest areas will be like. Some are huge, some are tiny. Some accommodate trucks more efficiently than others. Some have conventions for how trucks tend to park and where you should insinuate yourself when they are full. Late at night though when commercial traffic has to stop to stay legal there is a touch of 'anything goes' about most improvised parking spots. Off the main highway shoulder is the big rule. This usually involves parking on a slip road shoulder, either as the ramp curves in to the stop or as it leaves, but there are limits and you do have to make a bit of an effort to be safely out of the way of thundering traffic. It is always safer to park on the off-ramp since vehicles are coming past you much more slowly, but if you drive through a full lot to get to the off-ramp and the ramp is full too you're snookered until the next stop, which could be an illegal distance down the road.

My personal rule goes, if there's a truck already parked on the on-ramp it probably means that the proper spaces and the off-ramp are full. It also means that parking there is acceptable so I'll pull in behind it and hope for the best. On a really good day, another truck pulls in behind me, then I know I'm safe and legalish and I sleep a lot better.

This was a tiny rest area. Big scary red 'no parking' signs littered the on-ramp and the legal bays were full. Big scary 'no parking' signs littered the off-ramp. There was just about room for one truck between where the signs stopped and the ramp ended. It would have to do. The spirit of the 'no parking' signs remained but I wasn't parked directly next to one, I could act dumb if required. I slept badly, waiting for the knock on the window.

***

I was up a little before legal driving time for a flurry of wet-wipes by way of a wash. All this stopping late at night nowhere near a truck stop meant that the chances of a proper shower were minimal these days. The not-a-rookie-now had tighter delivery windows to meet. Once I was off and running for the day, even if I found time to swing into a truck stop for coffee, fuel or a wee, the pressure to cover enough miles before my fourteen hours expired meant that making time for a shower was out of the question. That's what your ten hour break would be for, if you were ever taking it for real. I was getting quite adept at the wet wipe flurry though, and tooth cleaning with a tiny mug of water. I had some nifty toileting arrangements too but I'll spare you the details.

A breakfast of trail mix and half an apple and I was ready for anything. With a few minutes left before I could legally turn a wheel I turned my attention to the cab floor. All that trail mix made it look more than ever as though a parrot lived there too. I set to with my prized little travel-sized dustpan and brush and removed most of the layer of scattered seeds.

Erie passed by and I turned south, making good time. I sent a satellite message to dispatch…'delayed 4 hrs at shipper, eta 17:00'. I reckoned that catching up on two and a half of my four hour delay and only being an hour and a half off target was pretty damned impressive. I'd even remembered to allow for slower driving once I turned east.

Pittsburgh hove into view and the Turnpike began. Tollbooths were less intimidating by then although they all varied a bit so I was never quite sure what I would be expected to do. I got flustered from time to time with all the bits of change and bits of paper and it amused the staff in the booths. Since I like to entertain, I chose to view the flusterment as an endearing quirk rather than a sign of incompetence.

The toll roads I'd got used to in Indiana and Illinois just wanted five dollars or so to enter. Pennsylvania seemed to like to give you a ticket when you started so that they could charge you by the mile when you left. Sometimes a person gave you the ticket, sometimes a machine, either way it was a nuisance having to pull to a stop, especially fully loaded. It took ages to work up through all those gears again to anything like a normal speed and as you left the booths the lanes all merged from half a dozen or more back down to two or three in a very short distance. People got impatient and zipped round you, becoming hard to avoid once a bit of momentum picked up. I started to regret choosing the Turnpike, it had better be a nice road to drive.

More cheeringly though, I was heading for the Blue Ridge Mountains. Having started the trip in true Laurel and Hardy style with my load bar shenanigans I felt obliged to add a little Blue-Ridge-related singing in the cab, which kept me entertained until I began to realise that I had made a huge mistake. The Turnpike was anything but nice to drive. I had assumed that a toll road would be cut through the landscape a little and relatively well maintained. Isn't that what the money is for?

Not only was it uppy and downy, it was one interminable mass of road works reducing most of its length to one lane in each direction. Moreover, these lanes weren't just coned off with little bollards, the workers were properly protected with temporary concrete barriers on both sides so that the edges of your lane were alarmingly close and alarmingly, well, concrete.

An optical illusion sets in when the side of the road rises up to meet you, you know it's wide enough but it looks as though it isn't and the instinct to swing from side to side is merciless. I ran through the mantra in my head from training days, 'raise your vision, look ahead, trust the sides, raise your vision, look ahead, trust the sides'. In your head you do actually know that there is room to pass through, you're doing it after all, but the moral fibre required to not look down so that you don't start to steer away from the concrete, for miles and miles and miles, is utterly exhausting.

There was a lot of up and down through the gears as well, the heavier the load the greater the effect of a grade on your speed, both up and down. The rules were the same as they'd been back in The Rockies but gear plates are heavier than mail, everything is amplified. The load holds you back and slows you even more going up, the wrong gear is more likely than ever to mean grinding to an embarrassing halt in the middle of the road. Going down, as the heavier load pushes you forward the gear you might have selected to hold back a Challenger load would be useless now. Added to which, it's not a great idea to try and change gears on a hill, the incline messes with the time it takes for the revs to lift or drop the right amount from one gear to the next, making any shift a risk for dropping out of gear completely.

In school they taught you rules for timing gear changes. The revs had to lift or drop by 300rpm and you did it exactly as they said it, when they said it, until you got the time interval into your head and feet. Eventually your muscle memory timed it for you, but as learners we were driving around with the same weight in the back all the time, and around the same streets. We could learn sixth for this ramp and fourth for that hill and get ready for them in advance.

Out in the real world the timing changed slightly for each weight you pulled, the single interval you had in your head needed to adapt from run to run. Then you learned the hard way that some corners needed one gear when empty and another when loaded and that some hills could be climbed by taking it down a mere half a gear when empty but don't try it when full or you'd be in trouble. The rules were gradually replaced by judgement, a slow and tiring process. I'd begun this learning process so long ago that mostly I did it by instinct these days but on the Pennsylvania Turnpike I realised that I was thinking about it more than usual. I'd not driven these sorts of grades at the limits of maximum weight before. Judging by the relative absence of crunching noises I was mostly getting it right but the extra concentration, added to the extra work and general heaviness of everything, was surprisingly tiring.

Somehow, annoyed, pissed off and regretting trusting the Turnpike I got across the Appalachians and into the tiny spit of Maryland that runs across the top of the Virginias.

Now here, just for a moment, I have to abandon tales of gearboxes and derring-do and meander down a diversion about how weird it is that American states look different from each other. You can drive about the UK and Europe and cross from one country to another without the landscape giving much away. What's more, when you look on a map the US state lines appear pretty arbitrary. It always surprises me therefore when I cross a state line and things suddenly change. There was a startling colour combination in the trees lining the roads in Maryland that I'd not seen anywhere else. A range of almost-silver shades of green. I took a photo but it didn't do the remarkable Maryland silvers any justice.

***

Making a mental note to return via Highway 15, I congratulated myself on still having an eta of five o'clock when I turned off the highway and took the road to Culpeper. Naturally it was at a standstill. The traffic was backed up for what seemed to be miles and the CB came into its own. The news wasn't good. A fatal accident closing off all lanes in both directions. Nothing to do but sit tight and tell dispatch I was stuck. I called on the phone, since I wasn't moving anywhere.

"We'll let them know, they're there until eleven, just get there when you can."

"Ok, but what about the pickup?" I was due to travel further south to Roanoke for a reload that day, I hadn't even looked it up on the map yet.

"They're there until midnight but you can pick up tomorrow morning if you like, the load has been ready since Monday and it's not due back until the third." This was grand news, I could sleep before trying to find the next people. "Call when you're loaded in Roanoke, it's only twelve bins, we'll send you somewhere else for more." This wasn't so good. It looked like I was going to be out all week, there might not be enough clean clothes. Or trail mix.

After twenty minutes or so the news on the CB changed. It meandered from, "The chopper's landed," via, "Someone must be still alive," through, "Chopper's leaving," to "Both southbound lanes are open now, northbound still closed, you're not going anywhere just yet driver." Amid thanks for the updates—well not from me, I just thought them—we gradually started to move and by six o'clock Betsy informed me I had arrived at my destination. I was outside a huge plant on a vast quantity of open land with a clearly-marked driveway for shipping and receiving. I risked driving along it uninvestigated. Big places with signs for trucks usually meant you'd be able to turn around.

I drove as far as a barrier by a little guard's hut. The hut was empty. It had a little paper note stuck to the window that had spent too much time out in the rain. Something about finding the guard at the main entrance to the building and using a phone. It was a pleasant enough evening, I shut off the engine and went walkabout. There was a fancy main entrance to the building with a place for staff to swipe ID cards, but no staff. And no guard. There was an elderly phone on the wall though and a little sign that said, "To contact security guard," so I lifted the receiver. There was a recorded message. I put it down. Was there any point in leaving a message? I didn't know. I picked it up again. And put it down again. I thought the conundrum over. If I was going to call dispatch and tell them the place was deserted they'd ask about that sort of thing wouldn't they? It would sound better to say, "I left a message and nobody came," than, "It said leave a message and I didn't". So I did.

I continued walking. A good reason to appear to be lost and looking for someone is that it gives you a chance to find the docks and scope out how the hell to set up for them without looking too much like you have no idea what you are doing. Since I was lost and looking for someone anyway, a tour round the outside of the building seemed like a sound idea.

I found some docks and a warehouse area round the back. The doors were open and the lights were on. I could hear some activity around machinery way over to the back but nobody buzzed me with a forklift. I found an office that said SHIPPING on the door. The lights were on and the door was open but it was deserted. It had phones though, I could call dispatch from there and sound more intelligent than from outside the front of the building. I could find a loo first though. Now I had a plan. Wander through the plant looking for the ladies, if accosted tell people I was trying to find the shipper, then return to the deserted office to make that call if there was still nobody to be found.

The lady with the fierce hair found me as I was telling dispatch, from the phone on her desk, that I was here but nobody else was. "You should have come and found me," she reproached, "I'm the only one here after five, I can't be everywhere." She was tiny, had the sort of glasses that are elaborate enough to count as jewellery, wore a sparkly salmon pink top and reminded me of one of my scarier aunts. I grovelled.

"I'm so sorry, I'm new at this and I've not been here before, I didn't know where to look."

"Didn't the guard tell you?"

"I couldn't find the guard, I'm still parked up by the barrier." She softened a bit. And walked me back through the building to show me where I should have looked for the guard. When he wasn't there and she tried the phone and got the recorded message as well she softened a lot more and declared it her mission for the evening to sort this out.

We made introductions. "I'm Ursula," she said, although that isn't how it sounded. What I heard was "I'm Oooors'la", which is the ugliest way I've ever heard anyone pronounce a pretty name...I thought for a fleeting moment she was unwell. Oors'la bustled and I followed on her heels like a puppy (which is hard to do when you are twice someone's size) until she found the hapless guard. He apologised, he was new too. He'd been told to patrol the building, nobody told him there would be deliveries. Once we'd all made friends, forgiven each other for first impressions and blamed absent ne'er-do-wells he raised the barrier and I drove round to the dock.

By the time I had made a decent job of reversing in Oors'la was my best friend. It turned out that she literally was the only person in the shipping department after five, since she it was who beetled in and out of my trailer, unloading it with a forklift. Somehow I expected from her demeanour that I was dealing with an office person but who am I to judge by appearance? She drove her forklift in fastidious manner, with pinkies raised, exactly as though she were having a polite cup of tea. I didn't know that was possible.

My scary aunt's little doppelganger may not have looked right in a forklift but she really knew her stuff, even down to the load bars. She thoroughly approved of my time and trouble fixing the spares to the walls instead of letting them fly about loose. I had treated her clutch plates as though they were kittens and she appreciated this.

When we were done my new pal told me all about the best way to drive to Roanoke, where the sneaky speed limit changes were, and to, "Be sure to come back and visit again soon." I left Culpeper, Virginia a lot sprightlier than expected and headed south.

ANOTHER INCONVENIENT
DUMPSTER

MY NEW pal Oors'la had predicted that Highway 29 would be busy in addition to being full of madly pointless speed limit changes. She also advised that Interstate 81 would be nose-to tail-trucks. She was right on all counts, particularly the difficulty in spotting the speed limit signs owing to them being both hidden behind foliage and completely non-intuitive. Usually there is at least a house heaving into view to provide something worth slowing down for, but no, this road arbitrarily sped you up and slowed you down merely to create some sort of entertaining activity between junctions. Or possibly a job creation scheme for the sign makers…but not the tree pruners.

I was heartily grateful for her advice and beginning to lose interest in trying to get to Roanoke by midnight. The nose-to-tail truck thing set me wondering how easy it would be to find a place to sleep. There didn't appear to be an abundance of truck stops in and around Roanoke itself, or on the way, which was likely to mean the rest areas would fill up fast.

I opted to stop early, about nine, and find a place to sleep in daylight before the mass truck-parking binge began. Stopping about an hour from the morning's destination would mean that I could take a legal ten hour rest, start at seven and be delivering by eight in the morning. Perfectly acceptable and a bit of a change from all the log book massaging, which was starting to piss me off. It may or may not Be Trucking but I was the one who was too knackered to think straight.

I found a rest area, parked relatively untroubled, sent dispatch a satellite update on progress with an eta for tomorrow and settled down for some serious rest. I was beyond tired. Too exhausted to eat even though I was hungry, too zoned-out to miss the shower I wasn't having and wanting very much to turn for home as early as I could the following day.

A return message came through to the satellite messaging machine. Had I exchanged one trailer for another at Culpeper or had they unloaded the one I'd driven in with? I replied that no, I hadn't switched trailers, they had unloaded while I waited and I was now off for my legal rest. Allegedly dispatch liked to be told when you were going to sleep so that they didn't disturb you with unnecessary messages. Yeah right. Half way through the night that awful incessant bleeping woke me up. It was dispatch wanting to know whether I'd delivered the Culpeper load yet. This led inevitably to some bad-tempered typing of the, "Don't you people bother to read the messages I bother to send you?" variety. Plus a spot of typing with a distinct, "Even if you didn't read my voluntary update, you could at least have read the replies I bothered to send to the stupid questions you've already asked," sort of tone. I was becoming a shirty trucker. I didn't get back to sleep.

***

Finding Roanoke, finding the shipper, loading up and sorting the paperwork all went remarkably smoothly in the morning. It was still before nine when I called dispatch to tell them I had four skids on board and was ready to come home. "We may have another load for you to add first, we're not sure yet. Call us in half an hour." I sat for half an hour in the customer's grounds waiting for orders but as the company's day wound up and cars and trucks arrived and left I started to feel a bit in the way. I called again.

"We still don't have a reload for you, give us another half an hour."

"I'm a bit of a nuisance sitting here, can I start heading home while I'm waiting?"

"We don't know which direction we'll be sending you yet, could be anywhere now you're that far south, find somewhere local to wait."

I wasn't getting happier. I remembered seeing a truck stop just as I'd pulled off the Interstate and decided to retrace my steps to try and find it. At least there would be coffee, breakfast and maybe a snooze while I waited. I was on the outer limits of usual Linamar runs, tales abounded among the drivers of being expected to wait for a day or two once they had you that far away from home. It was allegedly cheaper to keep you there doing nothing waiting for business than to bring you back half empty. For all I knew, South Carolina could be next.

I located the truck stop and it was bedlam. So many trucks were trying to get in and out that the road was gridlocked in both directions as far as I could see. It definitely appeared to be the only truck stop in the region, clearly yesterday's assessment of the local late-night parking potential had been spot on. Maybe I was gaining some experience.

I declared my decision of the previous night a stroke of genius and waited my turn to pull in, realising with a sinking feeling that I would be competing for parking space with people whose reversing was faster and more accurate than mine. Once I pulled in off the road though, I twigged that I had been somewhat brilliant. Hit a busy truck stop in the morning and more trucks are leaving than arriving! I found a 'pull-through' space and, grinning again, set off in search of coffee. The shirty trucker was learning. All I needed now was a pickup on the way home instead of further away and the trip would turn into some sort of success story.

After another of those, "I love your accent, come back and see us again," type conversations I called dispatch and they still had nothing to tell me. I snoozed for an hour or two and called again. I had decided that I would head for the shower if I had to sit there any longer, despite the fact that I would have to pay for it since it wasn't in the chain we used for refueling. Dispatch still had nothing to tell me. I whinged. Any early tendency to want Brownie points had been well and truly knocked out of me. They were working me hard and I'd bloody well have my say. They had a bit of a conflab and then told me to start heading home and call again in a couple of hours. I changed my tune and thanked them prettily. There was a J half-way up the 81. I'd get there, have a free shower and a decent meal…and then call.

***

Be careful what you wish for. The next pickup came through on the satellite just as I pulled in to the J. I was on my way to Saint Mary's, Pennsylvania. I looked it up. It was on the way home all right but not via any main roads. On the edge of the Allegheny Forest in Elk County, it was smack in the middle of the mountains. I would be driving across the Appalachians and then up through the Alleghenies and I had to be there by eight in the morning. It was now lunchtime. Forgoing the shower (thank goodness for baby wipes) I headed off, determined to get as far as I could in daylight.

As I drove I thought better of this plan. Once off I81 I would have very limited access to places to sleep. There would be nowhere safe to pull off the road once I was in the mountains proper. The route Betsy planned out for me included two short stretches of other Interstates, a bit of the Turnpike and then a smaller section of I80 further north. I would have to stop for a legal break on one or the other of those or not at all. The 80 looked as though it only had one rest area within reach of the stretch I needed, and that would involve going past my exit and having to double back again in the morning. So, I opted to stop on the Turnpike, earlier rather than later. It would mean a lot of driving in the morning but I could stop at six, say, then start at four in the morning and even allowing for bendy roads, hilly bits and slower speed limits I should be there on time.

The Turnpike, much maligned on the way over, turned up trumps for me on the way back, with a real service area just before I needed to turn off it to head north. It had easy pull-through parking spaces, decent coffee, and pizza and sandwich outlets for supper and breakfast. If I'd been able to unknot my stomach enough and work out what time of day my body thought it was I could have eaten well. As it was I opted for another nibble of trail mix and fell asleep wondering how long it would be before I would be able to eat properly on the road. I was tripping over my trousers a bit, they were getting longer as I got thinner. Didn't most truckers put weight on? I must be doing something wrong.

It was a four in the morning start though and, as ever, that made me happy. The brisk walk to collect coffee helped with waking up, whereupon I realised that it was decidedly foggy. I'd forgotten about early morning fog in my planning but I assessed it as I ran around the truck completing my morning routine of lights, tyres and other checkables. I reckoned it wasn't thick enough to cause a problem, it wouldn't slow me down too much. I'd forgotten about the effect of mountains on fog too though, and the road had only just started to climb. Driving off the highway and up into the foothills took me onto little winding roads through woodlands and past streams and as I climbed, the fog got thicker.

Terrible visibility, bends and hills all had me quickly exhausted with churning up and down through the gears and I made very slow progress even after climbing above the fog. With less freight on board I wasn't as heavy as I'd been the previous day but the grades were steeper off the Interstate. They had the sort of percentages that meant big signs demanding that trucks STOP at the top of hills to select the right low gear for getting down them safely. I hadn't seen that sort of thing since The Rockies. But I *had* seen that sort of thing before, and in winter on roads that were too slick for the Jake brake. Once I remembered that I'd done this stuff successfully in worse conditions and survived I perked up enough to take a few photos of a truly stunning dawn. And think a few beautiful thoughts.

I didn't pass a single rest area, service area or truck stop. None of the junctions were large enough for a joining ramp and if there had been a safe place to park in the night I would probably have missed it. I declared my decision of the previous day to sleep before leaving the Turnpike another stroke of genius and decided somewhat complacently to put it down to experience. There is, of course a fine line between natural confidence and hubris but we're getting ahead of ourselves here.

Saint Mary's Pennsylvania was in the middle of a mountain. I passed the 'highest point in the Alleghenies' to get there. I know that because there was a sign. I was a mere hour late. The foundry itself was a huge building but it didn't have any apparent driveways in or signs for trucks. I stopped by the side of the road opposite a little barrier with a hut and ambled in to ask directions.

"The shipping docks are just down there," the guard pointed down the road.

"I can't see a driveway."

"No, they're on the side of the building, you can just see a truck backing in now."

"What, that one reversing across the street?"

"Yes, you can turn around in the parking lot over there," he indicated a bit of waste land on the opposite side of the road to the foundry. The road was kinda busy. "The traffic gets a bit impatient but it's the only way." I thanked him a little warily, parked where directed and wandered across the road to fret about the docks. There were two of them, both offset to the right so that a right-angled reverse would have your blind side out in the traffic. They were also set back under a roof so that the usual, 'can't see the dock 'til you're in the building' nightmare applied as well. The guard was right, the only way in would be to back across the road.

The shipper was a charmer called Ray. He parodied my accent for a while as he bustled about checking papers. One of my shipments was apparently ready but the other one would have to be collected from somewhere else by somebody or other's little van, which would need to unload at the dock before I could pull onto it. I got a bit lost in the details but the salient clause, delivered in a James Bond sort of way, involved me waiting for an hour or so.

At least nobody cared that I was late. I quipped that I could wait an hour for them if they could wait an hour for me to reverse over the road. Ray promised, in a new accent worse than anything Dick Van Dyke ever produced, to come and collect me when they had the dock clear. He also undertook, sliding into a dialect from Frazier, to stop the traffic on his way back over the road for as long as it took. Anticipating embarrassment I headed off for a snooze. I'd been working for five hours already that day and had at least seven more hours' driving to get home.

That would have been too many hours driving in the US of course but crossing the border would give me two more hours of driving legality. Being in Canada and all. The hours of service sums were becoming second nature.

As was reversing, the embarrassment wasn't too bad in the end. There was a bit of jiggery-pokery with lining up under the roof but all in all, a tolerable effort.

"After all that about your backin'," Ray used the opportunity to try a little more Cockney, "an' you knew what you was doin' all the time." Gratified, I beamed.

"Ah, well, always under-promise and over-deliver," I attempted a terrible American accent, "It helps people have a good day." I drawl really badly.

Trailer loaded, skids strapped down, paperwork faxed and all in order I headed away from another foundry having made another friend. I was finally a real trucker. One who didn't screw up, delay people, apologise for being new or otherwise let the sisterhood down.

The drive from Saint Mary's to Buffalo and the border was one of the hardest physical things I have ever attempted. Mountains, little towns, villages, the only road north wound its way through what felt like every tiny community in Pennsylvania. Each little community had a sharp turn into a little main street with buses, children and shoppers all hell-bent on throwing themselves under my wheels. Then a sharp turn out again off into the hilly, bendy bits. As soon as the road widened out into some semblance of a highway, the construction began. This was still Pennsylvania, which still liked to protect its construction workers with concrete. Most laudable, as a construction worker I'd have been charmed by the concern.

By the time I hit the border I was feeling the effects of four days' worth of too much anxiety, too little sleep and even less food. My three customs dockets were stamped with no trouble, I remembered where I lived, breathed a sigh of relief, floored the throttle and rejoiced that being in Ontario meant 'nearly home'. All this adventuring was turning out to be a lot more tiring than planned.

***

Arriving at the Guelph plant awaiting my various skids of stuff, I thought my trip was over. Easily onto the dock, perfect paperwork, I was done within 20 minutes and ready to run the scant kilometre back to the yard to park up and go home. And sleep for 24 hours. But one should never relax too soon.

Without wishing to launch into a tedious lecture, that would never do, there are several ways that airbrakes can fail. The most spectacular of failures shouldn't ever happen, overheated brakes leading to the classic runaway truck are down to bad driving, no more, no less. But a leak in the air line can happen to anyone and what happens next depends a little where you are and how catastrophic the leak is.

The normal brake-pedal brakes work by compressed air being pumped into the brake chambers but the emergency/parking/handbrake thingy works when air is removed from the system, so that you can keep the vehicle still if all goes pear-shaped. That one's called a spring brake because, well, it's got a spring in it. Trouble is, below a certain air pressure the spring brake pops on anyway which you don't want all of a sudden on the highway. That's why a warning alarm goes off in the cab before things get that drastic.

I'd noticed that my low air warning alarm had started to go off at traffic lights a mile or so from Guelph and put it down to being tired and using too much welly on the brakes. While the truck sat on the dock being unloaded whatever was leaking air must have got a lot worse, with the result that the trailer spring brakes stayed applied when I tried to leave. Still in blaming self rather than vehicle mode I checked all the stupid mistakes I could have made, like trying to pull away while the dock clamps still had hold of the back bumper. Or forgetting to take the chocks out from under the wheels.

With all that checked though and the vehicle still not moving, it had to be an air leak. I sat for ages pumping the throttle to try and build up enough air pressure to release the brakes and I watched the gauges register next to nothing. I was in the way, other people were waiting to get onto the dock, unload and go home. This would be a very antisocial spot for a breakdown. Finally I built up just enough air to release the brakes. If I didn't use the brake pedal for the scant kilometre back to the yard and drove very, very carefully I could maybe park up and declare the truck out of service somewhere convenient.

I pulled off the dock and turned in front of the other trucks, ready to make the next turn, past the dumpsters, through the car park and out onto the road. But the car park was full of people in a hurry to get home themselves. A car cut me up and I had to brake. The trailer springs sprung again and I was now stuck at an angle across the car park.

I had one more go at revving like mad to get some air

pressure going. Then I released the clutch to see if I could get the truck to move. It moved. It leapt forwards and a smidge to the left continuing the turn I'd started and forgotten about, whereupon I realised that I'd taken the turn around the dumpster a little tight. Under normal circumstances I'd have had time to correct it. In my defence I maintain most stoutly that if the crappy, falling–to-bits-wreck of a bloody useless, smelly tractor they gave to the rookie hadn't inflicted a brake failure on me, that dumpster wouldn't have ripped the back door of my trailer completely off and chucked it somewhat embarrassingly on the ground. Or maybe it would, I was very tired and making some crap decisions.

I had no idea what to do next. I just stood there, nonplussed. What do you do when one of your trailer doors appears to be on the ground instead of on your trailer? Apart from wishing the last ten seconds could be rewound? Fortunately (in a manner of speaking) I had an audience. A couple of nice guys took over. They regaled me with tales of how many times everyone they knew had ripped a trailer door off and how it wasn't a big deal. I remained mortified. And useless.

They picked it up, popped it in the back of the trailer, strapped it to the inside wall so that a forklift could still get in and unload the rest of my freight in the morning and then followed me slowly back to the yard, in case the brakes gave trouble again. There were hugs and more reassurances, everybody does it! But I was devastated.

Linamar were sweet about it. As I sat in the drivers' room desperate to get home for a shower, some rest and some food but filling in accident forms instead, all manner of people told their horror stories for me. It began to look as though nobody at Linamar hadn't ripped a door off a trailer at some point. Even the safety officer whose job it was to assess the accident said, "It's only a door." He added, "You're doing fine, don't worry about it. You're getting to places on time, driving well, dispatch are happy and so are we." But I knew better. I knew that if I'd not been exhausted I'd have made a better set of decisions about my leaky brakes.

I took a couple of days off, since my truck was out of commission anyway, and thought things over. I had a feeling that the writing might be on the wall for this mad career.

CONVOY

IT DIDN'T get better. I popped back into work the following day, issues with accident forms and such. Apparently being knackered, starving, frightened and shocked means you don't fill forms in all that well. Who'd have thought?

Back in the drivers' lounge I sat miserably as everyone tried to cheer me up. All the people I'd run into during various other crises seemed to gravitate to the coffee machine while I was there. The chap with the cowboy hat and the huge moustache for example. He'd been my gallant rescuer during the first, and apparently still secret, dumpster-related trailer door incident. I'd expected the old hand who got me out of trouble at the time to use the knowledge not just against me but as ammo against all women truckers everywhere. But no, the perfect gentleman had breathed not a word. He'd said at the time, "Everybody's got to learn," and he said it again now. He added tales of woe and mayhem and twinkled kindly.

Newfie, who'd become my best friend on day one, gave me a hug. He launched into a hilarious tale of getting his truck stuck in the middle of Guelph the day before. He'd misjudged a turn ever-so-slightly and got one wheel stuck in a ditch. The road's camber tilted the trailer enough for it to bottom out in the middle of one of the busiest intersections the busy little town possesses. He'd blocked the road for half a day, requiring lifting gear and tow trucks to get moving again.

We all laughed our heads off at the image and agreed that this debacle had probably cost Linamar a deal more money than my trailer door would. There was plenty more agreement that these things happen. I almost started to think they might be right but I couldn't get over the mental image of the size of that dumpster…and the fact that I'd been too tired to see it. It could have been a person. Then I would have killed somebody.

***

I was still mulling over whether the less-than-load, auto parts delivery life was for me when the phone rang. It was ex-employer and much-beloved, adopted extended family member Bert. A lifelong trucker, he'd ambled into a car dealership one day after seeing a nice stretch limo on the forecourt. He'd bought it on the spot and exchanged the long-haul life for a business driving brides to weddings and high school grads to prom nights. I'd driven his limos for one glorious Ontario summer while trying to find my feet in this country the first time around. Our families were friends and I did tend to get the occasional, "we need a driver tomorrow," emergency call. I always helped out if I could but this call was a little bit different.

Bert had never lost his love of trucks. So, in the same way that I filled in for him when I could he filled in for his old pals too. On this occasion the trucking pals were short of not one, but two AZ drivers for a run to Montreal. Despite Bert's amusement at the very idea that females could or should drive such things (he'd once demanded to examine my licence at a family party, convinced I was making it all up) it was late on a Saturday and a driver was needed for the following day. Ten vehicles had to be moved and Bert was their ninth driver.

Would I like to bobtail the tenth tractor? Of course I would. Not only did it sound like fun, this appeared to be a foot in the door with a company who used drivers on an ad-hoc basis. Maybe there would be more, "would you like to help us out?" sort of work. They'd have to like me of course and I'd have to not screw up and break anything on my first run presumably but it still represented a possible way out of the 70-hour-a-week grind. And I was available anyway, my Linamar truck was still broken.

And this is how I suddenly found myself driving a heavy duty, 18-speed Peterbilt for someone I'd never met and who had no idea who or what I was or where I came from. Now, I've written about Petes before. They are reputedly the Rolls Royce of North American trucking, drivers are duty-bound to love them but I still don't get it. The layout of the cab makes for a commandingly impressive appearance reminiscent of some flight deck or other, but they are an ergonomic nightmare for the relatively normal-sized. Once you have adjusted your seat to reach the pedals and got over the bizarre lack of visibility you realise your arms are even more too-short than your legs, all the buttons and knobs and things you have to twiddle are located just out of reach. Although maybe normal-sized men have longer arms and legs than normal-sized women. Do they? It's possible. Thinking back thirty years to the day Rachael and I had to suit up to put a suspected Lassa Fever patient in the back of our ambulance, we'd made the mistake of asked for average-sized infection control suits. Because we were average sized-women. We'd spent ages rolling up the arms and legs to a point where we could actually walk about and function.

I digress. Bert and I dutifully turned up at Bert's pal's yard the following evening. The plan was to drive the ten tractors to Montreal overnight for delivery to an auction house early Monday morning. The company would be driving us back apparently. The tractors were ready and waiting for us, with neatly organised paperwork piled on the driving seats. Leafing through all the papers I was charmed to see that someone had gone to the trouble of hand-drawing a detailed map of where we had to go. The map looked as though it was going to help a lot, someone had gone to considerable trouble for us and I began to think these people might be a decent bunch to work for.

I was heartily glad to have driven a Pete back at Challenger with Dave the long-haired Angel addict, all I had to do was think back to Howard Stern on the radio and the locations of things that weren't where they should be came flooding back. Bert and I had arrived at the yard a little ahead of the other eight drivers, expecting to need some time to get settled and sorted, but with the neatly arranged paperwork plus my Howard Stern related recollections we were ready to hit the road in no more time that it would have taken to safety a familiar truck. We discussed waiting for the others but assumed that both our elderly bladders might require more stops along the way than the whiz kids and opted to set off early anyway. They would no doubt catch us up at some point on the road.

Very little went wrong. That makes for very little to write about. Road works, impossible signage and rude drivers are all normal for Montreal (I think I may have mentioned hating Montreal more than once) but it was all a little easier to handle without a trailer. We did have a slight getting-lost-related incident which took half an hour or so to sort out but I've worked with Bert before, this was hardly unusual.

"Actually, if you look at the map, I think it says we should have taken the next exit."

"What map?"

"There's a little map on the back of all the paperwork."

"Is there?"

"Didn't you look at the papers before we left?"

"No."

"Ah."

"Can you read it then? I've not got the right glasses…"

"Um, would you like to follow me then, instead of me following you?"

"No, I'll lead, just tell me where to go."

"Back to the highway, take the next exit, the one after we took, then there's a weird junction which looks like we have to go straight across but I think the road markings will be telling us to turn left…"

"You go first."

"Ok Bert." It's our secret of course.

Having intimated that if things don't go wrong there is

nothing to write about I should really add that trouble-free drives are great for pondering time, space and life as we know it. And something ponderably bizarre did happen. Nothing to do with driving, more a Twiglet moment with regard to the smallness of the world.

With the short notice I hadn't had time to dash to the library for more audio books for this particular run so I was dependent on the radio for company. As I think I've also mentioned before, the wilds of North America between cities can throw up a dire lack of decent radio stations. I was fine through the extended urban sprawl that merges east from Toronto, plenty of news and talk, but as the night wore on the listening options became rather thin. I took to setting the radio to scan and checking each offering that wasn't actually rapping at me for sources of interest.

And this is how I found, at about one-thirty in the morning, a programme called Coast to Coast hosted by some bloke in Nevada. I must have picked up a station in New York State that was rebroadcasting it, I wasn't far from the border. Now this Coast to Coast chappie specialises in investigating and discussing UFOs, life after death, government conspiracies and other unexplained phenomena so I settled in for a good giggle and a ponder about how gullible people can be. And then I heard a name, followed by a voice, that transported me back 35 years. They planned to interview, by phone, an author from England who had written a book about conspiracy theories. The book, Voodoo Histories, the author, one David Aaronovitch.

The name took me back to 1978. Specifically, the Manchester University Students' Union during that magical year. Some pals and I had formed the Custard Appreciation Society (MUCAS, natch) for a bit of a laugh. We thought we might be able to get some union funds for a properly constituted society and then we could spend it on parties and custard creams. I was the Trifle Secretary, mainly because my student flat had a fridge. To our surprise the laugh grew legs and the society got popular.

There were humourless types within the union hierarchy who considered that the point of being a student was to have votes condemning political misdemeanours the world over. Among these serious hacks suspicion was rife as to whether the Custard Appreciation Society was really a front organisation for some subversively right wing political elements. Chief among the suspicious union politicos, one Dave (I suppose David suits the now successful journalist better) Aaronovitch.

Perhaps if I'd not left the UK ten years ago I'd be used by now to someone I vaguely knew in university days being a relatively well-known pundit but this was news to me. There I was, somewhere between Toronto and Montreal, listening to the voice of someone I'd known 35 years ago in Manchester being interviewed by some nutter in Nevada and broadcast from somewhere in New York.

We've taken remarkably different paths to our fifties. And I haven't made trifle for years. But the weirdness of it all kept me pondering the passage of time and the growing up of people all the rest of the way. I enjoyed the interview and I will buy his book, it sounds good. I might even send him a copy of mine, after all he's in it. And I have a sneaking suspicion that he may have developed a bit of a sense of humour over the years so maybe he won't mind.

We arrived at the auction yard about half past five in

the morning. The guard spoke only French. Bert sent him to talk to me on the grounds that I was edumacated but my French education stopped with a barely scraped pass at O level. I think he was telling us that we couldn't park there but I chose to refuse to understand. "Les autres," I stumbled, dredging up one word at a time. "Venez ici…aussi." He looked puzzled. "Dix camions!" I waved my hands around dramatically. He started to look defeated.

As if to punctuate my words, a straggly line of identical tractors started to arrive and line up behind us. "Avec nous!" I ramped up the waving. With much irritated body language he gave up, opened the barrier and directed us to park in a line behind a bunch of JCB type things. Then, in a flurry of bad-tempered paperwork, ten of us were relieved of our trucks and the introductions and conversations began. Apparently we were supposed to have waited until eight o'clock to deliver the trucks, presumably that's what the cross guard had been trying to tell me.

There was general delight that we were now free to leave immediately and one of the somebodies-in-charge called our transport home to tell him we were ready to roll early. This chap, the eleventh man, had been dispatched the previous day and accommodated in a nearby hotel so that he would have had legal amounts of sleep to drive us all back. Thus disturbed he leapt into action and assured us all he was on his way. We snoozed in the backs of our respective cabs until he arrived, remarkably un-bad-tempered considering his unexpected early start.

I was anticipating a minibus of some sort, something like the uncomfortable bone-shaker Tri County had sent us to go skidding in, not a spanking-great, white, shiny, luxury super-stretch limo. We all piled in, settled down among the plump and fancy cushions, took our shoes off and curled up to re-snooze. It was heaven. Apparently this is normal. The chaps took a vote on where to stop for breakfast and settled on the Flying J just outside Montreal. Hooray, you can get a nice veggie omelette at a J, even if Canadians only make you one. I was unstressed enough to be getting hungry and dozed contentedly until we stopped.

The two chaps who were emerging as the bosses of this pleasant little outfit commandeered half the restaurant and organised the wait staff into pushing tables together so that all eleven of us could eat together. It was all delightfully chummy and I learned a little more French. Did you know that you have to order a 'mirror' egg in Quebec if you want it sunny-side-up? Sorry, that should be 'miroir'. Because it's shiny. Not that I like sunny-side-up eggs but if I ever run another B&B it might come in handy.

Once we'd all placed our orders for breakfast combos; steak and eggs, monster omelettes and the like, one of the boss chaps told the server to put it all on one bill. I looked at Bert, nonplussed. "They buy our breakfast?" I hissed. He grinned and nodded.

Plenty of coffee and brekky later and back on the road the atmosphere in the limo became positively festive. The questioning began. Who was I? What had I driven? How had I ended up in their convoy? I hedged and fluffed a bit but didn't tell any outright porkies and the fact that I'd driven their Pete effortlessly and without incident from a to b appeared to speak for itself. It wasn't long before the questions morphed into teasing, that's when you know it's ok. I have learned to start off pretty quiet in unknown corners of macho territory, you never quite know where the resentment might lie—who may or may not have 'issues'—but teasing means acceptance. Especially after the bit of conversation that went,

"I'm surprised they let us in so early."

"That might be my fault. I think he was trying to tell me we couldn't go in but I pretended not to understand."

"Do you speak French?"

"Only a bit, I kept on telling him there were ten of us until he caved in." Apparently this doesn't normally happen. The value of a girlie on the crew, especially in Quebec, started to sink in. This was turning into the sort of trucking I could cope with.

I thought the pleasant surprises were over but then a decent interval after brekky someone dug around under the pile of coats and bags and unearthed a huge cooler. It was placed carefully in the middle of the limo within everyone's reach. It was full of beer. Gobsmacked for a third time. "That'll help you sleep on the way back," soothed the guy who had mother-henned us around the truck stop. And we did. This was definitely the sort of trucking I can cope with.

They took my phone number and asked about availability for future runs. I could be a part-time trucker if I liked. The runs might not be frequent but I decided to take the chance. Much though I enjoyed the long-haul life and much though I hated to give in the exhaustion was killing me. Not to mention the alarming weight loss.

Linamar appeared quite sorry to lose me. I was doing fine they said, it was only a door after all and everyone does that. I was driving well, getting everything delivered on time. Did I want local work for a while? How could they keep me? I was touched, and very sorry. I knew I wasn't just letting them down, I was letting lady truckers down too. The 25-year-old me wouldn't have bailed but the 50-something-year-old knew I'd never cope long-term. If the industry standard was to view the legal maximum hours as a practical minimum and to assume that nobody really needed their sleep then I really was in the wrong job.

Part-time trucking, even if it was very part time, would have to do. There might be less to write about, what with all the not-much-going-wrong, but there already appears to be a bookful.

EPILOGUE

NEVER AN EX

YOU CAN be an ex-con, an ex-wife, an ex-athlete. You can be an ex-loads of things but there are other states of being which never leave you. Is one ever an ex-mother? An ex-doctor or nurse? An ex-gardener?

I don't drive trucks frequently these days, although I do have a tendency to point out the A and the Z on my driving licence with pride if ever required to show photo id. But I'm not an ex-trucker. I will never view the highways of North America, the motorways of Britain or the autobahns of Europe in the same way again. There are things that I *know*. I love the stuff of driving and the business of keeping roads safe enough to think that matters. I will never drive my four wheels the same way around eighteen ever again.

When people ask, as they do surprisingly often, what I learned in my truck I counter their question with some of my own. Questions such as, "When you're stuck behind a

341

truck on the highway, what do you do?" The answer is usually, "Get round him as soon as I can." I let the 'him' go and ask why.

"I can't see very far, he's in the way."

"You could drop back a bit."

"Yes, but I want to get past, I don't feel safe behind a truck."

"Why is that?"

"He might brake and I won't know why."

"That's true but who's going to stop first?"

We chat about brakes and physics. How your car will always brake faster than the truck, how you are massively safer behind the truck than in front of it, especially if your speed is about the same. We talk about how pulling round a truck without thinking about crosswinds can end up, how cutting in front of someone who could be carrying so much weight their brakes are effectively useless might turn out.

Then if the coffee and biccies haven't run out yet I'll ask something like, "Have you sat back and watched what trucks do on the highway?" Now we can discuss how to tell whether the truck in front of you is light or heavy so that you can decide whether to wait for a hill to overtake on and thus get by faster. (Here's a hint, next time you see a few trucks jockeying for position on the highway, observe them going up and down hills. It's kinda interesting.)

If my captive chatees aren't terminally bored by then—and thank goodness the world has people in it who can be converted by an overdose of enthusiasm, otherwise this might get to sound preachy—I move on to, "Do you ever read the little stickers on the backs of trucks?" Everyone's seen that one about, "If you can't see my mirrors I can't see you," and sometimes the little diagram of a car getting stuck under a truck turning right because they tried to pass on the inside. People actually start to get really interested in who can see what, where the rest of the blind spots are and how, oddly enough, most of the time the trucker will know if you're in the blind spot behind him...shadows and headlights work wonders.

The pennies drop into place and now it's kinda exciting that the truck in front of you can see miles further ahead than you can. If you know that he knows you're behind him and that he will tell you what to do if necessary by where he places his vehicle, everybody gets a bit safer. By all means leave him in the dust if you wish to but dropping back a bit, knowing what he can see and what he can and can't do might mean that you wait a few seconds longer and make the manoeuvre a little more safely. I'm sticking with *he*, I've decided that trucks are all male, even if their drivers aren't.

I've been a road safety fanatic ever since ambulance days, but when I signed up with Tri County it was to have some fun and earn some money. I had no idea how much more I would learn about road safety than I ever knew existed to be learned. Preachy? Maybe. Gregg and Jeff still sit on my shoulders and whisper in my ears every time I get behind a wheel.

Given half a chance I would clamber back into the cab tomorrow and head off over the horizon. I can still drive for eleven hours straight and right through the night if I have to which makes me popular on road trips with friends. I'd give anything to be lulled to sleep again by the unique and wonderful sound of dozens of diesel engines ticking over at a truck stop. But I have accidentally become a writer.

Word got around that I do wacky things to find out if a book can be written about them. Nowadays I get asked to do new wacky things all the time and sometimes I go off and do them.

But I'll never be an ex-trucker.

THANK YOU

For taking the time to read *Trucking in English*. If you enjoyed it, please consider telling your friends or posting a short review. Word of mouth is an author's best friend and much appreciated.

Sincerely, *Carolyn Steele*

ABOUT THE AUTHOR

Carolyn has been a psychologist, a paramedic, a proof reader and several other things, not all of them beginning with P. A trucker, for example.

She began writing the day she decided to try and see the world…doing both just to find out whether she could. Parts of her first book appear in the Rough Guides' third *Women Travel* anthology, an event which quite turned her head.

Born and bred in London, England, Carolyn and her son now live permanently back in Kitchener, Ontario. They ran a B&B there for five years and Carolyn is currently working on the tale of how that came about. They're more exciting than you'd imagine, B&Bs. Drugs, prostitutes and a murder for a start. And betrayal, incontinence and poached eggs.

Trucking in English is the third in her Armchair Emigration series. Book One, *A Year on Planet Alzheimer*, is available at Amazon and other online booksellers. *Bed and Breakfast* will fill the gap but first, some fiction. Carolyn's first novel, *Queenie's Teapot* is due for release in 2016.